D0706589

FEMINIST PERSPECTIVES

on SOR JUANA INÉS de la CRUZ

LATIN AMERICAN LITERATURE AND CULTURE SERIES

SERIES EDITORS

EVELYN PICON GARFIELD
University of Illinois

IVAN A. SCHULMAN
University of Illinois

BOOKS IN THE SERIES

AUTOR/LECTOR
Huidobro, Borges, Fuentes y Sarduy
By Alicia Rivero-Potter
1990

THE IMPENETRABLE MADAM X
By Griselda Gambaro
Translated by Evelyn Picon Garfield
1990

VIOLENT ACTS
A Study of Violence in
Contemporary Latin American Theatre
By Severino João Albuquerque
1990

FEMINIST PERSPECTIVES

on SOR JUANA INÉS de la CRUZ

edited by Stephanie Merrim

WAYNE STATE UNIVERSITY PRESS · DETROIT

COPYRIGHT © 1991 BY WAYNE STATE UNIVERSITY PRESS, DETROIT, MICHIGAN 48202. ALL RIGHTS ARE RESERVED. NO PART OF THIS BOOK MAY BE REPRODUCED WITHOUT FORMAL PERMISSION. MANUFACTURED IN THE UNITED STATES OF AMERICA.

95 94 93 92 91   5 4 3 2 1

LIBRARY OF CONGRESS CATALOGING-IN-PUBLICATION DATA

Feminist perspectives on Sor Juana Inés de la Cruz / edited by Stephanie Merrim.
  p.   cm.—(Latin American literature and culture)
Includes bibliographical references.
ISBN 0-8143-2215-8 (alk. paper)
  1. Juana Inés de la Cruz, Sister, 1651–1695—Criticism and interpretation.   2. Women in literature.   3. Feminism in literature.   I. Merrim, Stephanie.   II. Series.
PQ7296.J6Z656   1991
861—dc20   90-36787

GRATEFUL ACKNOWLEDGMENT IS MADE FOR PERMISSION TO REPRINT THE FOLLOWING COPYRIGHTED MATERIAL:

Asunción Lavrin, "Unlike Sor Juana? The Model Nun in the Religious Literature of Colonial Mexico," *University of Dayton Review* 16, 2 (Spring 1983). Reprinted by permission of the author.

Josefina Ludmer, "Tricks of the Weak," translation of "Tretas del débil," *La sartén por el mango,* ed. Patricia Elena González and Eliana Ortega (San Juan, P.R.: Ediciones Huracán, 1984). Copyright ©1984 by Ediciones Huracán. Translated and published by permission of Ediciones Huracán.

Dorothy Schons, "Some Obscure Points in the Life of Sor Juana Inés de la Cruz," *Modern Philology* 24, 2 (November 1926). Copyright © 1926 by the University of Chicago Press. Reprinted by permission of the University of Chicago Press.

The book was designed by Selma Tenenbaum

CONTENTS

CONTENTS

6

PREFACE

Quintessence of the Baroque, bridge to the Enlightenment, Sor Juana Inés de la Cruz has also been celebrated as the "First Feminist of the New World." Our volume begins to fill a gap in Sor Juana scholarship by exploring in literary and cultural terms the implications of this epithet. What did it mean for Sor Juana to be a woman writer and a woman writing?

That single question contains a wealth of divergent yet interlocking questions to which the essays collected herein attempt to do justice—both in the variety of issues the volume addresses and in the plurality of approaches it embraces. We examine, from differing woman-centered stances, the personal and intellectual climate in which Sor Juana lived and wrote, as well as each of the genres in which she employed her literary talents. As an introduction to the purposes of this volume and the directions it aims to elucidate, my "Toward a Feminist Reading of Sor Juana Inés de la Cruz: Past, Present, and Future Directions in Sor Juana Criticism" surveys key issues in Sor Juana criticism from a feminist literary perspective and suggests a blueprint for future studies.

The essays by Dorothy Schons and Asunción Lavrin reconstitute essential dimensions of Sor Juana's world. First published in 1926, Dorothy Schons's "Some Obscure Points in the Life of Sor Juana Inés de la Cruz" examines from the feminist viewpoint of its author's times the crucial biographical issues of why Sor Juana entered the convent and why she renounced humanistic pursuits at the end of her life. Though one might debate certain of Schons's conclusions, the article remains a landmark piece, the mother of feminist studies on Sor Juana. Schons suggests that Sor Juana passed from being an atypical to a typical nun; in drawing on the rich colonial literature by and about nuns, historian Asunción Lavrin's "Unlike Sor Juana? The Model Nun in the Religious Literature of Colonial Mexico" profiles the values and norms of religious life, which allow us to form a more incisive picture of Sor Juana's conformity and nonconformity.

Moving from social norms and values to their verbal expression, Josefina Ludmer's important essay on the *Respuesta a Sor Filotea de la Cruz* (Response to Sor Filotea de la Cruz), "Tricks of the Weak," suggests certain tactics by means of which the weak and subordinate, such as Sor Juana under the circumstances that provoked the *Respuesta,* express their resistance to oppressive structures. Knowing and not saying, valuing knowing over saying, annexing new spaces for knowledge— such are Sor Juana's gestures of resistance in the *Respuesta* to the power of others. My "*Mores Geometricae:* The "Womanscript" in the Theater of Sor Juana Inés de la Cruz" examines other mechanisms of indirection, which are less practices of resistance than the complex expression of internalized cultural norms oppressive to women (writers). I argue that, by refracting these norms and rewriting literary precursors, each of Sor Juana's major plays encodes the drama of the conflicted creative woman.

In their own distinctive ways, the remaining three essays continue to examine the essential question of Sor Juana's rewriting and modulation of received literary culture. Where the majority of previous criticism has focused on the influence on Sor Juana of prior models, we now begin to chart her purposeful difference. The first of the two essays on Sor Juana's masterwork, the *Primero sueño* (First Dream), Electa Arenal's contribution sees the poem as something of a Baroque concerto, a dialogue with the texts of its times and a prefiguring of twentieth-century feminist modes. Georgina Sabat-Rivers exposes Sor Juana's female/feminist interventions in the traditional tapestry of the *Primero sueño:* among them, the preponderance of feminine nouns and the revisionary importance attached to female characters. Ester Gimbernat de González, studying three of Sor Juana's love sonnets in which the poet adopts a man's voice to address "his" female beloved, asks, "What does the lover say to the beloved when the poet is a woman?"

The use of gender masks enables Sor Juana subtly to question the terms of the literary tradition—its hierarchies and values—to which she out-wardly conforms.

This volume hopes to engage in the feminist study of Sor Juana Inés de la Cruz not only the specialized but also the nonspecialized Hispanic scholar, as well as those with an interest in women writers and feminist criticism in general. To this end, we close with a Bibliographical Note, listing general critical sources sympathetic to a feminist understanding of the author's oeuvre and significant editions of her work in Spanish and in English, followed by a chronology of Sor Juana's life and works. All primary and secondary material in Spanish has been rendered into English, by Professors Lavrin, Arenal, and Elias Rivers (for Professor Sabat-Rivers) in the case of their own essays and by the editor in all other cases. We have provided literal prose translations of poetic works; translations of the *Respuesta* and the *Sueño* (except those of Professor Rivers) draw on the English versions of Margaret Sayers Peden and Luis Harss cited in the Bibliographical Note, with modifications in accordance with the context and emphasis of the particular essay.

I gratefully acknowledge the collaboration of contributors Electa Arenal, Ester Gimbernat de González, Asunción Lavrin, and Georgina Sabat-Rivers (to whom I also owe the impetus for my first forays into Sor Juana's works); the editors of this series, Evelyn Picón Garfield and Ivan Schulman; as well as Kathy Wildfong of Wayne State University Press—all of whom have given generously of their time and efforts in helping me bring this book to fruition. Ana-Cecilia Rosado contrib-uted to the final stages of the editing process with meticulous care and concern. Very special thanks go to Elias Rivers for his translation of Georgina Sabat-Rivers's essay. Rolena Adorno and Alan S. Trueblood have given me valued critical advice and support throughout the pro-cess, especially at crucial junctures.

This book—that is, my contribution to it—is dedicated to my sister, Andrea Merrim.

Stephanie Merrim, Editor

Toward a Feminist Reading of Sor Juana Inés de la Cruz:
Past, Present, and Future Directions in
Sor Juana Criticism

STEPHANIE MERRIM

> . . . quedando a luz más cierta
> el mundo iluminado, y yo despierta
> (leaving the world illuminated by a more
> certain light, and I awake)
> —Sor Juana Inés de la Cruz,
> *Primero sueño* (First Dream)

What inner forces and drive motivated Sor Juana
Inés de la Cruz, catapulting her into prominence as the "Tenth Muse"
and into the daringly incongruous position now understood as that of
the "First Feminist of America"?[1] What was the nature of her passions,
intellectual and erotic? Why did she abandon life at the viceregal
Mexican court to enter the convent of San Jerónimo? Quintessence of
the Baroque, bridge to the Enlightenment—how do Sor Juana's writings and thinking relate to the culture of her times? Did she exceed the
bounds of orthodoxy? Was she persecuted for being an intellectual or
for being a woman? Why, and to what degree, in the last years of her
life did Sor Juana renounce her humanistic literary endeavors in order
to pursue the religious "camino de perfección" (way of perfection)?

Such are the historical, literary, and biographical questions that
have intrigued readers and critics of the Mexican churchwoman-writer
over the centuries. Critical observations amassed around these and related issues have proved so considerable as to acquire a history of their
own: celebrating Sor Juana as a "phenomenon" in her own times, de-

generating into disregard or disapproval of her Baroque "excesses" by the neoclassical eighteenth century, and beginning the curve of ascendance with the nineteenth-century renascence of Sor Juana, as sparked by the Romantic cult of personality. Our century, with the aid of new and complete editions of Sor Juana's works,[2] has witnessed a proliferation and diversification (in methodologies and practitioners) of Sor Juana scholarship, which has now expanded to include notable works by non-Hispanic as well as distinguished women critics.[3] The publication in 1982 of Octavio Paz's monumental 650-page *Sor Juana Inés de la Cruz o las trampas de la fe* (English title, *Sor Juana*)[4] has incontrovertibly, and felicitously, altered the landscape of Sor Juana criticism, bringing it to new heights. Any further studies on Sor Juana will inevitably have to take this milestone work into consideration. Let us therefore begin by examining in some depth its premises and most significant formulations, which will serve both as a window onto the state of the art in Sor Juana criticism and as a gateway to our reading.[5]

A summa of the accumulated wisdom on the subject, by means of exhaustive research in conjunction with its author's own penetrating insight, Paz's book confronts, and attempts authoritatively to resolve, such intriguing issues surrounding Sor Juana's life, work, and times as we have presented above. Not only an attempt at resolution, Paz's study involves an ambitious project of *re-creation*, being a book of the world, of Sor Juana's world. As such, it takes on the contours of a hybrid work, necessarily combining, among many things, literary criticism, psychology, history, politics, and the history of ideas, largely in the service of Sor Juana's biography. Paz purports, he states, to have explained—

> to the degree that a human life *can* be explained—Sor Juana's conversion. I have tried to place personal circumstances within their intellectual context and to place both within the wider context of the society of New Spain, with its commotions and uprisings. I haven't denied the presence and importance of psychological and physiological realities. On the contrary: I have examined them quite closely. [Span., pp. 606–7; Eng., p. 469, trans. augmented]

Third, in its larger purposes, *Sor Juana Inés de la Cruz* presents itself as an essay of *restitution* of Sor Juana's works and world to their rightful place. As such, it engages in a dialogue with an essential aspect of the twentieth-century Mexican essayistic tradition, according to which Mexico cannot progress until it has understood and assimilated its own past, painful as that past may be.[6] With his work, Paz would restore a faded chapter of Mexico's history, that of its colonial (colonized) past:

> I believe I can say in conclusion: understanding the work of Sor Juana demands an understanding of her life and her world. In this sense my book is an attempt at restitution; I hope to restore to their world, to seventeenth-century New Spain, Sor Juana's life and work. In turn, Sor Juana's life and writings can restore to us, her readers of the twentieth century, the society of New Spain in the seventeenth century. Restitution: Sor Juana in her world and we in her world. [Span., p. 18; Eng. p. 7, trans. augmented]

As the above credo suggests, *Sor Juana Inés de la Cruz* subscribes to a notion of the past as an example for the present, of history as *magistra vitae,* and thus aspires to one final generic mode: the exemplary history.

Repetition and difference—Paz's book proffers striking reinterpretations of established critical debates on Sor Juana. Perhaps the most provocative is his attempt to penetrate the nun's most intimate psychology and hence to further our understanding of her attitudes toward learning and knowledge, the driving force of Sor Juana's life. Where Ludwig Pfandl, in his *Sor Juana Inés de la Cruz: La décima musa de México* (Sor Juana Inés de la Cruz: The Tenth Muse of Mexico),[7] notoriously and censoriously attributes the writer's literary producion to the narcissistic displacement onto literature of her "feminine" maternal instincts, Paz proposes a more subtle (if equally unprovable) psychic configuration: a triangle composed of Sor Juana's absent father, her grandfather, and her mother. As distinct from the archetypal Freudian family romance, Paz's interpretation has Sor Juana symbolically killing off her father rather than her mother, and assuming the masculine role. The masculine in Paz's reading of Sor Juana, we hasten to note, is identified with the world of learning (seventeenth-century Hispanic literary culture undeniably being a male-dominated world), to which she was first introduced through her grandfather's library. Pfandl views Sor Juana as a neurotic "intersexual," sublimating her "femininity"; Paz, with his complex Freudian sleight-of-hand maneuvers, demonstrates the recovery of the feminine in Sor Juana. The second phase of Sor Juana's psychic development, he argues, negates her supposed "masculinization": "Juana Inés converts the paternal fantasy into a phantom of her husband and transforms herself into his widow. . . . and the 'masculinization' is changed into 'feminization': in her mind Juana Inés takes her mother's place" [Span., p. 112]. Like her mother, who was

13

never married, in becoming a writer Sor Juana would remain single yet fertile, engendering creatures not of the flesh but of the mind.[8]

Whether this psychologistic reading, with the attendant effects on Sor Juana's literary production that we shall mention later, holds in absolute terms is practically impossible (at least for this writer) to determine. Paz weaves a convincing web, based on biographical and literary evidence, that in large part derives its authority from an impressive internal coherence. It is a compelling fiction and rather more ideologically palatable than Pfandl's.

Equally compelling, and more acceptable to the scholarly mind, is Paz's contribution to the question of Sor Juana's orthodoxy or incipient heresy. Irving A. Leonard, in his important *Baroque Times in Old Mexico*,[9] locates the epicenter of Sor Juana's thinking and writing in her conflict between the frozen forms of seventeenth-century church scholasticism and the new, empirical scientificism filtering into Mexico and to Sor Juana from non-Hispanic Europe. "Her attachment to the unorthodox kind of thinking," Leonard concludes, "became a compulsion against which she struggled constantly, fearful of its implications for her eternal security in its radical departure from ecclesiastical authoritarianism."[10] Throughout his book, supported by evidence too extensive to be presented here, Paz questions Sor Juana's direct knowledge of Enlightenment ideas. In their place, he brings to light the manner in which hermetic neoplatonism—an accepted and acceptable model—configured much of Sor Juana's thinking and writing. From this ancient and highly syncretic tradition, Paz demonstrates, Sor Juana derived many of her seemingly unorthodox ideas, including her problematical empiricism: "hermeticism postulated an empiricism, derived from its concern with magic and inseparable from the handling and observation of matter" [Span., p. 335].[11] With his argument, Paz at once contradicts those, like the priest and editor of her *Obras completas* (Complete Works), Alfonso Méndez-Plancarte, who would see in Sor Juana a faithful adherent to neo-Thomist scholasticism, as well as the proponents of her tormented heresy.

If not, at least in part, the torments of possible heresy, what motivated Sor Juana's renunciation in 1693 of secular learning? Paz's twofold argument here notably expands the scenario of Sor Juana's renunciation depicted in previous criticism[12] as it moves from the personal to the larger, convoluted circumstances of colonial society. Paz maintains that the publication by the bishop of Puebla, Manuel Fernández de Santa Cruz, of Sor Juana's *Carta atenagórica* (Athenagoric Letter, 1690), which attacked a sermon of Portuguese priest Antonio Vieyra, in fact

represented an attack on Fernández de Santa Cruz's rival, the archbishop of Mexico—Francisco de Aguiar y Seijas, admirer and friend
of Vieyra. Sor Juana, in this interpretation, began as the *accomplice* of
Fernández de Santa Cruz. Yet the presumptuous tone and defense of
women's rights in Sor Juana's response to Fernández de Santa Cruz's
prologue to the *Carta atenagórica,* her famous *Respuesta a Sor Filotea de
la Cruz* (Response to Sor Filotea de la Cruz, 1691), Paz argues, then
alienated the bishop of Puebla as well as Aguiar y Seijas *and* his sup-
porter, Sor Juana's confessor Antonio Núñez de Miranda—causing the
latter to withdraw from her his spiritual guidance and his support. At
the same time, dire events in Nueva España such as floods, famine,
and fierce public uprisings, had corroded the power of the colonial government and thus of Sor Juana's secular supporters. The church, on the
other hand, emerged from the struggles as an even stronger force than
before. Sor Juana found herself bereft of ecclesiastical or secular supporters and increasingly (Paz asserts strongly, though adducing no new
evidence) under siege by this same church—largely for her audacity as
a woman: "if she had been a man, the zealous Princes of the Church
would not have persecuted her. Deeper than the incompatibility between secular and religious pursuits was the perceived contradiction
between writing and being a woman" [Span., pp. 607–8; Eng., p. 470].
Embattled, perhaps falling prey to the superstitious climate aroused by
the evil omens of these hard times, Sor Juana withdrew from the secular world, seeking reconciliation with Núñez de Miranda and molding
herself to the more traditional outlines of a nun's life, which she had
previously eschewed.

In the end, then, Paz contends that Sor Juana's supposed conversion
in fact comprised an abdication, to be attributed to an overpowering
sense of isolation—"the increasing solitude in which she lived" [Span.,
p. 580]—which capped a life, again according to his depiction, marked
in so many of its aspects by solitude: the solitude of the phantom lovers
in her poetry, more ideas than flesh; the solitude of life in a religious
community of women whose values and pastimes she did not largely
share; the solitude of the struggle to exercise her search for knowledge;
and so on. Those traits that rendered Sor Juana outstanding, sui generis,
also rendered her "a monster, unique, a singular example. She was a
species in herself. Nun, poet, musician, painter, errant theologian,
embodied metaphor, living conceit, beauty in a wimple, syllogism in a
gown, a creature doubly to be feared: her voice enchants, her arguments kill" [Span., p. 359; Eng., p. 274, trans. augmented] and condemned her to solitude. A constant in the Tenth Muse's life, the

theme of solitude also pervades Paz's book as he repeatedly—perhaps ironically—contrasts the isolation of the nun's inner life with the important role played by her works such as the *Neptuno alegórico* (Allegorical Neptune) or the many short theatrical pieces, in the celebrations and spectacles that constituted the society's symbolic representations and reaffirmation. Thus, it becomes clear that in *Sor Juana Inés de la Cruz*, Octavio Paz once again rehearses the notions of "Mexican masks" and the alternation between solitude and communion familiar to readers of his other essays. With this, the last ruling theme of the book which we shall detail, it also becomes clear that Paz's study has both restored a lost chapter in Mexico's history and appended a new chapter to its author's essays.

Sor Juana Inés de la Cruz at once represents a milestone and a watershed in the critical reception of the Baroque writer's works: as it rounds off both Paz's own intellectual endeavors and the critical tradition surrounding Sor Juana, the study also paves the way for a more enlightened feminist understanding of its subject. For one thing, the work avoids the ideological blunders regarding its female subject, be they overt or implicit, so rife in other critical studies. As Electa Arenal has remarked, "Sexist criteria continually obtrude in books and articles that otherwise contain much of value on Sor Juana's times, her life, and her work."[13] On the most immediate level, Arenal notes the patronizing language in which critics have couched their discussions of Sor Juana, calling her a "damita intelectual" (an intellectual little lady), a "pobre monjita" (poor little nun), and the like.[14] Similarly, even the most hyperbolic panegyrics of the writer's work from the seventeenth century on, often contain a patent (for us) double edge, praising Sor Juana's achievements but viewing her as an anomaly of her gender. For example, in his prologue to the first edition of Sor Juana's *Inundación castálida* (Castalian Inundation, 1689), Fray Luis Tineo de Morales writes:

> Now let it fall to the most severe of Catos to say if by chance there is a single syllable of Sor Juana's which fails to elevate her to the exquisite lineage of the highest praise—Ideas, Wit, the extent of information, skillful discourse, that difficult facility typical of Argensola which gives the impression that there is nothing left to say? Well, if all of this together, in a most accomplished man, were a marvel, what is it in a woman? Is this not worthy of immortal applause?[15]

We can see how easily such attitudes feed into modern arguments such as Pfandl's notion of the woman writer's "unnatural" intersexuality, implicitly devaluing her literary production as freakish.

Other disturbing androcentric critical tactics involve what we might term the "domestication" of Sor Juana's person or life story and the "feminization" (in a traditional sense of the word) of her *écriture*. With regard to the first, it has proved remarkably difficult for critics to understand Sor Juana as an *intellectual* woman who dedicated her life to the pursuit of learning. According to Judith Thurman, "Critics even recently have found the particular quality of her intelligence inconsistent with her sex. She lived to reason. She lived *by* reason. She was, therefore, a flaw in the man-centered cosmos and they needed verbal epicycles to explain her."[16] Hence, I believe, the interminable and inconclusive debates about whether Sor Juana entered the convent in the wake of a lost love and whether her love poetry reflects life experiences. For example, as the influential Spanish critic Marcelino Menéndez y Pelayo wrote, "She was a most beautiful woman. . . . She was also a woman of the most vehement and passionate emotions. . . . [U]nder these circumstances it was unlikely that she not love and be loved."[17] In highlighting her "female" emotions and motivations, this external line of criticism domesticates Sor Juana, conforming her life story to a more conventional feminine mode. Another aspect of the attempt to create an "acceptable" profile for Sor Juana has involved the rewriting of her life into an exemplary religious tale. We find (particularly religious) writers—from Sor Juana's first biographer, Father Calleja, to Méndez-Plancarte[18]—emphasizing Sor Juana's "conversion" and adjusting her biography to the lines of hagiography, of saints' lives. A frequent error of such fictions (even found in an article entitled "Sor Juana Inés de la Cruz, Primera feminista de América"!, Sor Juana Inés de la Cruz, First Feminist of America)[19] is to situate Sor Juana's renunciation of secular pursuits immediately after her response in the *Respuesta* to the church's reprimand, when in fact two years intervened. While not always involving such egregious fabrications, domestications such as these reflect a need to transform the anomaly into an icon.

The abstruse Baroque nature of Sor Juana's style represents an analogous threat, to conventional notions of "women's" writing as emotive, sincere, transparent. As is well known, until the early twentieth century the Baroque itself was considered something of a literary perversion and transgression. The Baroque in the hands of a woman might seem to constitute a double transgression. Thus, be it as a reaction to the Baroque per se or to the Baroque as wielded by a female, we find a curious tendency in noted critics such as Menéndez y Pelayo and Karl Vossler to "feminize"—in their terms—Sor Juana's style, despite the staggering evidence to the contrary. Menéndez y Pelayo would reduce

Sor Juana to an unthreatening *poetisa* (female poet), praising the heartfelt simplicity of her writing: "almost all of it is spontaneous, straight from the soul. Which is why Sor Juana so often hits upon the felicitous expression, the unique expression, which is the true hallmark of sincerity in affective poetry."[20] In an equally incongruous maneuver, Vossler would deny the extraordinary crafting of Sor Juana's work: "In terms of external form her work makes no new contribution; instead, it is characterized by a certain feminine naturalness, a tendency to mixed and free forms and improvised dialogue, rather than careful crafting."[21]

Both of these tendencies—toward domestication and feminization—contrive a mask or metaphor for Sor Juana, making of her (in Frederick Luciani's words) "a literary figure who was literally a *figure*,"[22] with this figure defined in predictable and conventional terms. Octavio Paz, on the other hand, assumes a more modern perspective and appreciates the revolutionary and *intellectual* nature of Sor Juana's passions. Compare his following statement with Vossler's, and others presented above: "A new passion in the history of our poetry appears with the *First Dream:* love of learning. Let me clarify. The passion, of course, was not new; what was new was that Sor Juana used it as a poetic theme and invested it with the fateful intensity of erotic love" [Span., p. 504; Eng., p. 384]. Viewing Sor Juana as a feminist *avant la lettre*, at several points he discusses the feminist ideological content of Sor Juana's writings as well as the circumstances of her life which would have inspired her proto-feminist stances,[23] as arising from the fact that "Juana Inés quickly discovered that her gender was an obstacle, not natural but social, to her learning" [Span., p. 628; Eng., pp. 486–87]. Further, Paz serves as an apologist for Sor Juana and against the misconceptions of other critics. In a chiaroscuro contrast to the dark backdrop of twisted priests and mystical nuns that Paz paints, his Sor Juana emerges as a supremely rational figure, characterized by the "lucidity" that distinguished her actions and writing. Sor Juana, he argues against Pfandl and José Maria Cossío, was no dilettante; rather, her expansive thirst for knowledge corresponded to the polygraphic notions of the times [Span., p. 543; Eng., p. 419]. We have already discussed Paz's reactions to Pfandl's other contentions. Similarly (if perhaps misguidedly), the Mexican writer mounts an assiduous attack on those who see in Sor Juana's fervent love poems to her female protectors indications of her homosexuality. It was more appropriate, Paz submits, for a woman to express her feelings to another woman rather than to a man; poetic convention only provided an erotic language for men to address women (see Part IV, section II).

18

As the above summary suggests, Paz surpasses the all too common and facile feminist readings of Sor Juana's work that limit themselves to recounting her most militant or unmistakable statements on behalf of women. In so doing, he also lays the groundwork for more properly *literary* feminist analyses of her work. Perhaps his most original formulations in this vein—adding another layer to the solitude/communion dialectic—involve the nun's portrayal of male and female characters. In the sonnet that begins, "Detente, sombra de mi bien esquivo" (Stay, shadow of contentment too short-lived), Sor Juana admonishes her elusive lover that "poco importa burlar brazos y pecho / si te labra prisión mi fantasía" (little does it matter if you escape my arms and breast if my fantasy creates a prison for you). Paz invokes this poem as emblematic of Sor Juana's male characters, who are invariably shadows, incorporeal ideas; "fantastic" phantoms—in sum, absences recreated in the solitude of unreciprocated love.[24] "We can see Sor Juana's women," he writes, "her men are 'ghostly shadows'" [Span., p. 299; Eng., p. 226]. Much as Sor Juana's portraits of and heartfelt paeans to female figures exceed preestablished stereotypes and rhetoric, her revivals of certain female figures of classical lore are even more personal. In many of her writings Sor Juana resuscitates Egyptian, Roman, and biblical female figures as embodying the positive qualities she would attribute to women. Paz gives special attention to those figures, notably the Egyptian Isis, whom he presents as telling literary projections of the nun herself. As Paz would have it, telescoped into the *Neptuno alegórico*'s figure of Isis—goddess of wisdom whose name means "dos veces varón" [p. 232] (doubly man, p. 171) and who reconstructed the body of her dead husband, Osiris—is Sor Juana's own psychic dilemma of the masculine and feminine as well as its resolution through literature as discussed earlier.[25]

The preceding example, in particular, evinces both the potential and certain representative shortcomings of Paz's approach with regard to our project for a feminist reading of Sor Juana's work. As the critical reader will have deduced, though Paz has much to say of relevance to a feminist reading, his interest in female characters and the feminine in Sor Juana's oeuvre remains largely determined and circumscribed by the biographical focus of his book, his desire to reconstruct not just the world but also the mind of the writer. In other words, while the implications may be literary, the focus remains biographical. Within this framework, as in so many life-and-works studies, texts serve as documents, characters as masks—indices of the writer's absent *I*, bound to that *I* by the thread of the presumed identification between the writer's experience and his or her works. Paz, it is clear, in responding to and attempting to resolve the critical enigmas that have gathered around Sor Juana, can also fall into their methodological and substantive errors. For example, while criticizing Pfandl's psychological approach, Paz nonetheless unquestioningly adopts its Freudian tenets, employing them, as does Pfandl, in the debatable enterprise of explaining away the phenomenon of Sor Juana's life, her anomaly and incongruity.

Yet even within the biographical framework that he himself sets up, we note the unhappy fact that Paz fails fully to achieve a reconstruction of Sor Juana, that is, to draw "a general picture of the world into which Sor Juana Inés de la Cruz was born and in which she lived and wrote" [Span., p. 42; Eng., p. 24]. This is due to the fact that *Sor Juana Inés de la Cruz* provides insufficient information, be it social or literary, regarding the *woman's* world in which Sor Juana lived and wrote. In social terms, Paz centers his discussions of the woman's world on conventional life rather than piecing together, as he does in other contexts, the broad picture of the larger factors, social, legal, affective, and so on, which pressed in on and determined the lives of the cloistered nuns. Recent works, from several articles by Asunción Lavrin to Judith C. Brown's *Immodest Acts: Life of a Lesbian Nun in Renaissance Italy*,[26] confirm the degree to which convents, while allowing women a certain autonomy and female community, nonetheless entailed microcosms of the social structures so oppressive to women from which they would seem to represent an escape. Even less satisfactory are *Sor Juana Inés de la Cruz*'s negligible efforts to situate its subject's works either in a female literary tradition or within the context of women's writing.[27] The book makes relatively little mention of women writers, and that mostly in passing; Paz's discussion of female characters in male Golden Age literature lacks depth.[28] Such myopia stands out particularly in a work whose wide-ranging literary discussions spiral out from Mexico to Spain to the whole Western tradition. Paz looks at Sor Juana, profoundly, in his way, as a woman, but not as a woman writer.

K. K. Ruthven has written in *Feminist Literary Studies*, "Every critical method is a scanning device for picking up particular types of information which it logs by means of a technical vocabulary specially invented for this purpose. The point of inventing a new device is to reveal what was previously invisible, and in that way to articulate a new kind of knowledge."[29] In this spirit and with similar intentions we now approach the next phase of this essay, which involves laying further, and explicit, groundwork for a feminist reading of Sor Juana Inés de la Cruz's oeuvre.[30] From my foregoing discussion the reader will have gained a sense of the axial issues and possibilities for such a reading; in what follows, I will both build on and depart from what has already been written to suggest what have struck me (and I emphasize the personal, and thus circumscribed, nature of these observations) as productive directions for future investigations. Here I will essentially be mapping directions as well as asking questions, briefly outlining a working plan for a feminist reading—and, tacitly, inviting the reader further to develop these ideas—rather than proposing in any way a definitive strategy.

Two emblems, of sorts, preview the shape of my argument. The first is Paz's incisive formulation regarding Sor Juana's double-edged relationship to the female condition—"Sor Juana's contradictions: . . . a deliberate exaltation of the female condition that, simultaneously, expresses a no less deliberate will to transcend that condition" [Span., p. 232; Eng., p. 171]—which suggests the manner in which Sor Juana, also in literary terms, moves between two worlds. The second is the exquisite and unresolvable multivalence of the last lines of the *Primero sueño* (First Dream) quoted as the epigraph to this essay, in relation to the poem they conclude.[31] A coda, a surprise ending, (as has been widely observed) these lines contain the poem's first and only "yo" or "I" as well as its only first person feminine adjective, and thus indication of its female authorship. The last lines explode the poem. Do they set the feminine quest for knowledge, and perhaps, by extension, the feminine, on an equal continuum with the masculine? Or do they privilege the female, feminizing and/or personalizing the quest? The rich indeterminacy of these lines provides us with both the crux and the categories for our discussion, as we proceed to raise questions regarding Sor Juana's relation to male literary tradition, her relation to female literary tradition, and the representation of her own personal circumstances. Throughout, the purpose remains to awaken the feminine in Sor Juana criticism, to "restore" Sor Juana as a woman writer and as a woman writing.

How to arrive at a fuller understanding, perhaps even a theory, of the terms that Sor Juana negotiates with the male literary tradition? In Sor Juana's time and space, institutionalized literary culture (this, of course, is not to deny the existence of a women's writing, which we shall address shortly), the cultural hegemony, was overwhelmingly masculine. Then, even as now, the great masters—Lope de Vega, Góngora, Quevedo, Calderón—dominated the Spanish and Mexican cultural scene. In practical terms, we cannot forget that it was patron-

patronage

age and acceptance by the court that allowed our nun the considerable autonomy from conventual strictures so essential to her intellectual endeavors. In philosophical terms it might be said that, for Sor Juana, to accede to knowledge involved allying herself with the reigning (masculine) tradition.[33] Writing, then, at the very end of an illustrious era, Sor Juana bows to the weight of prior literary tradition: in one of her "ovillejos" she exclaims, "¡Oh siglo desdichado y desvalido / en que

que todo ya se hizo

todo lo hallamos ya servido / pues que no hay voz, equívoco ni frase / que por común no pase / y digan los censores: / ¡Eso? ¡Ya lo pensaron los mayores!" (Oh disgraced and destitute century in which everything we find has already served, for there is no word, pun or phrase that doesn't pass as a commonplace and of which the censors don't say: *That? It was already thought up by our elders!*).[33] Rather than denying the past, she self-consciously absorbs and recapitulates the century's literary languages through explicit imitations both stylistic and thematic, verbal allusions, hidden polemics, and so on. Thus, José Lezama Lima's famous characterization of the New World as a gnostic space or incorporative protoplasm[34] is well applied to Sor Juana—a ventriloquist whose voice is to a significant degree configured by other voices, other texts.

When essayed by a woman of Sor Juana's sensibility and self-consciousness, I believe that such "textual friendships"[35] take on a greater resonance, exceeding the condition of simple admiring imitation. Rather than projections, displacements of the self onto the other, they may entail "introjections" of sorts, wherein qualities belonging to an external object are absorbed and unconsciously regarded as belonging to the self.[36] Let me explain. Sor Juana, we have seen, adheres to male literary languages, eschewing that "negative" function of rejecting the ruling cultural values that Julia Kristeva would attribute to women's writing.[37] Further, in her poetry and thinking, Sor Juana both

androgyny of the soul

ascribes to a neoplatonic notion of androgyny according to which the soul has no sex ("las almas / distancia ignoran y sexo," souls transcend distance and sex),[38] and describes herself as androgynous ("y sólo sé que mi cuerpo, / sin que a uno u otro se incline, / es neutro, o abstracto, cuanto / sólo el Alma deposite," and I only know that my body, not inclining to one man or another, is neuter or abstract, solely the dwelling of my soul).[39] In writings such as her *Respuesta* and the *Autodefensa espiritual* (Spiritual Self-Defense), Sor Juana militantly defends a woman's right to education and, by implication, participation in the male order. All of this together, added to the example of her own literary life, but substantiates the obvious: that—as is entirely

22

natural in view of the context in which she wrote—rather than asserting or projecting women's "difference," both ideologically and literarily
Sor Juana sought to *negate* their difference, to introject or appropriate
the masculine realm for the feminine and to place them on the same
continuum. For Sor Juana, to write with the words of the ruling order
may well have entailed claiming the woman's equal rights to write in
that world; and signaled, as Virginia Woolf's notion of literary androgyny would have it, her belief that "it is fatal for one who writes to
think of their sex."[40]

The foregoing discussion by no means purports to deny Sor Juana's
originality as a writer vis-à-vis her literary precursors. In fact, now that
we have analyzed the similarity of Sor Juana's writings to accepted
forms of discourse, let us explore certain aspects of their difference
from tradition. In this regard, not only Paz's book but, notably, Georgina Sabat-Rivers's El "Sueño" de Sor Juana Inés de la Cruz: Tradiciones
literarias y originalidad (Sor Juana Inés de la Cruz's 'Dream': Literary
Tradition and Originality), as well as Marie-Cécile Bénassy-Berling's
Humanisme et religion chez Sor Juana Inés de la Cruz (Humanism and
Religion in Sor Juana Inés de la Cruz) document our author's inno-
vations with impressive authority, though without undertaking theoretical conclusions.[41] Arthur Terry has noted that Sor Juana's "best
verse succeeds precisely because her imagination is able to find new
patterns in traditional clusters of thought without accepting them
schematically."[42] Following Terry's remarks (as well as the excellent information provided by the longer studies) through to their logical conclusions, we might attempt to arrive at a more global and systematic
understanding of the shape(s) of Sor Juana's "swerves" from tradition through an investigation, for example, along the lines of Harold
Bloom's The Anxiety of Influence, which would ask: in *general* and to
what end does Sor Juana modify, complete, or selectively reject the
courses set by her strong precursors?[43]

More particularly, feminist criticism has taken up Bloom's notion of
the "swerve" from literary tradition, adapting it to the woman writer's
situation. Pre-twentieth-century women authors in particular, Sandra
Gilbert and Susan Gubar observe, "'swerved' from the central se-
quences of male literary history, enacting a uniquely female process of
revision and redefinition . . ." which allowed them self-expression, ostensibly within the bounds of the acceped code.[44] Such, we must note,
are the verbal stratagems of the oppressed in general, not just of women.
The Baroque of colonial Mexico, with its cryptic anagrammatic forms
and always contending with the shadow of the Inquisition, especially

invited such ciphering.[45] Whether the encodings of a woman writer or of a colonial Mexican, it is something of a truism by now that Sor Juana's Baroque, as manifested in the forbidden scientific explorations of the *Primero sueño*, surreptitiously filled the empty Spanish forms with audacious new content. Fleshing out this truism, we might seek out other messages ciphered into other texts, as well as examining in detail those verbal strategies, so akin to dreamwork,[46] by means of which Sor Juana processed her models in order to achieve self-expression within another's language. Is it her own tale, as Irving Leonard in his reading of the Fabio sonnets (and I, rather less directly, in my other essay in this volume) would have it, that Sor Juana is telling? To what degree and in what contexts does she deflect, as in the *Respuesta*, her own most dangerous thoughts onto others' words?[47] And, importantly, in what ways does Sor Juana avail herself of poetic topoi and conventional forms, such as the courtly love sonnet or portrait poem, only to subvert them to her own purposes? (I shall have more to say on this subject.) Such investigations should confirm what we will call, thinking of *El Divino Narciso* (The Divine Narcissus), the echolalic nature of Sor Juana's language: for Echo/Eco, the quintessenial trope, only manages to speak by repeating others' words. Like Sor Juana, as one critic puts it, Echo deconstructs words "into their hidden but operative ultimae."[48]

Also standing inside and outside of literary convention, as we began to see in examining Paz's reflections on the subject, is Sor Juana's treatment of female characters and her depiction of their passions. In reconstructing legendary female figures as the embodiment of knowledge, and particularly in the "Villancicos a Santa Catarina" (Villancicos to Saint Catherine), Sor Juana performs a revisionary reading of the female which should be understood as a necessary complement to the views expressed in the *Respuesta*. Sor Juana also flies in the face of conventions, past and present, to portray women as the locus of reason in the wars of love. Secular love, in our author's (anti-romantic) conception, is a battleground—invariably problematic, fueled by unreason, fraught with tensions—wherein males and females enact that eternal strife to which the Fall condemned them.[49] A battleground and an illness, marked by "desasosiego" (restlessness), "desvelos" (sleeplessness), "tibiezas" (indifference), and proceeding "hasta que con agravios o con celos / apaga con sus lágrimas su fuego" (until injuries or jealousy extinguishes its fire with their tears).[50] The female *yo* of the love poems rails against and attempts to defend herself from "mad love's" ravages, as in Décima 99 ("Que demuestra decoroso esfuerzo de la razón contra la vil tiranía de un amor violento," Which demonstrates the decorous efforts of reason against the vile tyranny of a violent love) which postulates, "En dos partes dividida / tengo el alma en confusión: / una, esclava a la pasión, / y otra, a la razón medida." (In two parts divided is my soul in confusion; one, a slave to passion, and the other, gauged to reason). The poem concludes in reason's favor, "Y así, Amor, en vano intenta / tu esfuerzo loco ofenderme: / pues podré decir, al verme / expirar sin entregarme, / que conseguiste matarme / mas no pudiste vencerme" (And thus, Love, in vain does your mad effort attempt to offend me: because I can say, seeing myself expire without surrendering, that you tried to kill me but couldn't defeat me).[51] In like manner, the third-person voice of the famed *redondilla* "Hombres necios" (Foolish Men) through biting logical argumentation exposes the absurdities of the male's double standard. As this last point suggests, both the content and the impeccably logical form of Sor Juana's poetry argue for the female as a bastion of reason: the poet "cannibalizes" the topic of love, using it as a pretext for philosophical debates and as a showcase for her own lucid reasoning.

Much remains to be said about the construction of the female as well as the male, and about notions of androgyny in Sor Juana. In this light, for example, one could consider the author's manipulation of gender switches (in voice and in characters), of the stock figure of the *mujer varonil* (manly woman) in her plays and other writings, of the courtly love tradition when addressed to a female by a female, or of patristic mariolatry—which Sor Juana reshapes to her own needs and beliefs.[52] All of this may well necessitate a further act of revision, that is, a re-viewing of the canon of Sor Juana's works in accordance to their relevance to a feminist reading. Such a reading would accord new prominence to works, notably to Sor Juana's devotional writings (which Paz finds "insignificant": "They are interesting neither as literature nor as examples of ascetic or mystical writing. Prose for devout old ladies" [Span., p. 550; Eng., p. 538]),[53] so important for their elevation of the female and previously considered to be of little interest. Further, it incites us to cross parochial critical lines, tracing the continuity between Sor Juana's religious and secular writings, between her prose, poetry, and theater.

To my mind, however, the most challenging act of revision facing us—practically a *terra incognita*—entails situating Sor Juana's work within the traditions of women's writing, both universal and within her own milieu. If, as Carolyn Heilbrun observes, feminist criticism is moving from an investigation of the constraints placed on the female

25

writer to an examination of women writers per se,[54] Sor Juana criticism, when cognizant of women's issues, seems to have run aground at the first stage. Substantive comparative studies of the following, among many other topics, are certainly in order: the vital role played by writing in the lives of Sor Juana and the twelfth-century nun Heloise as compensation for their effective impotence and bridge to the outside world; Sor Juana and Anne Bradstreet (1612?–1672) also dubbed the "Tenth Muse of America," and their literary tactics for the defense of women; the striking similarities between Sor Juana and Spanish satiric writer María de Zayas y Sotomayor (1590–1669);[55] perhaps even of Sor Juana and Virginia Woolf; and so on. As formidable a task as it may be to arrive at a working understanding of Sor Juana's literary production on its own terms, we should not shrink from such outreachings.

Virginia Woolf's celebrated pronouncement that "we think back through our mothers if we are women. It is useless to go to the great men writers for help, however much one may go to them for pleasure"[56] leads us to a consideration of Sor Juana's somewhat vexed relationship with women's writing as she probably knew it. I refer to what I perceive as the fascinating complexities of Sor Juana's manipulation of the diction, topoi, and forms of churchwomen's writing, that is, of the nun's *Vida* written at the behest of confessors. In Santa Teresa de Jesús's *El libro de su vida* (The Book of Her Life), *Su vida* (Her Life) of Colombian Madre Castillo, or the spiritual autobiography of Mexican Madre María de San Joseph,[57] to name but a few notable examples, we find hallucinated mystical discourse with its own stylistics, something of a "writing of the Other" laced with exclamations of incomprehension ("no sé," "no entiendo," "no sé decir," I don't know, I don't understand, I don't know how to say, and the like). As Saint Teresa wrote in her *Vida*, "Es menester tenga paciencia quien to leyere, pues yo la tengo para escribir lo que no sé . . ." (Whoever reads this must have patience, as did I in writing what I don't know . . .).[58] Transported, entering an oneiric realm which blurs the boundaries between the real and the unreal, the writer is at times possessed by the Spirit who speaks through her. The Spirit fragments her discourse, renders it chaotic and illogical, and inspires rich, bizarre poetic imagery. Recent studies, I might add, claim some of these traits (irregularity, discontinuity, the break with chronology, lack of authorial direction) as characteristic of women's autobiography in general.[59]

In significant ways, Sor Juana's *Vida,* her *Respuesta a Sor Filotea de la Cruz* (and, to a degree, the *Primero sueño*) represent the antithesis of such women's writing, its negation. In counterpoint to the divine chaos and illogic of others' *Vidas*, Sor Juana deploys her logical powers to construct an eminently reasoned *apologia pro vita sua*. In the *Respuesta*, and by implication the *Primero sueño*, she rewrites her life not *a lo divino* but *a lo científico* (not in divine but in scientific terms). Rather than reveling in not understanding, she dedicates herself to the quest for knowledge, philosophical and scientific; her quest involves a more absolute understanding of the real, rather than its progressive mystical negation. Sensuous, mystical imagery cedes to physiological and empirical. And finally, where other nuns depict themselves as the undeserving handmaidens of divine forces, Sor Juana audaciously equates herself with Christ, in that distinction has brought martyrdom to them both.

It is, of course, impossible to determine whether these pointed contrasts represent a conscious denial of Sor Juana's part of the conventions of spiritual autobiographies. We can, however, more safely maintain that in her *Respuesta* Sor Juana neatly exploits certain of these conventions, turning them to her own ends. The autobiographical thrust of the *Respuesta*, addressed to a superior, at least in part equates her document to the genre of the *Vida*. Yet here the addressee (Fernández de Santa Cruz) is a man assuming the guise of a woman, from which masquerade, and the greater intimacy it implies, Sor Juana derives many pungent ironic effects. More importantly, as I have detailed elsewhere,[60] Sor Juana employs the language and thematics of mystical possession as the keypins of her own self-defense. Disabusing herself of responsibility for her inclinations toward secular knowledge, Sor Juana attributes them instead to a God-instilled proclivity over which she has no control. The transports, the "sin razón" (unreason) and "no sé qué" (I know not what), and the mystical quest for ultimate knowledge found in other women's writings are all called into service here, perhaps ironically, to testify to Sor Juana's innocence and conformity to God's will. Purged of guilt and sanctified, the nun extends her own defense to that of women's right in general to knowledge. Thus, we see how the *Respuesta* both implicitly counters and explicitly avails itself of the forms of churchwomen's writing, with the end (akin to that discussed several paragraphs above) of asserting a woman's rights to participate in the male intellectual order.

Sor Juana, we might suggest, plays with more than a nun's language. In the *Respuesta*, the prologue to the *Carta atenagórica*, and the poems regarding her own fame, we hear the writer speaking with a conventionalized "woman's" voice—employing a rhetoric of humility, submis-

27

sion, and subordination. Is this yet another of the author's verbal stratagems? I maintain, following Annette Kolodny's formulation, that
often for the woman writer "the critical examination of rhetorical
codes becomes . . . the pursuit of ideological codes, because both em-
body either value systems or the dialectic of competition between
value systems."[61] In other words the woman writer's adherence to a
rhetorical code can involve an awareness of its relation to an ideological system. Now, both the *Respuesta* and the *Carta atenagórica* were to
a degree public documents, in the sense that they were written to or
about public figures (and later publicly circulated). That the "female"
voice they adopt is also a public stance, adjusted to patriarchal expectations, can be established tellingly through comparison with the only
piece of the nun's personal correspondence at our disposal, Sor Juana's
Autodefensa espiritual. Recently unearthed in Monterrey by Aureliano
Tapia Méndez (and reprinted in the third edition of Paz's book as well
as in the English version), the *Autodefensa* is a personal letter written
by Sor Juana to her confessor, Antonio Núñez de Miranda, approxi-
mately ten years before the *Respuesta* in which she breaks with him,
complaining of another act of persecution, his public defamation of
her person. Though in many ways a blueprint for the *Respuesta*, and
touching on several of the same topics,[62] the language and argumentation of the *Autodefensa* are shockingly different. Rather than the unc-
tuous rhetoric of subordination, here we find assertive and biting in-
vective with no subterfuges; these few pages effectively deflate the
many concerted efforts on the part of exegetes to render Sor Juana a
servile saintly nun. Sor Juana's true voice? A Sor Juana with no mask?
Whether or not this is the case, the *Autodefensa* attests to Sor Juana's
ability to wield vastly different verbal registers in addressing similar
themes.

The contrasting registers and argumentation of these in other ways
twin autobiographical documents, the *Respuesta* and the *Autodefensa*,
compel the critic to come to terms with an important premise underlying the foregoing discussion of the nun's autobiographical acts. Contrary to such scholars who would contend (in keeping with the "feminization" of her writing) that Sor Juana ingenuously "represents herself
with transparent simplicity,"[63] we have begun to expose the complexity and sophistication with which she crafts her self-representations.
Coming full circle back to the issue of life and works so central to Paz's
analyses, let us argue for an understanding more befitting Sor Juana's
ingenuity of the autobiographical indirection in her works. Paz himself, though (as his analyses betray) waffling on the subject, does not

deny this gap or *écart*. At various moments in his book, for example, he emphasizes that Sor Juana did not write directly confessional poetry, since the poetic norms of the times precluded direct confession. Instead, the writer conformed personal experience to poetic convention.[64] With a similar sense of the distance between world and word, we might chart the shape and purposes of that space in Sor Juana's autobiographical works focusing, for one thing, on the construction—or deconstruction—of her *yo* or "I." As the marked distinctions between the *Autodefensa* and the *Respuesta* indicate, Sor Juana configures her "I" strategically. Molded in accordance with the circumstances, the addressee, and her specific argumentation, far from a transparent self-representation her "I" becomes another prime weapon in Sor Juana's self-defense. The mercurial "I" of the *Respuesta*, for example, assumes a new mask at each step, passing from *comedia* character to courtly lover (of learning) to chaste pastoral nymph.[65] Oscillating dramatically as well between self-exaltation and denigration, the catachrestic "I" pointedly testifies to the nun's instability, to her possession (as detailed above).

Dorothy Schons describes the Sor Juana of the *Respuesta* as a "house divided against itself."[66] Her statement, as does the imagery of possession already noted, anticipates Susan Gubar's characterization of the woman writer's anxiety of authorship: "If artistic creativity is likened to biological creativity, the terror of inspiration for women is experienced quite literally as the terror of being entered, deflowered, possessed, taken, had, broken, ravished—all words which illustrate the pain of the passive self whose boundaries are being violated."[67] And this, in turn, brings us to our final area of reflection for a feminist reading: the consideration of Sor Juana's uneasy attitude toward creativity, writing, fame, knowledge—as perhaps motivated by her situation as a woman writer. Many and famous are the poems that treat such topics, notably Sonnet 146 (which begins, "En perseguirme, Mundo ¿qué interesas?" In pursuing me, World, what do you gain?), Romance 2 (which begins, "Finjamos que soy feliz, / triste Pensamiento, un rato," Let us pretend that I am happy, for a brief time, sad thought), and Romance 51 (entitled, "En reconocimiento a las inimitables Plumas de la Europa, que hicieron mayores sus Obras con sus elogios: que no se halló acabado," In recognition of the inimitable Pens of Europe, which enhanced her Work with their praise: found unfinished). These poems poignantly express Sor Juana's anguished and conflictive attitude toward writing, the burdens with which it has presented her, her sense of being unworthy of fame. Parallel dilemmas, as I attempt to establish in chapter 5 of this volume, are built into the negative female characters of the writer's dramatic production (if, as Paz would have it, Sor Juana's female characters represent masks—attempts to move from confession to art—we must consider the dark masks as well).

Karl Vossler accepts Sor Juana's stated reticence toward fame at face value: ". . . Sor Juana never accepts the success and the recognition of her talent by others as something natural or deserved."[68] Paz, on the other hand, would see her reticence as a rhetorical stance, holding that Sor Juana actively sought public recognition. I, too, while subscribing to the authenticity of her crisis, have pointed out earlier the rhetorical dimension of the "fame" poems. This is indeed a slippery territory, a balancing act on the shifting grounds of irony. Rather than attempting to resolve the matter in favor of one or the other position, we might add further depth to the problem by proposing a consideration of the manner in which Baroque topoi dovetail with Sor Juana's conceivable anxiety of authorship. *Desengaño* (disillusionment), the fleeting rewards of worldly achievements and fame, the illusory nature of worldly knowledge—more than a literary language, the Baroque was a philosophy that in all likelihood molded the worldview of those it touched. Conversely, it is just as probable that Sor Juana found these formulations aptly suited to her own concerns as a writer and seeker of knowledge under sometimes hostile circumstances. Internalized and appropriated, the Baroque worldview would place a tragic philosophical interpretation on the writer's personal conflicts.

The tragic dénouement of Sor Juana's life, whatever its immediate causes, bears compelling testimony to the weight of the real or perceived injuries to which her writings, despite their layers of ambiguity and irony, give voice. In its end, attributable less to her own weakness of character than to the force of patriarchal structures, Sor Juana's life story descends into martyrdom, deviating from the straight path of feminist illumination and anagnorisis. So, too, as we have seen, does her literary production weave a uniquely deviant, convoluted path between masculine and feminine modes. If not always exemplary on the thematic level, the twisting course of Sor Juana's vast and complex literary universe does present an exemplary challenge to the feminist critic. "Women writing are not," it has been argued, "*inside* and *outside* of the male tradition; they are inside two traditions [of the male and female] simultaneously."[69] Baroque and thus syncretic, a woman writer, Sor Juana epitomizes this cultural model. In approaching Sor Juana Inés de la Cruz, then, I believe that the feminist critic will find a rich opportunity not forcibly to resolve long-standing questions but rather to elucidate the many-layered and intermeshing spheres of the literary worlds in which she wrote and whose conflation brought her works to such admirable heights.

NOTES

1. Title awarded Sor Juana in Mexico in 1974 and anticipated in an early article by Dorothy Schons (as well as by others), "The First Feminist in the New World," *Equal Rights*, October 31, 1925, pp. 11–12.

2. See the Bibliographical Note in this volume for the references to new editions.

3. Among the distinguished women critics, we note Anita Arroyo, Marie-Cécile Bénassy-Berling, Josefina Muriel, and Georgina Sabat-Rivers. We refer more specifically to their works throughout this essay and in the Bibliographical Note.

For detailed discussion of the reception of Sor Juana's works, see Francisco de la Maza, *Sor Juana Inés de la Cruz ante la historia* (Mexico: UNAM, 1980), which traces and documents the critical tradition up to 1900; and Anita Arroyo's chapter, "Sor Juana y la crítica," in her *Razón y pasión de Sor Juana* (Mexico: Porrúa, 1952, 1971), pp. 152–73.

4. Octavio Paz, *Sor Juana Inés de la Cruz o las trampas de la fe* (Barcelona: Seix Barral, 1982). Page references to Paz's book will henceforth be included in the body of the essay. The English versions are largely taken from Margaret Sayers Peden's translation of Paz's book, *Sor Juana* (Cambridge, Mass.: Harvard University Press, 1988), and page references to the English are also included in the body of the essay. Since the English version is a revised edition of the original, not all of the material I quote from the Spanish appears in it. Those citations that are a mixture of Peden's translations and my own are identified as "trans. augmented"; those entirely my own list only the page reference for the Spanish edition. My sincere thanks to Maud Wilcox of Harvard University Press and Enrico M. Santí of Georgetown University for making available to me a prepublication copy of the translation.

5. Needless to say, I do no purport to wield or to comment on the entire, vast (and often disappointing) critical bibliography on Sor Juana's works. I base my arguments on works with a distinctive viewpoint which have significantly influenced directions in Sor Juana criticism.

6. This intellectual tradition arose from the debates of the Mexican *Ateneo de la Juventud* (Atheneum of Youth), beginning in 1914, and persist to this day. Pedro Henríquez-Ureña, Julio Jiménez Rueda, Samuel Ramos, Alfonso Reyes, José Vasconcelos, and Leopoldo Zea (among many others) contributed significantly to the early stages of the polemic. For a representative sampling of their ideas, the reader may consult *El ensayo mexicano moderno*, ed. José Luis Martínez (Mexico: Fondo de Cultura Económica, 1958). In particular, Paz's renowned *El laberinto de la soledad* (1951), his *Posdata* (1970), and Carlos Fuentes's *Tiempo mexicano* (1972) develop the lines of thought propounded by the Ateneo writers.

7.   Ludwig Pfandl, *Sor Juana Inés de la Cruz: La décima musa de México*, ed. by Francisco de la Maza (Mexico: UNAM, 1963). Given the (largely negative) importance that we will be attaching to Pfandl's argument, let us quote at length a passage (p. 91) in which Pfandl summarizes his views on Sor Juana:

> Her declaration that she entered the convent because she considered herself absolutely unsuited for marriage; the decisive role that the myth of Narcissus played in her poetry and personal life; the possibility of interpreting a whole series of her almost incomprehensible love poetry as emanating from a narcissistic auto-eroticism; the unmistakable degeneration of her innate desire to learn into a formal tendency to brood; the peculiarity of this counterproductive and wretched mania, which, when correctly interpreted, clearly converts her ridiculous and absurd mental games into sad and serious documents of psychic content and stimuli; and the singularity of her principal work, the *First Dream*, which in its latent (not manifest) content is certainly overloaded with fantasies and dreams, simply and comprehensibly indicated through symbols of procreation, birth, and maternity—these and other similar indications, concepts and images aborted and removed from the true line of the normal path of the spirit, assuredly render Sor Juana an instructive and extreme case of a psychoneurotic double life, which, in our opinion, lives inside our nun in contradiction with her own being.

8.   This argument is to be found in Part II, section 2, and Part III, section 4, of Paz's book.

9.   Irving A. Leonard, *Baroque Times in Old Mexico* (Ann Arbor: University of Michigan Press, 1959; cited in the Bibliographical Note).

10.   Ibid., p. 185.

11.   See, particularly, Part IV, section 5, of Paz's book.

12.   I duly note, however, that both Leonard and Schons (in her article reprinted in this volume) anticipated Paz's argument by examining the political and social circumstances of the times in Mexico. In note 3 of my study of Sor Juana's theater (chapter 5 herein), I provide further references to recent interpretations of Sor Juana's "conversion."

13.   Electa Arenal, "The Convent as Catalyst for Autonomy: Two Hispanic Nuns of the Seventeenth Century," in *Women in Hispanic Literature: Icons and Fallen Idols*, ed. by Beth Miller (Berkeley: University of California Press, 1983; cited in the Bibliographical Note), p. 182.

14.   Ibid., pp. 181–82.

15.   Quoted in de la Maza, *Sor Juana Inés de la Cruz ante la historia*, p. 60.

16.   Judith Thurman, "Sister Juana: The Price of Genius," *Ms. Magazine*, April 1973, p. 14. Though introductory and more journalistic than scholarly, this article contains incisive formulations and is to be recommended.

17.   Marcelino Menéndez y Pelayo, Introduction to *Antología de poetas hispanoamericanos*, Vol. I (Madrid: Real Academia Española, 1927), p. lxix. Similar meditations are to be found in the first part of Ezequiel A. Chávez's *Sor Juana Inés de la Cruz: Ensayo de psicología* (Mexico: Porrúa, 1970).

18.   P. Diego Calleja, *Vida de Sor Juana*, first published in Sor Juana's post-

humous *Fama y obras pósthumas* (Madrid, 1700) and available separately in a limited modern edition with annotations by E. Abreu Gómez, published in Mexico by the Antigua Librería Robledo, 1986. Similarly, in our era, Gabriela Mistral writes of Sor Juana's "conversion": "This, for me, is the most beautiful hour of her life, and without it I would not love her." "Silueta de sor Juana Inés," *Abside* 15, 4 (October–December 1951): 505.

19. Carlos E. Castañeda, "Sor Juana Inés de la Cruz, Primera feminista de América," *Revista de la Universidad de México* 29 (1933): 378.

20. Menéndez y Pelayo, *Antología*, p. lxxi.

21. Karl Vossler, *Escritores y poetas de España* (Buenos Aires and Mexico: Austral, 1947), p. 115.

22. Frederick Luciani, "Octavio Paz on Sor Juana Inés de la Cruz: The Metaphor Incarnate," *Latin American Literary Review* 15, 30 (1987), p. 10.

23. See Span. pp. 628–29 and Eng. pp. 486–87 of Paz's study for a summary of these circumstances.

24. See particularly Part V, section 1, of Paz's book. Marie-Cécile Bénassy-Berling, in her *Humanisme et religion chez Sor Juana Inés de la Cruz: La femme et la culture au XVIIe siècle* (Paris: Editions Hispaniques, 1982), and Arthur Terry, in "Human and Divine Love in the Poetry of Sor Juana Inés de la Cruz," *Studies in Spanish Literature of the Golden Age*, ed. by R. O. Jones (London: Tamesis, 1973), pp. 297–313, discuss the vicissitudes of reciprocated and unreciprocated, divine and human, love in Sor Juana's works.

25. See Part III, section 4, of Paz's book.

26. Asunción Lavrin, "In Search of the Colonial Woman in Mexico: The Seventeenth and Eighteenth Centuries," in her edited collection, *Latin American Women: Historical Perspectives* (Westport, Conn.: Greenwood Press, 1978), pp. 23–59. See also her excellent Introduction to the volume, as well as her "Female Religious," in *Cities and Society in Colonial America*, ed. by Louise S. Hoberman and Susan M. Socolow (Albuquerque: University of New Mexico Press, 1986), pp. 165–95 and "Women and Religion in Spanish America," in *Women and Religion in America*, ed. by Rosemary Radford Ruether and Rosemary Skinner Keller (San Francisco: Harper and Row, 1983), II, pp. 42–78. Judith C. Brown, *Immodest Acts: Life of a Lesbian Nun in Renaissance Italy* (New York and Oxford: Oxford University Press, 1986). For a historical recreation of the repressions of seventeenth-century Mexican religious life, the reader may consult Fernando Benítez, *Los demonios en el convento: Sexo y religión en Nueva España* (Mexico: Era, 1985).

27. In all fairness, we must note that these are clearly not Paz's goals. His understanding of feminism, as evidenced in the study and in keeping, to a degree, with Latin American tradition, is obviously more political and ideological than literary.

28. On the provocative subject of female characters in Golden Age literature, Paz has this to say: "Seventeenth-century Spanish literature is not rich in female characters; of course, there are women in Cervantes and in Lope de Vega—sometimes adorable, at other times horrible creatures. But these are isolated cases" [Span., p. 400; Eng., p. 304]. I refer the reader to Melveena McKendrick's *Women and Society in the Spanish Drama of the Golden Age: A Study of the Mujer varonil* (London: Cambridge University Press, 1974) for a more appropriate treatment of the subject.

29. K. K. Ruthven, *Feminist Literary Studies* (Cambridge: Cambridge University Press, 1984), p. 24.

30. My notion of feminist criticism with respect to this essay is broad-based and fluid but gravitates toward those critical postures that are more practical than theoretical in nature, and which are relevant to the context and concerns of a seventeenth-century Hispanic writer such as Sor Juana. The kinds of questions I ask and the directions I propose in this essay will give the reader a better sense of what is meant here by feminist criticism.

31. Paz, as might be expected, would resolve this ambiguity. In viewing the impersonality of the bulk of the poem as an expression of Sor Juana's notions of androgyny and her own ungendered state, he plays down the impact of the coda: "This information doesn't alter the impersonality of the poem" [Span., p. 481]. In philosophical terms, his argument may be well taken; in poetic terms, I believe that it is counterproductive to explain away the rich dynamics of the dramatic ending.

32. Paz incisively notes in this regard, "How, in a civilization by and for men, can a woman obtain to learning without making herself masculine?" [Span., p. 94].

33. Sor Juana Inés de la Cruz, *Obras completas de Sor Juana Inés de la Cruz*, Vol. I (*Lírica personal*), ed. by Alfonso Méndez Plancarte (Mexico: Fondo de Cultura Económica, 1951). Ovillejo 214, lines 39–44. All quotations of Sor Juana's poetry are taken from this edition and volume.

34. José Lezama Lima, "Sumas críticas del americano," in *La expresión americana* (Santiago: Editorial Universitaria, 1969), pp. 112 ff.

35. I owe this felicitous phrase, as well as many other insights, to my colleague at Brown University, Professor Alan S. Trueblood, Golden Age scholar and translator of Sor Juana.

36. Elizabeth Wright, writing about Melanie Klein, in *Psychoanalytic Criticism: Theory in Practice* (London and New York: Methuen, 1984), p. 80.

37. Ann Rosalind Jones, "Writing the Body: Toward an Understanding of *l'Ecriture femenine,*" in *The New Feminist Criticism*, ed. by Elaine Showalter (New York: Pantheon, 1985), p. 363, quotes Julia Kristeva: "If women have a role to play . . . it is only in assuming a *negative* function: reject everything finite, definite, structured, loaded with meaning, in the existing state of society."

38. Romance 19, lines 111–12.

39. Romance 48, lines 105–8.

40. Virginia Woolf, *A Room of One's Own* (New York: Harcourt, Brace and World, 1957), p. 108. As Sor Juana noted in her *Autodefensa espiritual*, "pero los privados y particulares estudios ¿quién los ha prohibido a las mujeres? ¿No tienen alma racional como los hombres? ¿Pues por qué no gozará el privilegio de la ilustración de las letras con ellos?" (but private and individual study, who had forbidden that to women? Like men, do they not have a rational soul? Why then should they not enjoy the privilege of the enlightenment of letters with them?) [p. 642; trans. p. 499].

41. Georgina Sabat-Rivers, *El "Sueño" de Sor Juana Inés de la Cruz: Tradiciones literarias y originalidad* (London: Tamesis, 1976). Reference to Bénassy-Berling's book is provided in note 24 above. Jean Franco's excellent *Plotting Women: Gender and Representation in Mexico* (New York: Columbia University Press, 1989) appeared after this book was written. See her Chapter 2, "Sor Juana Explores Space," for a sophisticated theoretical and textual analysis of the nun's interventions in the

"language games" [p. 25] of her times: Professor Franco examines the ways in which Sor Juana "destabilizes" the male and female literary languages of her times.

42. Terry, "Human and Divine Love," p. 303.

43. Harold Bloom, *The Anxiety of Influence: A Theory of Poetry* (New York: Oxford University Press, 1973). Bloom presents these questions in a far more detailed and technical fashion.

44. Sandra M. Gilbert and Susan Gubar, *The Madwoman in the Attic: The Woman Writer and the Nineteenth-Century Literary Imagination* (New Haven: Yale University Press, 1979), p. 73. Such "swerves," in Gilbert and Gubar's interpretation [p. 73], created "palimpsestic" works "whose surface designs conceal or obscure deeper, less accessible (and less socially acceptable) levels of meaning." "Thus," they comment, "these authors managed the difficult task of achieving true female literary authority by simultaneously conforming to and subverting patriarchal literary standards."

45. As Mariano Picón-Salas observes of the New World Baroque, on p. 127 of his *De la conquista a la independencia* (Mexico: Fondo de Cultura Económica, 1944; cited in the Bibliographical Note): "The form is cryptic, exceedingly ornate and obscure, for two reasons: because they have nothing to say or don't mean to say anything, or because they are guarding themselves from danger with the most complex tangle of forms."

46. Akin to dreamwork, as understood by Freud, in the sense that one seeks an acceptable set of images to express a dangerous personal content.

47. See Arenal's "The Convent as Catalyst for Autonomy" for a discussion of these tactics in the *Respuesta*.

48. John Hollander, *The Figure of Echo: A Mode of Allusion in Milton and After* (Berkeley: University of California Press, 1981), p. 12.

49. As Sor Juana wrote paraphrasing Genesis in her *auto sacramental, El cetro de José* (*Obras completas*, Vol. IV, p. 205), "Quebrantará, altiva, / tu cuello orgulloso; / y a su carcañal / le pondrás estorbos" (Arrogant, the woman will break your prideful neck, and at her heel the man will place obstacles).

50. Sonnet 184, lines 7–8.

51. Décima 99, lines 21–24, 45–50.

52. See Electa Arenal's excellent, "Sor Juana Inés de la Cruz: Speaking the Mother Tongue," *University of Dayton Review* 16, 2 (Spring 1983): 93–102. On p. 101 of the article she characterizes Sor Juana's special mariolatry as having "accomplished what a twentieth-century North American feminist theologian insists women must do to legitimize and authorize themselves—to go beyond the father." My essay in chapter 5 in this volume contains further discussion of Sor Juana's mariolatry.

53. Paz, in keeping with his analysis of Sor Juana's forced "abdication," likens these writings to Soviet confessions made under duress, finding them impersonal and formulaic [p. 602].

54. Carolyn G. Heilbrun, "A Response to *Writing and Sexual Difference*," in *Writing and Sexual Difference*, ed. by Elizabeth Abel (Chicago: University of Chicago Press, 1982), p. 293.

55. Interestingly enough, in the poem that concludes the "Desengaño sexto" (Sixth Disillusionment) of María de Zayas's *Desengaños amorosos* (Amorous Disillusionments), we find a woman's lament, verging on satire, of men's follies, perhaps anticipating Sor Juana's "Hombres necios." The first stanza, for example, reads: "Si

amados pagan mal los hombres, Gila, / dime ¿qué harán si son aborrecidos? / Si no se obligan cuando son queridos, / ¿por qué tu lengua su traición perfila?" (If, when beloved, men pay badly, tell me Gila, what will they do when detested? If they feel no obligations when loved, why does your tongue trace their perfidy?). See the essay by Georgina Sabat-Rivers in this volume (chapter 7) for further discussion of Sor Juana and María de Zayas.

56. Woolf, *A Room of One's Own*, p. 79.

57. Kathleen A. Myers has recently studied and edited the first volume of María de San Joseph's spiritual autobiography in "Becoming a Nun in Seventeenth-Century Mexico: An Edition of the Spiritual Autobiography of María de San Joseph," unpublished dissertation, Brown University, 1986.

58. Santa Teresa de Jesús, *La vida. Las moradas*, ed. by Antonio Comas (Barcelona: Planeta, 1984), p. 280 (Chapter II of *Las moradas*).

59. On p. 17 of "Women's Autobiography and the Male Tradition," in her edited collection *Women's Autobiography* (Bloomington and London: Indiana University Press, 1980), Estelle C. Jelinek writes: "irregularity rather than orderliness informs the self-portraits by women. The narration of their lives is often not chronological and progressive but disconnected, fragmentary, or organized into self-sustained units rather than connecting chapters. The multidimensionality of women's socially conditioned roles seems to have established a pattern of diffusion and diversity when they write their autobiographies as well." She cites Santa Teresa's autobiography as an example of such writing [p. 18].

60. "*Narciso desdoblado*: Narcissistic Stratagems in *El Divino Narciso* and the *Respuesta a Sor Filotea de la Cruz*," *Bulletin of Hispanic Studies* 64, 2 (April 1987): 111–17.

61. Annette Kolodny, "Dancing Through the Minefield: Some Observations on the Theory, Practice and Politics of a Feminist Literary Criticism," in Showalter, ed., *The New Feminist Criticism*, p. 147.

62. Tapia Méndez's *Carta de Sor Juana Inés de la Cruz a su confesor: Autodefensa espiritual* (Monterrey: Impresores Monterrey, 1986) reprints Sor Juana's letter and sets portions of it side by side with similar passages of the *Respuesta*.

63. Ernesto Chinchilla Aguilar, "El siglo XVII novohispano y la figura de sor Juana Inés," *University of Dayton Review* 16, 2 (Spring 1983): 59. In contrast to such an interpretation, I refer the reader both to Josefina Ludmer's contribution to this volume (chapter 4) and to Rosa Perelmuter Pérez's outstanding article, "La estructura retórica de la *Respuesta a Sor Filotea*," *Hispanic Review* 51, 2 (Spring 1983): 147–58.

64. Paz states, "her most intimate experiences tend to conform to and be transfigured within traditional forms," *and* "those experiences are presented in canonical forms and take on a representative quality" [both quotes on p. 370, Span. version; Eng. version, p. 279]. Paz also writes in this connection, "It is clear that an author's life and work are related, but the relation is never simple: the life does not entirely explain the work, nor does the work explain the life. There is a blank zone between the two, a gap" [Span. version, p. 13; Eng. version, pp. 2–3, trans. augmented].

65. Luciani, "Octavio Paz on Sor Juana."

66. Dorothy Schons, "Some Obscure Points in the Life of Sor Juana Inés de la Cruz," chapter 2 in this volume.

67. Susan Gubar, "'The Blank Page' and the Issues of Female Creativity," in Abel, ed., *Writing and Sexual Difference*, p. 86.

68. Vossler, *Escritores y poetas de España*, p. 113.

69. Elaine Showalter, "Feminist Criticism in the Wilderness," in Showalter, ed., *The New Feminist Criticism*, p. 264. This essay also appears in Abel, ed., *Writing and Sexual Difference*.

Some Obscure Points in the Life of Sor Juana Inés de la Cruz

DOROTHY SCHONS

The biography of Sor Juana Inés de la Cruz is yet to be written. Though much has appeared on the subject, many things still remain unexplained. Material of the period in which she lived is very limited. The fact that she was a nun made her figure less in the works of her contemporaries than would otherwise have been the case, and the period of literary stagnation following her death contributed still further to the oblivion in which she rested. When interest in Sor Juana finally revived in Mexico, it was already too late to preserve the documents that existed in the convent of St. Jerome and elsewhere. The laws of reform and the final closing of convents and monasteries scattered books of inestimable value. It is possible, however, even at this remote date to glean a few facts from the meager material that has come down to us. The present article is an attempt to answer in the light of contemporary books and manuscripts a few questions asked over and over again by her many biographers.

One question often raised is: Why did Sor Juana go into a convent? Why did she not remain in the world where she was admired for her beauty and her mental attainments? It will be remembered that Juana became lady-in-waiting to the Marchioness of Mancera, whose husband was the Viceroy of Mexico from 1664 to 1673. Endowed with a pleasing personality and gifted with unusual talents, she quickly attracted powerful friends at court, and met the outstanding people of her time. One would naturally expect that her life would here reach its climax in a blaze of glory. But in 1667, when not quite sixteen, she suddenly retired from the court and entered a convent. Why?

Some of her biographers believe that she must have taken this step because of an unfortunate love affair. Amado Nervo says:

> Some say . . . that a certain man . . . found his way into her heart, inspiring great affection; others add that this gentleman was of too high a rank for Juana, a noblewoman but a poor one, to rise to his level; others say that he died in the flower of his youth, just when their two united hands were to be blessed with the tie that binds forever. Juana de Asbaje, inconsolable, sought relief in study and retreat.[1]

This romantic legend has long been connected with Juana's name. The story is based on nothing more substantial than the fact that her works contain a large number of love lyrics. This is insufficient evidence on which to build a case.

A few have accepted Juana's own explanation of the decisive change in her life and have declared that she entered a convent to find a place where she could devote herself to her intellectual interests. It must be remembered that she was one of the most unusual personalities developed in the New World, and is hardly to be judged by ordinary standards. José Vigil, one of the first to appreciate her remarkable personality, says:

> Many have conjectured that Sor Juana's resolution to enter monastic life may have arisen from an ill-fated love. . . . I believe, nevertheless, that such an opinion is based on an incomplete knowledge of the Mexican writer's character.
>
> I understand Sor Juana to be one of those superior souls . . . incapable of succumbing to common weaknesses.[2]

According to her own confession, she had been, from the age of three, a most enthusiastic devotee of learning. She had devoured any and every book that came within her reach. At the age of fifteen she had already established a reputation as the most learned woman in Mexico. That she sought refuge in her books because of a broken heart is impossible. It was because of her learning that she gained a position at the viceregal court. Her books were her first love, and they were probably one of the reasons that impelled her to seek the seclusion of a cloister.

One looks in vain for religious motive underlying this important step in her life.[3] She even hesitated because she was afraid that convent life would interfere with her intellectual labors. She herself says that she did not wish any

> ocupación obligatoria que embarazase la libertad de mi estudio, ni rumor de comunidad que impidiese el sosegado silencio de mis libros. Esto me hizo vacilar algo en la determinación, hasta que alumbrándome personas doctas de que era tentación, la vencí con el favor divino.[4]

> (obligatory occupation that would inhibit the freedom of my studies, nor the sounds of a community that would intrude upon the peaceful silence of my books. These desires caused me to falter some while in my decision, until certain learned persons enlightened me, explaining that they were temptation, and, with divine favor, I overcame them.)

The biographer of her confessor testifies that she hesitated before taking the step.

> She felt that she had been called to the state of retreat by God . . . but was restrained by the fact that it seemed a necessary condition of this state to abandon the books and studies in which she had placed her affections since her very first years. She discussed her vocation, and fears, with the venerable Father Antonio Nuñes. . . . The Father had already heard of the talents and singular gifts which the heavens had deposited in this child . . . and he approved . . . of her vocation . . . encouraging her to sacrifice to God the first fruits of her studies, if she thought that they would be an obstacle to her perfection.[5]

Juana knew that the religious state might interfere with her labors. In spite of this fact, however, she finally decided to become a nun. There must have been, then, another and a more powerful reason that caused her to take the veil. What was it?

Most of Juana's biographers have examined this point in her life with the eyes of the present instead of with the eyes of the past. To understand Juana's motives one must go back to the period in which she lived, and study the social conditions of her time. She lived in a most licentious age. A careful study of contemporary writers shows that moral conditions in Mexico were very bad. The presence of many races, of adventurers, of loose women and worse men brought about conditions that were possibly unequaled elsewhere in the world. How bad they were the following entry in a contemporary chronicle shows:

> On the 12th died Br. Antonio Calderón de Benavides, native of Mexico, one of the most singular clerics that this archbishopric has known: in addition to being gallant, of pleasing face and very wealthy, it was commonly held that he had remained a virgin.[6]

Had this not been an astonishing fact, the chronicler would not have taken the pains to record it. The male element of the population was under no restraint (even the priesthood was no exception) and roamed at will, preying on society. Not only immorality, but depravity and bestiality reigned. Things came to such a pass that the Inquisition brought the attention of the civil government to this state of affairs. In a letter written by the inquisitors in 1664 we read:

> looking at the cases of the last three or four years which have principally involved clergy, we find implicated in this crime a large number of ecclesiastic and secular individuals. . . . if this cancer isn't remedied soon . . . it seems that it will be very difficult to halt later on . . . if it isn't remedied by the Holy Office, it doesn't seem that secular justice will suffice to do so.[7]

The civil government, however, refused to interfere. The church was therefore forced to devise ways and means of combating this evil. If they could not fight it through the men, they could fight it through the women. By building convents and houses of refuge and putting women in them they hoped to improve matters somewhat, and protect women at the same time.

In all of this the attitude of the church toward women was medieval. They were looked upon as an ever present source of temptation to men. Ecclesiastics who did not wish to be tempted avoided them. The biographer of Francisco de Aguiar y Seixas, Archbishop of Mexico from 1682 to 1698, says:

> [His Honor the Bishop] believed in the importance of guarding his eyes to preserve his chastity; he made sure that women not visit him except under the most urgent of circumstances, and even then, when their visits were necessary, he refused to look at their faces . . . various times we heard him say that if he found out that any woman had entered his house, he would order the bricks upon which they had stepped to be removed.

And this horror, and aversion to women, lasted his whole life, as he consistently preached against his female visitors and their finery. . . . He considered it a great gift from God that he was nearsighted.[8]

Juana's confessor, Antonio Núñez, was just as discreet. His biographer says that his motto was "Regarding Women: to guard my eyes, not to let myself be touched or have my hand kissed, not to look at their faces, or clothing, nor visit a single female. . . ." And that he might not be tempted, he says: "When walking the streets he always kept his eyes to the ground, as he did when visited by women. . . . To avoid any chance of . . . women touching him, or kissing his hands . . . he always kept his hands covered with his mantle."[9] Many similar instances could be cited.

It was in such a world that Juana grew up. On the one hand, extreme license; on the other, extreme prudery. Out of such a state of society the famous *Redondillas* were born. Is it not this very attitude and these very conditions that she challenged so boldly in "Hombres necios, que acusáis a la mujer sin razón" (Foolish men, who fault women for no reason)? Is it not the terrible dissoluteness of the men of her time that she epitomizes with the words "Juntáis diablo, carne y mundo" (In you are joined devil, flesh, and world)?

To remedy this state of affairs, the church began to build *recogimientos* (shelters, houses of retreat). Some of these were for *mujeres malas* (loose women); others for widows, orphans, and single women. The Bishop of Puebla, Manuel Fernández de Santa Cruz, built a number of such *recogimientos* in his diocese, but they would not accommodate all the women clamoring for admission. His biographer writes:

Once the doors of his Palace were open, women in search of their Pastor began to enter them . . . many women wanting to keep the Flower of their purity intact, women who had managed to do so up till then, . . . but, distrustful, were afraid of losing it, either because they were very poor or because they were pursued for their beauty.[10]

Of the Bishop's efforts on their behalf the same writer says:

Having set up the Convent in the manner described above, don Manuel determined to put into effect the remedy required for the defense of the purity of poor nobles and beautiful young maidens; and although the City already contained a Colegio de Vírgenes

(College of Virgins) in which could be protected those manifestly in the worst danger, both the limited capacity of that College and the number of candidates, so increased that even the most capacious cloister would prove too small, it occurred to his generous soul to purchase a certain site on which to erect a College for the Flowers of Virginity; but since each day his attentive ears heard more and more clamors of poor young maidens, he was obliged to create for them two Colleges, walled Gardens, where removed from the examination of the bold, they could preserve the innocence of their virginal purity.

From these Colleges, as from flowering Gardens, many young maidens went on to blossom, transplanted into religious Convents where, maintaining their virtuous reputations, they ascended with zealous steps to the peaks of perfection; others, subjecting themselves to the ties of Matrimony, did justice to their good education. . . .[11]

This was the state of affairs in the diocese of Puebla. In Guadalajara and other places conditions were the same. How about Mexico City? The biographer of Domingo Pérez de Barcía says:

One can hardly deny the heroism and grandeur of the work of cloistering women, who voluntarily retreat, fleeing from the World and its dangers, so as not to fall prey to its bonds nor stumble over its precipices, finding themselves vulnerable—due to the freedom of their lives or to the necessity of selling their beauty to the detriment of their honesty, using their bodies to the perdition of their souls. Our City of Mexico found itself lacking this great work, and so needy of it to attend to the abundant supply of women who, unable to find places in the convents, wept in the outside world, in manifest danger. . . .[12]

He goes on to say that various attempts were made to establish *recogimientos,* but lack of funds always prevented the realization of the project. A Jesuit, Luis de San Vitores, even wrote a book on the need of a *refugio* (shelter),[13] and finally, with the help of Father Xavier Vidal, a house big enough to accommodate six hundred women was built. But money was lacking for the maintenance of the place, and so Payo Henríquez de Ribera, Archbishop of Mexico from 1668 to 1680, was obliged to give the house to the Bethlemites for a hospital.[14]

During this time Juana was living at the viceregal court in *la publicidad del siglo* (worldly limelight). She was the talk of the town because of her brilliant attainments. What her situation was she describes clearly in *Los empeños de una casa* (The Trials of a Noble House):

> Era de mi patria toda
> el objeto venerado
> de aquellas adoraciones,
> que forma el comun aplauso,
> . . . .
> llegó la superstición
> popular a empeño tanto,
> que ya adoraban deidad
> el ídolo que formaron.
> . . . .
> que habiendo sido al principio
> aquel culto voluntario,
> llegó después la costumbre,
> favorecida de tantos,
> a hacer como obligatorio,
> el festejo cortesano,
> . . . .
> Sin temor en los concursos
> defendí mi recato
> con peligros del peligro,
> y con el daño del daño.
> . . . .
> Mis padres en mi mesura,
> vanamente asegurados,
> se descuidaron comigo:
> ¡qué dictamen tan errado . . .[15]

(I was the revered object of all my native land, of that adoration created by popular acclaim, . . . Popular superstition reached such a point that they worshipped as a deity the idol they had created. . . . And what at first had been a voluntary cult, then became the habit, adopted by so many, of making courtly homage to me an obligation. . . . Fearless in social gatherings, I defended my maidenly reserve, endangered by the danger, harmed by the harm. . . . Wrongly confident of my composure, my parents left me alone: how mistaken they were!)

She was a curiosity, a veritable *monstruo de la naturaleza* (phenomenon of nature), and must have been the object of persistent and in many cases unwelcome attentions. If ordinary women were in danger, the beautiful Juana Inés certainly was. To be sure, she had the protection of the Viceroy. But how long would the Marquis of Mancera retain that office? In a change of administration what would be her fate? Her family was poor, and besides, in her day the chimney corner for the spinster member of the family had not yet been heard of. Moreover, she was a *criolla* (creole) living at a Spanish court. She was therefore at its mercy. That her position was not safe, we may gather from the biography of her confessor:

> Father Antonio . . . aware of the singularity of her erudition, as well as her not unconsiderable beauty, both of which attracted the curiosity of many who might wish to meet her and would be happy to court her, used to say that God could not visit a worse scourge upon this land than to allow Juana Inés to remain in the worldly limelight. [16]

He goes on to tell why she left the convent of St. Joseph and adds: "she had no choice but to leave, and to find another port where, with less danger of illness, she could take refuge and find herself free from the many waves which threatened her." [17] Her biographer, Father Calleja, expresses the same idea. She realized, he says, that "the good face of a poor woman is a white wall on which every fool will want to leave his mark: even the restraint of honesty becomes a risk, for there are eyes for which ice is an even greater attraction. . . ." [18] And she herself says of this step: "con todo, para la total negación que tenía al Matrimonio, era lo menos desproporcionado y lo más decente, que podia elegir en materia de la seguridad . . . de mi salvación" (but given the total antipathy I felt for marriage, I deemed convent life the least unsuitable and the most honorable I could elect if I were to insure my salvation). [19]

It was, undoubtedly, necessary for her to retire from public life at court. There was no *recogimiento* where she might live until she could decide definitely on her future occupation. She was, therefore, practically forced to choose convent life, or be at the mercy of the world. Juana Inés was, perhaps, even lucky to get into a convent, for there was not room for all who applied. With the powerful influence, however, of the Viceroy and of Father Núñez, a haven was found for her. The influence of the latter in this decisive step is not to be overlooked. He it was who finally persuaded her and hastened the ceremony lest the devil should tempt, meanwhile, his beloved Juana Inés.

We may safely conclude that the deep, underlying reason for Juana's retirement from the world is to be found in the social conditions of her time. She was persuaded to take the step, too, in the hope of being somewhat favorably situated for a continuation of her intellectual labors. And when she came under the influence of that powerful *norte de la Inquisición* (guiding light of the Inquisition), the pious Father Núñez, she accepted his advice and took the veil. That she tried convent life a second time shows what serious and what pressing reasons she had for taking the step. *

Another question that has been discussed is: Why did Juana, when she was at the height of her fame, renounce fame? It seems impossible at first glance that Sor Juana, having made herself famous, having earned the title of *la décima musa* (Tenth Muse), and having published in Spain two volumes of poetry, should suddenly renounce her intellectual labors, her mathematical and musical instruments, her library of four thousand volumes, and everything that for her made life worth living to devote herself to a life of cilices and scourges, fasts and vigils. She had lived in the convent of St. Jerome a quarter of a century. She had lived on terms of intimacy with the most prominent people of the city. In Spain she had been the object of dozens of laudatory poems and articles. But for the second time in her life she suddenly retired from the world, and this time it was to lead the life of an ascetic, the life of a martyr. Why?

The blame for this strange renunciation has been generally laid at the door of the Bishop of Puebla, Manuel Fernández de Santa Cruz. A few attributed it to the Inquisition or to Father Núñez. Others have frankly declared it inexplicable. To understand the situation, let us go back and review briefly the preceding period in the life of Sor Juana.

In the year 1680 a new viceroy, the Count of Paredes, came to Mexico. The *cabildo* (town council) of the cathedral asked Juana to write a poem for one of the *arcos* (arches) erected in his honor. Placed thus in the limelight, it is not surprising that a friendship developed between Juana and the Count and Countess of Paredes. This was the beginning of a brilliant and happy period for the gifted nun. Her new patrons encouraged her in her literary ambitions. It was for them that she wrote some of her best works. During their residence in New

---

* We have not included the brief section of this essay that deals with the origins of Sor Juana's last name, a subject of more limited interest—Ed.

Spain, Sor Juana devoted more time than the church approved of to worldly things. The Viceroy and his wife were frequent visitors at the convent. The nun became very popular in court circles, and was the object of many attentions, of gifts, of letters, of poems. She was in constant contact with the world. She was in such demand socially that she could hardly find time for her literary work. In the spring of 1688, however, her patrons returned to Spain. With their departure Juana lost her most powerful protectors in New Spain. Though on friendly terms with the Conde de Galve, viceroy from 1688 to 1696, there was not the strong personal bond that bound her to his predecessor. It is to the Countess of Paredes that we owe the first volume of Juana's works.

The period just sketched had disastrous consequences for Sor Juana. Her worldly life brought down upon her the criticism of the more sinister, the more fanatical element in the church. Father Núñez broke off all relations with her. Oviedo says in this connection:

> It was the fond wish of Father Antonio that such singular gifts be dedicated solely to God, and that such a sublime intelligence graze only on the divine perfections of the Husband that she had taken. And though many have erred, persuaded that Father Antonio forbade Mother Juana the decent exercise of Poetry, sanctified by so many great servants of God, male and female, he did curtail as much as he could its circulation, her constant communication with the external world, by word and writing; and, fearing that her great fondness for studying might decline into the extremes of a vice, and rob her of the time that the saintly state of Religion rightly demands . . . he counseled her with the best arguments he could that, grateful to the heavens for the gifts with which it had enriched her and forgetting the world, she should place her thoughts . . . in the heavens themselves.
>
> Seeing that he could not attain what he desired, Father Antonio withdrew his attentions entirely from Mother Juana. . . .[20]

Father Núñez was one of the most powerful ecclesiastics in New Spain. Because of his learning he was popularly known as the "encyclopedia of the Jesuits." There is plenty of evidence to show that all important cases of the Inquisition passed through his hands. The break,[21] therefore, between him and Sor Juana was a most serious matter. The fact that Father Núñez disapproved of her conduct must have ranged against her some of the other intolerant churchmen of the time, such men as José Vidal and the Archbishop himself.

47

The latter was something of a fanatic. His character was very different from that of his predecessor, the much esteemed Fray Payo in whose honor Juana wrote several poems. Her relations with Aguiar y Seixas must have been quite different, for she never mentions him. If the biographer of the Archbishop is to be trusted there was probably a good reason why he and Juana were not on intimate terms. He says:

> In order to prevent sins, it is very important to attack their roots: the Archbishop took great care to do so. One principal cause of many sins are comedias and bullfights; hence his Honor truly hated these and other similar festivities attended by many people of all types, both men and women. He preached with great acrimony against these bullfights and comedias, and he stopped them whenever he could: when we made our visitations he ordered that in the Saints' celebrations, even of patron saints, there be no such festivities.
>
> Another of the Archbishop's efforts to banish vices and instill virtues was to try to put an end to profane books, both comedias and other types; and to distribute devotional works. From Spain we brought some fifteen hundred copies of a book entitled *Consuelo de pobres* (Consolation of the Poor) which deals particularly with charity, to distribute among the rich and exchange for bad books; and we carried out our plan. He persuaded the booksellers not to sell comedias; he got several of them to exchange what comedias they had for the above-mentioned devotional works: and then he burned the comedias. . . .[22]

That Aguiar was a bitter enemy of the worldly life of the times is shown by the following extract from a contemporary:

> Monday, February 27. The Vice-Queen and her husband were to visit the Caves of San Agostino, at the invitation of the Treasurer of the Mint; but they declined, in order to please Monseigneur the Archbishop, who condemned such diversions as scandalous.[23]

Life in Mexico changed under his administration. It took on a gloomier aspect. Many festival days were abolished,[24] and an effort was made to reform the habits and customs of the people.

Under such an archbishop Juana passed the last days of her life. That Juana wrote *comedias* and even published them must have been a crime in his eyes. In Mexico during his administration no *comedias* and almost no secular verse were finding their way into print.[25] Conditions in Mexico were quite different from what they were in Spain, though even in Spain a movement which opposed the theater was gaining ground. Conditions in Spain, nevertheless, were liberal as compared with those that obtained in New Spain. What the difference was becomes plain when we consider that the books of Sor María de Jesús de Agreda which were taken off the Index abroad (even the celebrated *Mística Ciudad de Dios* [Mystical City of God] being cleared by the Pope)[26] were prohibited in Mexico by an edict of the Inquisition in 1690.[27] Moreover, the fact that Sor Juana's works appeared in Spain is significant. This was due to the strict censorship[28] on books that existed in New Spain, rather than to other difficulties of publication such as expense and scarcity of paper. The fact that of all her works the most popular one in Mexico was a religious work, the many times reprinted *Ofrecimientos para un Rosario de quince Misterios* (Offerings for a Rosary of Fifteen Mysteries), is also highly significant. One is forced to the conclusion that the publication of her collected works would have been impossible in Mexico. The fact that she published them in Spain must have widened the breach that was gradually establishing itself between her and the church. The first volume of her works appeared in Madrid in 1689. It contains a large number of secular poems: lyrics of love and friendship, satirical verse, and burlesque poems in the Italian manner. Whether the book came back to Mexico I do not know. But enough information about it must have traveled back to make things slightly uncomfortable for Juana.

At about this same time Sor Juana committed another crime in the eyes of the church. She wrote a refutation of a sermon preached in Lisbon by the brilliant Jesuit, Antonio de Vieyra. The latter had set up his own opinion in opposition to that of the Church Fathers, Aquinas, Agustín, and Chrysostom. Juana defended the Church Fathers with logic and erudition. Her refutation found its way into the hands of Manuel Fernández de Santa Cruz. He had it published late in 1690,[29] together with a letter, the famous letter signed "Sor Philotea de la Cruz." In it he said in part:

> Para que V. md. se vea en este Papel de mejor letra, le he impresso, y para que reconozca los tesoros, que Dios depositó en su alma, y le sea, como más entendida, más agradecida . . . pocas criaturas deben a su Magestad mayores talentos en lo natural, con que executa al agradecimiento, para que si hasta aquí los ha empleado bien . . . en adelante sea mejor.
>
> No es mi juizio tan austero Censor, que esté mal con los versos, en que V. md. se ha visto tan celebrada. . . .

No pretendo, segun este dictamen, que V. md. mude el genio, renunciando los Libros; si no que le mejore, leyendo alguna vez el de Jesu-Christo. . . . Mucho tiempo ha gastado V. md. en el estudio de Filósofos, y Poetas; ya será razón que se mejoren los Libros.[30]

(I have printed this document so that Your Mercy may read yourself in clearer lettering; likewise, so that you may acknowledge the treasures that God has placed in your soul, and thus, being more aware, you be more grateful to Him . . . few creatures are more indebted to His Majesty for greater natural talents, or incur such a debt of gratitude to Him; for if heretofore you have used your talents well . . . henceforth they should be employed even more wisely.

My judgment is not so severe a censor as to disapprove of the verses for which Your Mercy has found herself so celebrated. . . .

I do not intend with this judgment that Your Mercy alter your natural inclinatios by renouncing Books, but rather that you better them by occasionally reading the book of Jesus Christ. . . . You have spent much time in the study of philosophers and poets; now it would be well for you to improve the quality of the books.)

This is the letter that has long been held responsible for Sor Juana's renunciation. It is quite clear from the letter that the Bishop did not really approve of her secular writings, but it is also clear that he did not ask her to give up her literary labors. All that he asked her to do was to devote herself to religious works. He was himself a lover of learning, and had during his youth written three books of commentary on the Scriptures. He is said to have brought many books for the Colegio de San Pablo in Pueblo. What gave the letter such force was that it was printed along with the *Crisis,* and that in it he asked her to pay less attention to *las rateras noticias del día* (petty news of the day). It amounted to a public censure.[31]

Of the cause and effect of this letter, the biographer of the Bishop writes as follows:

Mother Sor Juana Inés de la Cruz was greatly celebrated here in New Spain . . . both for the abilities and sovereign understanding with which God had gilded her, and for her gift of knowing how to write and compose . . . verses: for this reason she was visited by many people, and of the first ranks: her fame spread like wildfire . . . ; word of it reached our most loving Bishop . . . , and, . . . pained . . . that an individual of such outstanding gifts should be so misguided, and given over to the world, . . . he resolved to write her the letter that follows. . . .

This letter had its desired effect. . . .[32]

More than two years were to elapse, however, before Juana's renunciation. It does not seem possible, then, that this letter was the cause
of the steps she took. It was another sign of the times, however, and a
thorn in the flesh of the brilliant nun.

In March, 1691, Juana wrote an answer to the famous letter. Her
letter is astonishingly frank. One wonders how she dared so reveal her
innermost soul. Her answer could certainly have done nothing to
mend matters.

Meanwhile, the *Crisis* was receiving wide publicity. In 1692 it was
published in Mallorca. In the same year it was reprinted in the second
volume of her works, and in the following year it appeared again in the
second edition of that volume.[33] It was received with great enthusiasm
in Spain. Why did it arouse a storm of criticism in Mexico? Was it
heretical? It was so considered there. In her answer to the Bishop
Juana wrote:

> Si el crimen está en la Carta Athenagórica, ¿fue aquélla más que re-
> ferir sencillamente mi sentir . . . ? . . . ¡Llevar una opinión con-
> traria de Vieyra, fue en mí atrevimiento, y no lo fue en su Paterni-
> dad, llevarla contra los tres Santos Padres de la Iglesia? . . . ni falté
> al decoro, que a tanto varón se debe . . . ; ni toqué a la Sagrada
> Compañía en el pelo de la ropa. . . . Que si creyera se había de pu-
> blicar, no fuera con tanto desaliño como fue. Si es (como dice el
> Censor) herética, ¿por qué no la delata?[34]

> (If the offense is to be found in the Athenagoric Letter, was that
> letter anything other than the simple expression of my feeling . . . ?
> . . . That I proffered an opinion contrary to that of Vieyra—was
> that audacious of me, and was it not so of him to speak against the
> three Holy Fathers of the Church? . . . I maintained at all times the
> respect due such a virtuous man . . . ; I did not touch a thread of
> the robes of the Society of Jesus. . . . Had I believed the letter was
> to be published I would not have been so inattentive. If [as the cen-
> sor says] the letter is heretical, why does he not denounce it?)

We gather from this that it was declared heretical. In Spain, however,
Navarro Vélez, *Calificador del Santo Oficio* (Censor appointed by the
Inquisition), declared that it contained nothing contrary to the faith.[35]
That it was so strongly condemned in Mexico is due to the fact that
conditions there were different. The Jesuits were all powerful. They
were practically in control of the Inquisition. Father Vieyra was a
Jesuit, and it was felt that the *Crisis* was an attack on that order. How
Father Núñez felt about it one can easily guess. Juana had brought her-

self face to face with the Inquisition. At the time she wrote her reply she had not been brought to trial. No record has been found to show that she ever was. It is not likely that the Inquisition would have waited more than two years to do so. It does not seem possible, then, that it was directly responsible for her renunciation.

Did Juana, upon receiving the Bishop's letter, immediately stop writing about secular things? Not at all. Early in 1691 she wrote a *silva* celebrating a victory won by the armada of Barlovento against the French off the coast of Santo Domingo. This was published the same year by Carlos de Sigüenza y Góngora in his *Trofeo de la justicia española* (Trophy of Spanish Justice). In 1692 she was still sending manuscripts abroad for the second edition[36] of the second volume of her works. It seems likely that early in 1692 she was still writing some poetry and collecting it for that volume. Sometime in 1692 or 1693 she also wrote a poem thanking her newly found friends in Spain for the laudatory poems and articles which appeared in her second volume. This poem was never finished, and is probably her last work.

Sor Juana's renunciation took place in 1693.[37] In March, 1691, when she wrote her answer to the Bishop, she was not yet ready for her great sacrifice. She still defended herself vigorously, claiming for herself the right to study. The letter is, in fact, a defense of the rights of women, a memorable document in the history of feminism. In the light of it, her renunciation is even more startling than it would be had the letter never been written. Yet in it she reveals, too, a struggle in which she was as a house divided against herself. What it was and how insidiously it undermined what a lifetime had built up, the following passage will make clear:

> Pues aún falta por referir lo mas arduo de las dificultades; . . . faltan los positivos [estorbos] que directamente han traído a estorbar, y prohibir el ejercicio. ¿Quién no creerá, viendo tan generales aplausos, que he navegado viento en popa, y mar en leche, sobre las palmas de las aclamaciones comunes? Pues Dios sabe que no ha sido muy así, porque entre las flores de esas mismas aclamaciones se han levantado, y despertado tales áspides de emulaciones y persecuciones, cuantas no podré contar, y los que más nocivos y sensibles para mí han sido, no son aquéllos, que con declarado odio y malevolencia me han perseguido, sino los que amándome, y deseando mi bien . . . me han mortificado y atormentado más que los otros, con aquel: *No conviene a la santa ignorancia, que deben, este estudio; se ha de perder, se ha de desvanecer en tanta altura con su mesma perspicacia, y agudeza.*

¿Qué me habrá costado resistir esto? ¡Rara especie de matirio! donde yo era el mártir, y me era el verdugo.

. . . .

todo ha sido acercarme más al fuego de la persecución, al crisol del tormento; y ha sido con tal extremo que han llegado a solicitar que se me prohiba el estudio.

. . . .

. . . fue tan vehemente y poderosa la inclinación a las letras, que ni ajenas reprensiones—que he tenido muchas—, ni propias reflejas—que he hecho no pocas—, han bastado a que deje de seguir este natural impulso que Dios puso en mí: Su Majestad sabe . . . que le he pedido que apague la luz de mi entendimiento dejando sólo lo que baste para guardar su Ley, pues lo demás sobra, según algunos, en una mujer; y aun hay quien diga que daña.[38]

(For still to be related is the most arduous of my difficulties—still unreported are the more directly aimed difficulties that have acted to impede and prevent the exercise of my study. Who would have doubted, having witnessed such general approbation, that I sailed before the wind across calm seas, amid the laurels of widespread acclaim? But our Lord God knows that it has not been so; He knows how from amongst the blossoms of this very acclaim emerged such a number of aroused vipers, hissing their emulation and their persecution, that one could not count them. But the most noxious, those who most deeply wounded me, have not been those who persecuted me with open loathing and malice, but rather those who in loving me and desiring my well-being . . . have mortified and tormented me more than those others, saying *Such studies are not in conformity with sacred innocence; surely she will be lost; surely she will, by cause of her very perspicacity and acuity, grow heady at such exalted heights.* Imagine what it took for me to resist this? A strange sort of martyrdom indeed, in which I was both martyr and executioner!

. . . .

all this has brought me closer to the fire of persecution, to the crucible of torment; and to such lengths that they have even asked that study be forbidden to me.

. . . .

my inclination toward letters has been so vehement, so overpowering, that not even the admonitions of others—and I have suffered many—nor my own meditations—and they have not been few—have been sufficient to cause me to forswear this natural impulse that God placed in me: the Lord knows . . . that I have prayed that He dim the light of my reason, leaving only that which is needed to keep His Law, for there are those who would say that all else is unwanted in a woman, and there are even those who would hold that such knowledge does her injury.)

We gather from this that she was the object of constant persecution, and to such a degree that she began to ask herself if, after all, she was wrong. Should she give up her literary labors and devote herself to the *camino de perfección* (way of perfection)? This was the struggle that was going on in her soul and that reached a climax in 1693. It had probably been going on a long time before it came out into the open with the publication of her works. She must have had many enemies. What she suffered we can but guess. Slowly but surely the criticisms of friends and enemies destroyed her peace of mind. Even so, it is doubtful if Sor Juana would ever have given up her books and studies had not events in Mexico so shaped themselves that she felt upon her an inward compulsion.

It now becomes necessary to take a look at what was happening in Mexico between 1691 and 1693. In the summer of 1691 rains and floods were beginning to cause terrible suffering. A contemporary writes:

> The trials suffered in Mexico during those thirteen days are unimaginable. No one entered the city because the streets and causeways were impassable. There was no coal, firewood, fruit, vegetables, poultry. . . . Grain couldn't grow because of the excess of water . . . and none of the things I have mentioned were to be had, except at the highest prices. . . .
> The high level of Lake Texcoco on July 22 led the fearful to shout that *Mexico was being flooded.*[39]

The crops were ruined and by the end of the year the city was in the grip of a famine. By the beginning of 1692 conditions were so bad that the Viceroy asked that secret prayers be said in convents and monasteries for the relief of the city. Many a day there was no bread. Moreover, the supply of grain in the *alhóndiga* (public granary) was getting low. The populace began to threaten violence, blaming the Viceroy and his government for their sufferings. Finally, on the night of June 8, 1692, the Indians marched upon the viceregal palace and stormed it, setting fire to it and the surrounding buildings. The Viceroy and his wife took refuge in the monastery of St. Francis. Everybody sought monasteries and other places of security. The soldiers were helpless. Hordes of Indians pillaged the plaza and the surrounding neighborhood. Nothing could be done to stop the terrible riot. Bells rang all night. In the nunneries and monasteries prayers were said. Jesuits and

Franciscans went in procession to the plaza in an effort to quiet the rioters, but they were hissed and their images were treated with disrespect. After days and nights of terror, during which the churches ceased to function, the civil government succeeded in restoring order. Weeks and months of *azotados* (whippings) and *ahorcados* (hangings) kept alive the memory of the tumult. Famine continued to take its toll, for there was no bread. Disease followed. Toward the end of the year the *peste* (plague) was general throughout the land. Those were dark days for Mexico. Why had this affliction visited the country? The consensus of opinion was that it was a punishment for the sin, the license and irreligiosity that had reigned in Mexico. Robles says:

> The causes of this havoc are said to be our sins, which God would punish through the instrument of the weakest and most frail, such as the miserable and defenseless Indians, as His Divine Majesty has done in other times, according to divine and human histories. . . . May God look upon us with eyes of compassion! Amen.[40]

Sigüenza y Góngora says, speaking of the floods: "The word among the populace these days regards the storm in the mountains, the destruction of the fields, and the flooding of the outskirts as punishment for recent festivities. . . ."[41] He says, furthermore: ". . . I have no doubt that my sins and everyone else's incited [God] to threaten us like a Father with a whip of water, followed by the punishment of hunger, with little effect on our erring ways. . . ."[42] Another contemporary writes: ". . . though we have so benign a prince for a Viceroy, . . . our sins are so many that his sanctity and zeal have not sufficed to keep us from the punishment of God's justice, such as we are experiencing now."[43]

The tragic events just narrated gave point to the remonstrances addressed to Juana on the score of her failure to walk in the *camino de perfección*. Where she had before stopped to reflect occasionally on her duty in the matter, now, with suffering and death on every hand, her own heart, her own conscience, must have taken a hand. It is not unlikely that she blamed herself somewhat for the sad state of affairs in Mexico. Death was everywhere. It took two of her lifelong friends, Juan de Guevara and Diego de Ribera.[44] It laid a heavy hand on the convent of St. Jerome, where ten nuns died[45] between April 24, 1691, and August 5, 1692. And in September, 1692, news came from Spain of the death of her beloved patron, the Count of Paredes. Life was becoming stern. But it was not too late. She could yet make amends. It is something of this spirit that shines through the fanaticism of the last two years of her life. Stern religious counselors had turned her eyes inward upon herself. Could outward compulsion alone have worked such a change? Does it not bespeak inward conviction? Sor Juana had very much a mind of her own. The Inquisition could have made her give up her books, her instruments, her literary labors, but it could not make her *volar a la perfección* (fly toward perfection). Inner conviction was needed for that.

Does not Juana herself express this in the *Petición que en forma causídica presenta al Tribunal Divino la Madre Juana Inés de la Cruz, por impetrar perdón de sus culpas* (Petition in forensic form presented to the Divine Tribunal by Mother Juana Inés de la Cruz, begging forgiveness for her sins)? In it she says:

> . . . en el pleyto que se sigue en el Tribunal de vuestra Justicia contra mis graves, enormes, y siniguales pecados, de los cuales me hallo convicta por todos los testigos del Cielo y de la Tierra, y por lo alegado por parte del Fiscal del Crimen de mi propia consciencia, en que halla que debo ser condenada a muerte eterna, y que aun esto será usando conmigo de clemencia, por no bastar infinitos Infiernos para mis inumerables crimenes y pecados; . . . reconozco no merezco perdón . . . con todo, conociendo vuestro infinito amor e inmensa misericordia, y que mientras vivo, estoy en tiempo, y que no me han cerrado los términos del poder apelar de la sentencia . . . con todo, por quanto sabéis vos que ha tantos años que yo vivo en religión, no solo sin Religión, sino peor que pudiera un Pagano; . . . es mi voluntad volver a tomar el Hábito, y pasar por el año de aprobacion. . . .[46]

> (. . . in the case by the Tribunal of your Justice against my grave, enormous and unequaled sins, of which I find myself convicted by all the witnesses of Heaven and Earth, and in view of the allegations of my conscience's own Prosecutor, which finds that I be condemned to eternal death, which itself would be an act of clemency, for infinite Hells would not suffice for my innumerable crimes and sins; . . . I recognize that I deserve no forgiveness . . . yet knowing your infinite love and immense mercy, and that as long as I am alive there is time, and that the chance to appeal the sentence is still open to me . . . withal, as God knows, for many years I have lived in religion not only without Religion, but worse than a Pagan might live; . . . it is my will once again to take the veil, and to undergo the year of approbation. . . .)

Undoubtedly force of circumstances joining hands with many parallel influences had brought about a crisis in Juana's life; not one cause, but many, working toward a common end, gradually broke the strong spirit and made her accept the martyr's role.

How did Juana carry out her penitence, for such it was? Oviedo says, speaking of this and of Father Núñez's part in it:

> Mother Juana was alone with her Husband, and . . . love gave her strength to imitate Him, zealously attempting to crucify her passions and appetites with such a fervent severity of penitence that she had need of the prudent care and attention of Father Antonio to take her by the hand, so that her life not end at the hands of her fervor. And Father Antonio used to say, praising God, that Juana Inés was not running but rather flying towards perfection.[47]

Everything she had she sold for the relief of the poor. The same writer says:

> . . . she rid herself of her ample library, only reserving for her own use a few slim devotional works as an aid to her saintly intentions. She also removed from her rooms all the unique and exquisite musical and mathematical instruments she had, as well as any valuable or esteemed jewels given to her in admiring tribute and acclaim by those who celebrated her talents as prodigious; and reduced everything to *reales*, sufficient to relieve and aid many of the poor.[48]

This, too, confirms the theory that the suffering in Mexico had much to do with her renunciation. She was joined in her charitable enterprise by Aguiar y Seixas, who also sold his library for the relief of the poor.

Two years later her penitence reached the heights of the heroic when, during the plague that invaded the convent of St. Jerome, Juana labored night and day nursing the sick, comforting the dying, and laying out the dead. Her fragile spirit, broken by the storms that had beaten about her, gave up the unequal struggle, and she who had once been the object of hatred and jealousy died in the odor of sanctity, revered and loved by all.

NOTES

1. *Juana de Asbaje* (Madrid, 1910), p. 78.
2. *Discurso pronunciado en la velada literaria que consagró el Liceo Hidalgo a la memoria de Sor Juana Inés de la Cruz* (Mexico, 1874), pp. 48–49.

3. For a discussion of this side of the question see Nemesio García Naranjo, "Biografía de Sor Juana Inés de la Cruz," *Anales del Museo Nacional de México, segunda época*, Vol. III, No. 1 (Mexico, 1906):567–68.

4. "Respuesta de la poetisa a la muy ilustre Sor Philotea de la Cruz," *Fama y obras posthumas* (Barcelona, 1701), p. 18. References hereafter will be to this edition. [For the reader's convenience, we have modernized all citations from Sor Juana's works. English versions of citations from the *Respuesta* are adapted from Margaret Sayers Peden's translation, *A Woman of Genius*, cited in the Bibliographical Note—Ed.]

5. Juan de Oviedo, *Vida y virtudes del Venerable Padre Antonio Nuñes de Miranda* (Mexico, 1702), p. 133.

6. Antonio de Robles, "Diario de sucesos notables," *Documentos para la historia de Méjico, primera serie*, Vol. III (Mexico, 1853), under date of July 12, 1668.

7. José Toribio Medina, *Historia del tribunal del Santo Oficio de la Inquisición de México* (Santiago de Chile, 1905), pp. 321–22. Part of this document is unprintable.

8. José Lezamis, *Breve relación de la vida, y muerte del Doctor D. Francisco de Aguiar y Seyxas* (Mexico, 1699). See chapter entitled "De su castidad, mortificación y penitencia."

9. Juan de Oviedo, *Vida y virtudes*, pp. 153–54.

10. Miguel de Torres, *Dechado de príncipes eclesiásticos* (Puebla, 1716), p. 123.

11. Ibid., pp. 124–25, 150. Also see José Gómez de la Parra, *Panegyrico funeral de Manuel Fernández de Santa Cruz* (Puebla, 1699), p. 64.

12. Julián Gutiérrez Dávila, *Vida y virtudes de Domingo Perez de Barcia* (Madrid, 1720), pp. 27–28.

13. Ibid., p. 30.

14. Ibid., p. 31.

15. *Segundo tomo de las obras de Soror Juana Inez de la Cruz* (Sevilla, 1692), Act I.

16. Juan de Oviedo, *Vida y virtudes*, p. 133.

17. Ibid., pp. 134–35.

18. "Aprobación," *Fama y obras pósthumas*.

19. *Fama y obras pósthumas*, p. 18. As for matrimony, it is possible that the Viceroy had already selected a husband for her. This seems to have been the regular procedure, at any rate, and Juana had no reason to suppose that he would not select one in her case. Doña Oliva Merleti, a lady-in-waiting at the court, entered the Capuchin order in preference to marrying a man selected for her by the Marquis of Mancera. See Ignacio de Peña, *Trono mexicano en el convento de Capuchinas* (Madrid, 1726), p. 213.

20. Juan de Oviedo, *Vida y virtudes*, pp. 134, 136.

21. It is impossible to fix the exact date of this rupture. It must have taken place at some time during Juana's greatest worldly activity, i.e., between 1680 and 1690.

22. José Lezamis, *Breve relación*, chapter entitled "De la oración, contemplación, amor de Dios y del próximo del Señor Arçobispo."

23. Gio. Francesco Gemelli Careri, *Giro del mondo, sesta parte* (Naples, 1700), p. 169. He visited Mexico in 1697.

24. Francisco Aguiar y Seixas, *Edicto pastoral sobre los días festivos* (Mexico, 1688).

25. Less than 25 percent of the books printed in Mexico City were secular in character. These figures are based on tables developed from Medina, *La imprenta en*

México (History of Printing in Mexico), for the period between 1682 and 1698. From 1666 to 1682 about 32 percent of the books were secular. These figures are only approximate since Medina is not complete, and beside, some of the material for the period has, undoubtedly, been lost. Of these secular works some were official documents, some were *gacetas* (gazettes), and a few were scholarly works. There was very little of a purely literary character.

26. Emilia Pardo Bazán, "Prólogo," *Vida de la Virgen María según Sor María de Jesús de Agreda* (Barcelona, 1899), p. 7.

27. Antonio de Robles, "Diario," under the date of September 24, 1690.

28. The censorship in Mexico during the seventeenth century has not yet been studied. For methods used during the sixteenth, see Francisco Fernández del Castillo, "Libros y libreros del siglo XVI," *Publicaciones del archivo general de la nación*, Vol. VI (Mexico, 1914).

29. Her refutation was reprinted under the title of "Crisis de un sermón" (Critique of a Sermon) in the second volume of her works.

30. *Fama y obras pósthumas*, pp. 2–4.

31. The signature, "Philotea de la Cruz," is pregnant with meaning. The name itself means "lover of God." The Bishop pretended that the letter was written by a nun of that name in the convent of the Holy Trinity. There may have been a nun of that name. But why did the Bishop choose that name? One of his predecessors in the bishopric of Puebla, the famous Juan de Palafox y Mendoza, published in Madrid in 1659 a book called *Peregrinación de Philotea al santo templo y monte de la Cruz* (Pilgrimage of Philotea to the Holy Temple and Mount of the Cross). He says it was written in imitation of a "Philotea Francesa" because it had seemed to him "not to be a useless imitation, but a spiritual and holy one: that a Spanish Philotea instruct others by showing himself to be a humble follower of the Cross. . . ." The books of Palafox were very popular. It is probable that Fernández de Santa Cruz had this book in mind when he wrote Sor Juana. If so, the significance of the signature could not have been lost upon her.

32. Miguel de Torres, *Dechado*, pp. 416, 421. The 1772 edition says that it was her *estudio de libros profanos* (study of profane works) that called forth the letter.

33. The subject of the *Crisis* was kept alive until 1731, when a defense of Father Vieyra's sermon, written by Sor Margarita Ignacia, a Portuguese nun, was translated into Spanish by Iñigo Rosende in a volume entitled *Vieyra impugnado* (Vieyra Impugned), published in Madrid.

34. *Fama y obras pósthumas*, pp. 50–51.

35. Juan Navarro Vélez, "Censura," *Segundo tomo de las obras de Soror Juana Inés de la Cruz*, Sevilla, 1692.

36. This edition, published in Barcelona in 1693, has on the title page: "añadido en esta segunda impression por su autora" (added by the author for the second printing). It also contains some *villancicos* dated 1691.

37. Both Oviedo and Calleja testify to this. The date can be established by the fact that in February and March, 1694, she signed her *Profesión de la fe* (Profession of Faith) and the *Renovación de los votos religiosos* (Renewal of Religious Vows). To do this she must have served her year as novice. Her *Petición*, undated, says: ". . . es mi voluntad bolver a tomar el Abito, y passar por el año de aprobacion" (it is my will once again to take the veil, and to undergo the year of approbation). This must have been written early in 1693.

38. *Fama y obras pósthumas*, pp. 15, 26–27, 34–35; our emphasis.

39. *Copia de una Carta de don Carlos de Sigüenza y Góngora a don Andrés de Pez acerca de un tumulto acaecido en México* [MS], August 30, 1692.

40. Antonio de Robles, "Diario," p. 97.

41. Letter by Sigüenza y Góngora cited in note 39.

42. Ibid.

43. "Copia de una carta escrita por un religioso grave," *Documentos para la historia de México, segunda serie*, III (Mexico, 1855), p. 311.

44. *Sucesos*, 1676–96 [MS], under date of April 11 and September 7, 1692.

45. *Libro de Prophessiones* (Book of Professions).

46. *Fama y obras pósthumas*, pp. 129–31.

47. Juan de Oviedo, *Vida y virtudes*, p. 137.

48. Ibid.

CHAPTER **3**

Unlike Sor Juana? The Model Nun in the Religious Literature
of Colonial Mexico

ASUNCIÓN LAVRIN

Sor Juana Inés de la Cruz, towering figure of viceregal culture in New Spain, is remembered as a poet, a woman, and a
nun. While she has been subjected to careful scrutiny and evaluation
as a poet and as a woman, her role as a nun has received much less
attention. This is despite the fact that she lived most of her life as a
nun and that, in her own words, her profession gave her the freedom
she wished to devote herself totally to writing. We know that Sor
Juana's choice to live as a nun created a constant tension between the
secular train of life which she still led within the convent and the pre-
scribed discipline of the cloisters. The unrestrained flights of her creative imagination clashed, at critical moments in her life, with the confining boundaries that strict adherence to religious life should have
meant for her. Reflecting on Sor Juana's words, we may question
whether the religious state was indeed appropriate to the purposes for
which she chose it. If it was not designed to give women peace and
quiet to write and learn, what then were the expectations women had
from life as professed nuns, and what was expected from them once
they entered the convent? In what ways was Sor Juana an atypical
nun? In order to answer these questions I propose that we survey the
available colonial literature on and by nuns, such as biographies, auto-

biographies, sermons, pastoral letters, and books of religious instruction and religious meditations, to reconstruct the world of the cloisters in which Sor Juana lived. These sources will help us elicit the norms, attitudes, and values of religious life, and the moral and intellectual forces that were so important to the church and to the persons living within it.

The question of training and vocation for religious life should be discussed first, as it has raised some controversy among historians, and because Sor Juana's own profession remains a controversial subject. Some historians assume that vocation for religious life was not always completely sincere and that families disposed of their unmarriageable daughters by putting them into a convent. Profession, it is claimed, was less expensive than marriage, since it required a smaller dowry. Thus, a family saved money by sending one or several daughters to a nunnery. On both economic and intellectual grounds, this interpretation fails to present a convincing and true-to-the-period picture. The endowment of a nun ranged from two thousand to four thousand pesos in the seventeenth and eighteenth centuries. In addition, profession in most convents involved other expenses, such as clothes, purchase of a cell for the nun, provision of slaves or servants, and possibly an endowment that would provide the nun with an annual sum of money for her living expenses. The number of families who could afford these expenses was relatively small. Pious endowments were created to help some families defray the expenses of their daughters' profession. Sor Juana's own dowry and profession expenses were paid by two benefactors, Don Pedro Velázquez de la Cadena and the Jesuit Antonio Núñez.

Although studies of the mean values of marriage dowries for colonial Mexico are scarce, available information indicates that the dowries of most brides was roughly between one thousand and five thousand pesos.[1] Furthermore, the dowries of many women were often promised but not given at the time of the marriage, while the dowries of nuns were generally deposited in cash and less commonly mortgaged as a lien on a family's properties. With the exception of a number of discalced orders that did not require an endowment, although they took it when offered, profession was not a cheap affair.

On the subject of religious vocation, we must not underestimate the powerful religious character of the sixteenth and seventeenth centuries in Spain and its colonies. Spain produced a large number of distinguished theologians such as Melchor Cano, Francisco de Osuna, Luis de Granada and Domingo de Soto. Among the saints, let us remember Santa Teresa de Jesús, San Juan de la Cruz, San Pedro Alcántara, San

Juan de Avila, San Ignacio de Loyola, and San Francisco de Borja. In Spanish America, Santa Rosa de Lima, Santo Toribio de Mogrovejo, San Martín de Porres, Santa Mariana de Jesús, and the *beato* (lay brother) Sebastián de Aparicio represent the strong currents of spirituality characteristic of the age. From the time of the Catholic Kings, the political unification of Spain had also entailed religious unification and reformation. Both the regular and the secular clergy came under the crown's scrutiny in its drive to create a more dedicated and less corrupt church. The transformation of the regular clergy into a more militant religious body moved by stronger spiritual forces was one of the ecclesiastical landmarks of the sixteenth century. The Society of Jesus, the reformed Carmelite Order of Santa Teresa, and the new Conceptionist Order founded by Beatriz de Silva and approved in 1511 by Julius II are the fruits of this internal revitalization.[2] Later in the century, the Council of Trent (1545–1563) regularized and systematized the behavior of the members of the secular church, giving a clear sense of direction to Roman Catholicism, then facing the challenge of Protestantism.

Another important characteristic of the sixteenth century was its strong drive toward mysticism. This impulse had its roots in the reforms of the Franciscan Order and the flowering of the concept of *recogimiento,* the withdrawal of the self to reach God through mystical contemplation. *Recogimiento* was best expounded by Francisco de Osuna, author of the *Abecedario espiritual* (Spiritual Primer) and other books which became widely read and accepted throughout Spain.[3] Santa Teresa accepted the concept of *recogimiento* as soon as she read Osuna. In Spanish America, a century later, Sor Josefa de la Concepción de Castillo, perhaps the best female mystic writer of the colonial period, mentions Osuna as one of her readings.[4] These are only two examples of the many followers of *recogimiento* in Spain and the overseas possessions. Although *recogimiento* was an important element in mysticism, it was not the only path followed in the sixteenth and seventeenth centuries. San Ignacio de Loyola advocated intense mental prayer blended with an active life in the world. His *Exercises* became one of the staples of devotional activity in the seventeenth and eighteenth centuries and a genre much imitated in this period. The more conservative members of the church continued to adhere to prayer and devotional acts, while the most radical adopted Erasmian and *alumbrado* (illuminist) concepts of receiving God by grace, or by mystical contemplation alone in the case of the *alumbrados,* without any need for devotional works or the mediation of the church. Both before and after the Council of Trent, these two paths were considered heretical, which explains the concern of the church with so-called mystical advocates. The Counterreformation church stressed the role of prayer and spiritual exercises, the cult of the Virgin Mary and saints, and the role of the church as an intermediary between mankind and God. Mysticism and *recogimiento* did not disappear in the seventeenth century. The discalced orders, for example, adopted canons of prayer and austerity with roots in *recogimiento,* and a number of theologians writing in that period followed its tenets. However, there was in that century a return to more classic forms of spirituality, based on concepts such as the need to uproot vices and replace them with virtues through attendance of religious ceremonies (mass, the eucharist, etc.), prayer, and acts of penance and devotion.[5] The blend of these trends is reflected in the works written for and by nuns and in the norms of religious life adopted by convents in the seventeenth and eighteenth centuries, which will be examined later. To ignore this heritage and to deny that it translated itself into the founding of convents and the pursuit of religious life by the many who felt it as a true vocation is to distort and misinterpret the character of the period.

In considering the prevailing religiosity and the formation of a religious vocation, we must also consider the usual education of girls. This was largely confined to a solid indoctrination in the principles of the faith, training in the so-called womanly occupations, and, as an additional although not common ornament, reading and writing. An educated woman who passed beyond mere literacy to the reading of literary or historical texts, or who knew Latin and had some notion of mathematics, was an unusual individual in the sixteenth and seventeenth centuries. Knowledge beyond these narrowly defined parameters was not for women.[6] On the other hand, few boundaries were set to their piety. Thus, while intellectual training was weak, the biographical sources of professed nuns cite early indoctrination by pious parents and the teaching and practice of a religious life from their earliest years. Parents interned their daughters in convents either for their education or simply to have them raised under strict religious orthodoxy. Some parents hoped that their daughters would receive their religious call and follow a religious life, since it carried a considerable degree of social prestige. Father Antonio Núñez, a confessor to Sor Juana and author of several religious tracts, indicated that the purpose of raising a girl in a convent was to make her fall in love with religious life through the living example of the nuns in the community.[7] Exposure to devotional practices at home, or to life within the cloisters, could not fail to produce a natural inclination to it. The religious call that many women felt was a sincere reaction to their religious and educational training.

Several examples of religious upbringing will help illustrate the situation that led many women to profess willingly. The parents of Micaela Josefa de la Purificación, discalced Carmelite in the convent of Puebla, were extremely pious and "raised her in perpetual enclosure, with good examples and healthy advice." As a young girl she would dress in a nun's habit and at age fourteen started seeking profession, practicing discipline and silence and fasting. She professed at age seventeen, in 1669.[8] Sor María Josefa Lino de la Canal, of the rich Canal merchant family, daughter of a Knight of Calatrava, was the founder of the convent of La Concepción in San Miguel Allende. She was under the spiritual guidance of the same confessor from the time she was six until she was thirty-one. He left a testimonial of her life, stating that ever since she was a little girl she lived in a separate room in her home, like a nun in her cell, and that to practice humility she shared the domestic duties of the house's servants.[9] Sor Encarnación de Cárdenas, a Yucatecan, of the distinguished Cárdenas-Escobar family, entered the convent of La Concepción in Mexico City at fourteen as a pupil, professing five years later.[10] Isabel de la Encarnación, a discalced Carmelite in the convent of Puebla, felt a religious vocation from age nine. At that tender age she started exercising herself in acts of spiritual and material penance. She professed in 1606.[11] Mariana de San Miguel, in the words of her biographer, Sor Ana María Josefa de la Purificación, also behaved as a nun since her childhood. She lived apart from the rest of her family, with little personal communication even with her sibling. This was regarded as a rehearsal for the edifying life which she later led in the convent.[12] Sister María de Jesús, a nun in the Conceptionist convent of Puebla, came from the rich Tomellín Campo family. Her mother had been raised in a convent and had left it to marry as an act of obedience to her parents. She raised her daughter in a very religious atmosphere, which accounts for the latter's refusal to obey her father when he attempted to arrange a marriage for her. Defying his will, but with the tacit approval of her mother, María de Jesús professed in 1599.[13] Sor Ignacia Gertrudis de San Pedro, daughter of an employee of the Royal Exchecquer, lived in the convent of Santa Clara in Mexico City from the age of three and a half. Needless to say, at the appropriate time she took the veil.[14] Sor María Magdalena de la Soledad entered the convent of Regina Coeli of Morelia, accompanied by her sister, when she was seven years old. Her biographer adds that

"the good example and virtues of the parents of our Magdalena in-
clined her since childhood to the perfection of the religious state."[15]

Another important factor in the education of women was the influence confessors had over them from their youngest years. Sor María
Inés de los Dolores, born in Puebla in 1659 and blinded at the age of
seven, was placed under the guidance of a confessor shortly after this
accident. She is described as soft wax upon which he impressed his
teaching. At the age of nine she made a vow of chastity, promising to
devote herself solely to God.[16] This is just one example, among many,
of the preeminent role confessors played in shaping and strengthening
the religious vocation of many women, prior to and after profession.[17]

Let us turn to Sor Juana and examine her statements about her
childhood and profession. Sor Juana made it abundantly clear that a
strong religious vocation was lacking in her. What she had was a "vehement" and "overpowering" inclination toward learning, a natural
impulse that neither the admonitions of others nor her own meditations sufficed to restrain. At the age of three this inclination set her on
fire with a desire to learn rather than to engage in religious exercises.
Unlike other professed nuns who ached for a life of retreat, sacrifice,
and complete devotion to God, Sor Juana admitted, after twenty-two
years of religious life, that the "spiritual exercises and company of a
community were repugnant to the freedom and quiet I desired for my
studious endeavors." She professed knowing that life in a convent entailed certain conditions "most repugnant to my nature: but given the
total antipathy I felt for marriage, conventual life was the least unsuitable and most desirable I could elect, given the security of salvation
I desired."[18] She used the term "repugnant" twice over, which should
leave no room for doubt that her profession was more an intellectual
than a religious decision. This profession, however, was an act of her
own will, which she never regretted. Why not? Sor Juana might have
had doubts about living in a community, but these doubts were mostly
egotistic, insofar as she dreaded the thought of being disturbed by
others when she wished to be alone to do what she wanted most to do.
On the other hand, Sor Juana was a devout and sincere believer, who,
like most other people of her times, was deeply concerned with the
salvation of her soul. Conventual life was acceptable because it was
regarded as a secure road to perfection and salvation, and as a Catholic
she was willing to endure those "certain conditions," repugnant as they
might be, in order to save her soul.

Nor should the influence of her confessor, Antonio Núñez, be un-
derestimated. He aided her in making up her mind about profession

and materially helped her to enter the two convents where she tried
religious life before her final profession. Father Núñez's biographer relates that, taking into consideration Sor Juana's beauty, talent, and
charm, Núñez considered that "God could not have visited a greater
scourge upon the Kingdom than allowing Juana Inés to remain in the
limelight of secular life."[19] Some will see a strong misogynist strain in
this statement. Although not denying that indeed there is a significant
degree of misogynism in a theology that wishes to separate outstanding
women from society, in my opinion Father Núñez was also expressing
religious attitudes of the period. For a Jesuit of that century, the combination of so many felicitous virtues in a woman was not a mistake of
nature but a challenge to the church. Such perfection should be devoted to God rather than wasted in secular life. Life as a professed nun
was the most perfect state. The consecrated virgins were God's most
beloved objects. Sor Juana could only do harm to the world from
within it because her assets would allow her to dominate many men.
The dominant woman was not acceptable to seventeenth-century religious thinkers and educators.[20] Within the convent, contained and re-
oriented toward the search for spiritual perfection, Sor Juana would
not only not hurt others but would be able to use her superior abilities
for the highest possible goals. Sor Juana was highly influenced by
Núñez throughout her life. He remained her advisor for many years,
always trying to separate her from secular distractions. Even though he
left her for several years, when she suffered her last spiritual crisis she
called him back. Doubtless, Sor Juana was tied to this man by strong
religious bonds, as were other nuns to their own confessors.

Other professed nuns who entered the convent with untested vocations remained due to a strong will or to the inflence of their spiritual
directors. Sor Mariana Josefa Nepomuceno, the founder of the Capuchine convent of Nuestra Sra. de Guadalupe in Mexico City, was
born in Puebla in 1751. She fell in love with an army officer, who
proved to be married in Spain. Her youthful emotional disappointment
led her to seek admission to the Capuchine convent of San Felipe de
Jesús, despite her mother's opposition. Having professed at age nine-
teen, she suffered numerous "temptations" to leave the convent but
eventually succeeded in overcoming them. Later in life she would help
out in the convent's kitchen to make up for the many nights she had
spent dancing and attending theatrical performances.[21] Throughout
most of her youth it did not occur to Luisa de Santa Catarina, born in
Michoacán in 1682, to become a nun. After the death of her parents,
she administered her inherited properties and refused several marriage

offers. Her decision to become a nun was the direct result of the influence of her confessor, Fr. Juan L. Aguado. She underwent a "horrifying novitiate" and many times thought of leaving the convent, but she never did, eventually becoming reconciled to her state.[22] Anna Antonia de San Buenaventura, a nun in the Dominican convent of Santa Rosa de Lima in Valladolid, was referred to as a proud and less than promising novice. However, under the guidance of a Jesuit confessor, she mended her ways and became a model nun.[23] Doubtless, a poorly defined vocation for religious life—despite intense religiosity—caused these nuns a great deal of mental anxiety. Many such women as those mentioned above populated the nunneries of Mexico and Spanish America. However, to admit the difficulties of religious life for a number of nuns is not the same as stating that most nuns lacked a vocation or the strength to carry out their duties. Sor Juana, despite her confessed lack of vocation, withstood the annoyances involved in communal life and remained in the convent like thousands of others.

One important difference between Sor Juana and others, however, is that the vast majority of nuns at times made heroic efforts to achieve the goals of religious life, and wrote copiously about them. Sor Juana made only minor references in her writings to her experience within the convent, mostly discussing those instances in which she was prevented from carrying out her studies. In order to learn about what constituted life within the cloisters, we must turn to the writings of other nuns, to pastoral letters and books of religious edification.

The essence or model of religious life is difficult to describe, as some convents were stricter than others in their internal discipline, and because certain nuns constantly attempted to exceed the rules in their desire to achieve perfection. Religious life began with the final profession as a nun of black veil. This profession entailed four vows: poverty, chastity, obedience, and enclosure. According to Antonio Núñez, the vows consecrated the nuns totally to God in what he termed "a perfect holocaust."[24] Poverty and obedience meant the renunciation of material possessions and the surrender of personal will to the will of superiors. Enclosure prevented the nun from ever setting foot in the outside world again. Virginity precluded any carnal knowledge, since the bride of Christ had to remain untouched by human sin. Guarded in the garden of God, the nun was supposed to lead a contemplative life devoted to the task of the salvation of her soul through prayer and acts of discipline and obedience. Her prayers could also benefit the souls of others by interceding on their behalf with Christ, God, the Virgin Mary, or the saints.[25] This was the ideal of religious life.

The reality of conventual life in New Spain, as revealed by historical records, shows that the ideal was difficult to achieve. Although most nuns renounced their share in the family's inheritance, this was done in many instances after the allocation of sufficient funds to assure them of a comfortable living in the convent. As institutions, convents did not renounce worldly possessions. Whereas many of them remained relatively modest in their holdings, others eventually accumulated a significant number of properties and liquid capital. Even those convents with relatively small incomes spent large sums of money, donated by patrons, on their buildings and ornaments. Nuns held property in the form of cells, slaves, and clothes. They drank enormous amounts of chocolate and even kept their own cooks. In the seventeenth century, some convents allowed nuns to introduce ornate habits in rich fabrics. The celebration of religious feasts with special receptions for visitors such as friends and members of the family, were not unusual in Sor Juana's times. Thus, when she received members of the viceregal court or her friend Sigüenza y Góngora in the convent, she was following a common practice of her times, if an irregular one according to the strict interpretation of the rules of most orders.[26]

Obedience was put to the test on numerous occasions when the nuns challenged orders from their superiors or fought with each other.[27] The vow of chastity was also put to the test as nuns were subjected to numerous temptations in the form of advances from unscrupulous confessors or lay male friends. Even though the recorded incidence of amorous involvement is notably low, personal internal struggle against the so-called temptations of the flesh was experienced and described by many nuns, or by their confessors, who considered them acts of the devil to try the nuns' vocations. Visions of lewd young men or of lascivious infernal figures tormented even some of the most devout nuns.[28]

These failures in carrying out the ideal religious life were to be expected and regarded as natural, given the fact that human affairs were, after all, imperfect in essence. Thus, the struggle for perfection was one of the purposes of religious life. Physical and spiritual discipline, prayer, meditation, self-effacement, and the constant restraining of human desires were some of the means to achieve perfection within the religious state. According to Father Núñez's advice, the most important duties of a nun were the fulfillment of her vows and of the rules of her religious order, the practice of her daily prayers (which he called the hands and feet of souls), and attending to all community acts, since they facilitated the achievement of perfection in her state. In his words, to achieve her religious goals the nun had to wage a constant war against herself as a fallible human being. Like many other spiritual directors, he envisioned religious life as a trying experience, calling it "a perpetual cross, a continuous martyrdom of the soul and the body."[29]

Archbishop Lanciego y Eguilaz (1712–28), in a *Carta pastoral a sus amadas hijas* (Pastoral Letter to his Beloved Daughters) printed in 1716, recommended prayer as the food of the soul and, in addition, the subjection of all passions and the watchful restraint of the senses. Religious profession, in his words, was undertaken by the nun to communicate with God and to consecrate herself to Him. Only through continuous religious exercises could a nun achieve perfection.[30] Nearly a hundred years later, in 1804, Sor María Vicenta de la Encarnación wrote a play for the profession of a sister in religion. Its symbolic actors were the Devil, the Flesh, the World, Religion, Patience, Vocation, Constancy, Perseverance, Christ, and his bride, the nun.[31] The Devil commissions the World to tempt the novice; Christ supports her, calling on Vocation and Perseverance, but to test the love of His promised bride, He allows the Devil to tempt her. After continuous harassment Religion protects the novice from the attack of the enemies of Christ as she reappears and promises to relieve the novice from the fatigues of the battle by consecrating her as one of her brides. This elegant small piece carried the message that religious life involved a continuous struggle, testing the mettle of the nun's vocation. The message had changed little throughout the colonial period.

The struggle for perfection, the leitmotif of religious life, took place within the individual nun, and it was supposed to remain within her. Outwardly she should be humble, meek, and self-effacing. Sor María Petra de la Trinidad, a Capuchine in the convent of San José de Gracia, Querétaro, was once found in the farthest corner of the convent's vegetable garden, where she lay covered with branches and leaves, persuaded "with saintly sincerity, that she would become a worm."[32] This kind of debasement of the self is missing in Sor Juana. The adulation of the most notable men of her time, and of the members of the viceregal court, could hardly have kindled a sense of humility in her. Rhetorical disclaimers of her own worthlessness aside, she was well aware of her intellectual capacity, and only under great duress did she suffer orders from her own superiors to suppress her writings or change their character. Only after she underwent her final spiritual transformation in 1693 do we find in her writings expressions of personal humiliation which bear strong resemblance to those found in the works of other nuns. Thus, we read in the *Petición causídica* (Forensic Petition): "Juana Inés de la Cruz, the most unworthy and ungrateful creature of all created by Your Omnipotence . . ."[33] She also asked to have the following phrase written in the book in which her death would be recorded: "I have been the worst one. I beg the forgiveness of all my sisters, for the love of God and His mother. I, the worst one in the world, Juana Inés de la Cruz."[34] Sor Juana had started to write like a model nun. Even if we follow Ezequiel Chávez in believing that these writings were not really authored by Sor Juana but simply signed by her, in carrying out this act she joined the company of the typical female religious writers of the seventeenth century.[35]

Suffused with the melancholic character of the struggle against the weakness of the self and the temptations of the world and the devil, the writings of colonial nuns are often joyless narratives of souls in a perennial state of spiritual siege. They fight back with discipline and prayers, but the sense of despondency is overwhelming. One of the best examples of this kind of literature is the work of Sor Sebastiana Josefa de la Santísima Trinidad, a Franciscan nun (d. 1757) in the convent of San Juan de la Penitencia, Mexico, who left a little-known collection of unpublished letters and poems. She is depicted by her biographer as an example of chastity, docility, and religiosity, and her letters offer the somber picture of a person who is far from finding inner peace.[36] She describes herself as unworthy of her confessor's spiritual care, expressing constant doubts about herself: "I am untrustworthy, the way I see myself, I would like to take my own life because I cannot tolerate the violence of my fearless surrender to my own appetites: all is lost. I do not know what could free me from myself." Torn between her desire for perfection and her own perceived imperfection, she was overwhelmed by a constant sense of guilt: "Nothing can console me. I cry helplessly because I cannot bear this any longer; but concealing the grief in which I live, I attend Choir. At times it is hard to stop my tears, but if this is the will of God, may He give me comfort and expand my oppressed heart, for my chest is bursting from holding it all in."[37]

One of her poems expresses a consuming desolation, in a style strongly resembling that of Santa Teresa, although lacking her masterly touch:

Qué alivio puede caber
En quien vive padeciendo
Si el remedio de mis males
Lo tendrán sólo muriendo
. . . .
Sácame de aquesta muerte,

Mi Dios, y dame la vida
No me tengas impedida
En este lazo tan fuerte
Mira que peno por verte,
Y mi mal es tan entero
Que muero porque no muero.[38]

(What relief may be given to one who lives suffering? The remedy to my afflictions will be found only in death. . . . Relieve me from this death my God, and grant me life. Do not constrain me in these tight bonds. Know that I crave the sight of you. And my suffering is so total that I die because I do not die.)

Other nuns have left poems written in a similar vein. For example, a poem quoted by the biographer of Sor María Ignacia de los Dolores, who lived with a professed sister in the convent of San Lorenzo, Mexico, reads as follows:

Tristezas, penas, dolores,
Y todo lo que me envías
Que lo merezco, y es nada,
como tu gracia me asista
. . . .
Que si padezco en tu gracia,
El tormento es alegría:
Y sin ella los consuelos
Son abismos de desdicha.[39]

(Sadness, suffering, pain; and whatever you send me, I deserve, and it is nothing if your grace assists me. . . . If I suffer in your grace, the torment becomes joy; without it, all consolation becomes an abyss of misery.)

Sor María de Santa Clara, in a book of spiritual exercises written for other nuns, tersely summarizes the spirit nurturing these sorrowful experiences: "If the Husband is surrounded by offenses, the Bride should not be surrounded by laughter. Religious life is undertaken to assume the sufferings of the Husband."[40]

Not all nuns wrote of tormenting experiences all the time. Some seemed to have achieved a serene enjoyment of life through religion at some points in their lives. Among these are Sor María Marcela, a Capuchine nun in Querétaro, and Sor María Agueda de San Ignacio, of the Dominican convent of Santa Rosa de Santa María in Puebla, both of whom lived in the eighteenth century. Sor María Marcela's autobiography remains in manuscript form. She professed in the wake of an unhappy courtship, and after a difficult novitiate she seemed to have encountered rest and peace in her religious life. The serene tones of her writings contrast strongly with the anguished expressions of Sor Sebastiana Josefa de la Santísima Trinidad and are closer to mysticism than to asceticism. The change in her life is described as follows:

> All my illness ceased naturally, without medicine. . . . All became quiet, tranquility, enjoyment, as when one returns weary from a trip full of risks, hunger, exhaustion and calamities, and arriving at her own cherished country, rests, and enjoys her most beloved possession.[41]

The cloisters did not strike her as a prison but rather as "a palace and wide meadow where the soul and the heart may expand themselves, full of such consolation that the soul feels like a rock in its element." There is an almost Franciscan spirit in some of her expressions: "I found my God within myself. I found Him in all creatures. Everything that I saw led me to God: flowers, trees, fruits, water, the Sun. . . . The flights of the soul were continuous."[42]

Sor María Agueda de San Ignacio is a relatively neglected figure in the religious literature of colonial Mexico. During her lifetime she received some recognition, as her works were printed at the expense of the Bishop of Puebla, Pantaleón Alvarez de Abreu. Four titles form the core of her work: *Leyes del amor divino* (Laws of Divine Love), *Maravillas del amor divino* (Marvels of Divine Love), *Devociones* (Devotions) and *Ejercicios* (Exercises).[43] A dual character of asceticism and delicate mysticism is found in her works. She does not linger solely on the intimate and personal experience of the search for God—in that sense she is not a total mystic. She was under the direction of a Jesuit confessor, and her writings bear more resemblance to the exercise genre than to *recogimiento* expression. She dwells on such themes as the imitation of Christ, the cult of the Passion of Christ, and the cult of Mary. The latter is best expressed in *Maravillas del amor divino* in which Mary is presented as the intercessor for sinners. Mary provides the milk of her special knowledge and love, in which humankind would find prudence and hope. Through her we all know Christ. The *Leyes del amor divino* were those that nuns, as brides of Christ, should follow to be more pleasing to Him and to achieve final union with Him. Through prayer and the contemplation of God the soul reaches the unitive state. Writing of the complete attention that nuns should devote to Christ, the third law of divine love, she says:

> Thus, the loving wife who does not leave the sight of her beloved is reborn into a new life of grace, and grows so much in it that she comes to enjoy a unitive Presence with God, which is an admirable thing, and a very particular grace; she may even attain total transformation.[44]

All the laws of divine love have the ultimate aim of achieving a mystical union with Christ, which María Agueda describes as follows:

> The soul finds itself as if free of its passions, and without impediment joins its beloved. Thus, not only the soul feels this divine union but also the body feels that it is possessed by the beloved. . . . Everything seems like fire in the fire. . . . The inflamed will loves without knowing how, because it is led by God himself, and in Him it is living transformed, but not by itself; it lives, but not its own life; it lives the life of the beloved. And it may well be said, as in Saint Paul: "I live, but not by myself, for I live in Christ."[45]

Thus, even though her work is largely concerned with exercises, measures, and rules, her ultimate goal, in spirit and expression, is mystical.

To understand the nuns' writings we must place them within the context of classical and Spanish spirituality. Since Saint Augustine, theologians and mystics have described the different stages of the human ascent to God. The classic interpretation of this ascent was through *vías* (paths): the purgative, illuminative, and unitive, expressed through vocal, intellectual, and affective prayer. The soul must divest itself of worldly cares (purgative) in order to achieve knowledge of God (illuminative) and reach final union with Him (unitive). These paths or stages did not have to be experienced in succession; they could be felt at different times or in different manners throughout life, although the movement of ascent—or, as others put it, inward descent to the core of the soul—was essential to reach the ultimate goal.[46] Melquíades Andrés suggests that Spanish writers of the sixteenth and seventeenth centuries emphasized the "austerity and perfection and nakedness of the spirit" in order to rid the soul of its worldly needs. He adds that internal and external mortification, and the search for perfection are characteristic of Spanish culture in the sixteenth century.[47]

It is obvious that seventeenth and even eighteenth-century feminine religious literature was deeply influenced by sixteenth-century spirituality, either through confessional advice or the nun's own reading. Within this context, the themes of the road to perfection, and of humility, poverty, obedience, chastity, mortification, and the rest, which appear in writings by or for nuns, become easily understandable.

In addition to those cited here, many other nuns engaged in writing during the colonial period. Sor Juana did not emerge from a vacuum. Writing was a common enough activity within the cloisters. However, prior to Sor Juana, none of the works of these women seems to have been published or to have received much public attention. Nor has their character or number made any impact on the literary and intellectual history of New Spain, although they could constitute a significant source of information on the religious mentality of the age and the feminine religious experience. Some of these works were written at the instigation of the nuns' confessors, and this confessional character has apparently condemned them to oblivion. In their times they were regarded as a means of refining the self and ultimately achieving its perfection, but not as literary pieces. Nuns were not supposed to write for pleasure. Even so, the variety of these works is surprising: autobiographies, biographies, histories of convents, plays, poetry, and personal letters. Most remain in manuscript in the archives of Mexico and Spain; others have been lost forever and are known only through excerpts or references in other works. For example, on returning to Spain Bishop Juan de Palafox (Puebla) took with him a copy of Sor Agustina de Santa Teresa's biography of Sor María de Jesús, of the convent of La Concepción in Puebla, which he never published. The eventual biographer of Sor María de Jesús, Br. Francisco Pardo, chaplain of the cathedral church of Puebla, knew this work, but called the author "una pobrecita iletrada y humilde religiosa" (a poor unlettered and humble religious).[48] One of the first nuns to profess in the Carmelite convent of Puebla, Sor Melchora de la Asunción, was apparently a very talented woman. After professing she assumed the expected humility of her state and "dio en encubrir su talento, haciéndose simple" (tried to hide her talent and to appear as a simpleton). Her confessor, however, forbade her to cover up her abilities, with the argument that the Carmelite Order needed her talents. As gifts of God, those abilities would be used in His service. She was described as wise and discreet; she engaged in correspondence with the order in Spain to learn more about matters of religion, on which topic she was consulted by many persons. The Carmelite Fathers considered her one of the "best talents of

Spain."[49] Whether this statement is an exaggeration we may never know, as not a single piece of her writings or her letters has yet been discovered. Thus, either through self-imposed religious humility or through the snobbish disregard of male religious authorities, the work of many nuns remains ignored or forgotten.

Within that context we can appreciate how fortunate we are that Sor Juana did not start her life as a writer within a convent but rather under lay patronage of the highest caliber. Even though some of her purely religious works do not differ significantly in content and purpose from most of the works written by other nuns, some key religious elements are missing. Her *Villancicos*, written on request for special religious celebrations, such as the consecration of the church of the convent of San Bernardo (1690) or for the feast of San Pedro Apóstol, are light and happy works, suited to musical expression and devoid of any theological complexities. Most of them praise Mary—he may be added to the list of cultivators of the Marian cult—the Queen, the beautiful, the favorite of God. *El Divino Narciso* (The Divine Narcissus) is a delightful pastoral allegory on the triumph of Christ through the redemption of humankind. The *Loas* are straightforward intellectual exercises in composing poetry on religious themes, quite similar in technique to those written for secular purposes. The *Ofrecimientos para el Santo Rosario de Quince Misterios* (Offerings for the Holy Rosary of Fifteen Mysteries) and the *Ejercicios devotos* (Devotional Exercises) for the nine days before the feast of the Incarnation, are Sor Juana's most religious and thus most exceptional works, and not often commented upon.[50] In the *Ejercicios* Sor Juana extols the qualities of the Virgin Mary, destined to be the mother of Christ, and pure since her own creation. A meditation for each day is followed by an offering to Mary and a request for her protection. It ends with the prescription of specific exercises, such as prayer and a pious resolution for every day. The *Ofrecimientos* are litanies for Mary and her suffering as she saw Christ being crucified and buried, and requests for her guidance and protection.

In these works Sor Juana came closer to what was expected from her as a nun. They were more unconditionally pious and devotional than anything else she wrote. These probably were the type of writings that Antonio Núñez and Bishop Fernández de Santa Cruz would have liked Sor Juana to write more often. However, one misses in them the clever theological analysis of the *Carta atenagórica* (Athenagoric Letter), which brought her condemnation from the bishop, and in the end we must conclude that although they meet the demands of formalized religion and are a serviceable aid to others in the road of perfection, they are not original in either purpose or execution.

Reminded as we are by these works that Sor Juana is a devout Catholic and a professed nun, there are still elements in the religious works produced by other nuns—or about them—that are missing from her writings and set her apart from them. Sor Juana never experienced visions or supernatural events or the "mystical" experiences that abound in the religious literature of the seventeenth and eighteenth centuries. In contrast, a typical nun, such as María Petra Trinidad, had numerous ecstasies and was supposed to have forecast her own death. As miraculous acts resulting from her faith, Sor Agustina Nicolasa María de los Dolores, abbess of the Capuchine convent of San Felipe de Jesús in Mexico, predicted the death of several persons, had visions of the Virgin, and several times found the cupboard of the convent replenished. Isabel de la Encarnación had numerous visions of demons who constantly tortured and tempted her. María de San José, founder of the Augustinian convents of Santa Mónica of Puebla and Oaxaca, also had numerous visions of the devil, as well as of the Virgin, prior to and after her profession. Fray Agustín de Vetancurt, in his *Melologio*, biographies of Franciscan monks and nuns written at the end of the seventeenth century, candidly narrates the innumerable miracles of some of the nuns cited in his work.[51] Even Carlos de Sigüenza y Góngora in his history of the convent of Jesús María, *Parayso occidental* (Occidental Paradise), concedes the apparition of the devil under different guises and the state of ecstasy reached by many nuns of that institution.[52] María de Jesús, nun of La Concepción in Puebla, had visions from the time she was a little girl and acquired the stigmata during one of her ecstasies. She was also credited with being transported to other lands of gentiles and pagans and with mystical travels to Ethiopia, Spain, and France.[53] These are typical expressions of seventeenth-century religiosity, and we need not accept them as verifiable to note that a nun who not once bothered to mention such circumstances in her writings must have been quite atypical.

Another element missing in Sor Juana's writings are narrative acts of penance and purification. Rigorous disciplines for the punishment of the flesh, described in meticulous detail, are hardly ever absent from the biographies of colonial nuns. The aim of penitence was the subjection of the flesh to the spirit or, in other instances, the imitation of the sufferings of Christ. Juan Benito Díaz de Gamarra y Dávalos, biographer of Sor Josefa María Lino de la Santísima Trinidad, while refusing to mention any "miracles" in the life of his subject, spared few details in the description of her discipline and her sicknesses. He explained that penance was the just reward for sinning: "The virtue of penance is a sincere rejection of sin and a strong desire to punish it and repair the injury made to God."[54] Without this kind of mortification nuns could not preserve the purity of their state. The imperfections of the human condition had to be fought and eliminated. Fasting, putting bitter substances in food, eating leftovers or only bread and water, wearing metal instruments that tore the flesh, beatings with ropes, and punishment by other nuns were all daily occurrences in the cloisters. Sister María Agueda de San Ignacio, the author mentioned above, used pliers to pinch the delicate parts of her body in penance. Once, carried away by fervor, she twisted the pliers so hard that she removed a piece of flesh from her arm. Others, like Sor María Leocadia of the Capuchine convent of Puebla, ulcerated their bodies wearing *cilicios* (hair shirts).[55] To be sure, not all spiritual directors approved of such excesses. Antonio Núñez wrote against the immoderate use of *cilicios* or instruments of mortification, since "notable manglings" could also be construed as acts of pride: "Solid virtues do not consist in extraordinary discomforts, wakes, *cilicios*, and other penitences." Yet he only criticized the excesses. He assumed that suffering was an intrinsic part of religious life. One of his maxims was: "A painless virtue does not count; the more it torments me, the more I appreciate it."[56] Perhaps not every nun practiced such excesses, but the fact that they were cited as examples for the edification of Christian women obliges us to conclude that they were essential to the religious pathos and imagery of the period.

Abstention, mortification, renunciation, and *humiliation* are all key words in the religious vocabulary of the colonial period. They point to the total loss of personal will and the obliteration of the self in Christ and God. A preacher thus summed up the aim of religious life for a nun in 1803: "Not to reflect except upon not examining; not to think except upon not inquiring . . . all the nun's discretion and prudence should consist in not possessing any."[57] He went on to state that reason should only be exercised by the nun to approve orders she received: "The lights of reason should serve to obscure one's own judgment. This means to leave everything for God: reason and will, desire and thought."[58] Archbishop Núñez de Haro (1771–1800), had the following advice for the nuns of his archbishopric: "Try to be humble, chaste and complaisant, amiable, charitable and disinterested. In these virtues resides the perfection to which you should aspire, and they suffice to reach a high degree of sanctity." The nun should say to herself: "The more I debase myself, the more I see myself despised, the less I seek the applause the world esteems, the more I will resemble Jesus my Savior, my Supreme King . . . my adored Husband. I will suffer forgetfulness and spite with joy. I will thus free myself from self-esteem and vanity, which have obliged me to do and say so many things alien to my profession."[59] For the last word, let us return to Sor Juana's confessor, Antonio Núñez, who advised his pupils "to cut the adornments of talent with the knife of mortification."[60]

Against this background, is it very difficult to understand the constant criticism and pressure under which Sor Juana lived on account of her talent and her writings? Consider that Sor Juana's greatest pride were her intellectual gifts and that the main theme of the *Respuesta a Sor Filotea de la Cruz* (Response to Sor Filotea de la Cruz) was the defense of her right to learn, to judge, and to think for herself. It is also easy to see that she was besieged after the publication of the *Carta atenagórica*—but not why she surrendered and reverted to a life patterned after the models discussed here. In 1693, as a result of a religious crisis that no biographer has managed adequately to explain, she recalled Fr. Antonio Núñez, who at that point claimed the final victory. He began to redirect her. Sor Juana became humble and pious. She presumably rediscovered how to be "alone with her Husband, and considering Him nailed to the cross for the sins of men, her love gave her strength to imitate Him, zealously attempting to crucify her passions and her appetites with such fervent severity in the penitence, that she needed the prudent care and attention of Father Antonio, to take her by the hand, so that her life not end at the hands of her fervor. And Father Núñez used to say, praising God, that Juana Inés was not running, but rather flying to perfection."[61]

Was Sor Juana a typical or an atypical nun? She was both at different times in her life. She did not seem to have had an overpowering vocation for religious life, but she was a dutiful nun who complied with the daily routine, performed the conventual assignments to which she was appointed, obeyed her superiors, and befriended her sisters in religion. She was not typical insofar as she failed to engage in the practice of the ascetic rigors that seemed to have been so common among certain orders. And yet, during the last years of her life, she seemed to have lived as the typical nun of religious literature, in a self-holocaust of humility and penitence. Did she surrender or did she find her ultimate vocation through her faith, as had others before her? This question will undoubtedly elicit several contradictory answers, but there is no doubt in my mind that the "model nun" overpowered the exceptional genius in the last years of her life. However, the Sor Juana who is best known and most remembered is the atypical nun: the one who would not write solely on religious topics but would let herself speak with many voices; the one who would challenge long-held attitudes on women's behavior with the power of her logic; the one who would allow her mind the total freedom of its own inquisitiveness.

NOTES

Hagiography, the lives of saints, *beatos,* and so on, is a much neglected historical-literary genre which could provide much factual information on the lives of persons in religious institutions and the religious life of many seculars deeply committed to the church. The mingling of fact and fancy, of usable historical data with less reliable information such as revelation and ecstasies, has discouraged many historians from utilizing these sources. This is regrettable, since even the nonfactual material could help determine religious beliefs and religious imagery. Psychohistorians and *mentalité* historians could also find much material of interest in these works. It is also important to point out that even at the time of their writing, hagiographic works were not uncritically accepted by the Catholic church itself, which subjected claims of beatitude and sanctity to close scrutiny and enforced a rule whereby books on saints, *beatos* or simply pious individuals, had to print a disclaimer stating that the facts related therein lacked the final authentication of the church. Pope Urban VII issued several dispatches (dated March 13, 1625; July 5, 1631; and July 5, 1634) that obliged all biographers of religious persons to disclaim support of any author's assumption of sanctity or divine intervention until and unless it was backed by the church. The material printed had to be understood as an example of virtue for the faithful. An example of such a *Protesta* reads as follows: "I protest that none of the things of which I write have infallible authority, but are based on the faith of the human authorities who wrote about them . . . and I also declare that any cult-sounding word such as Saint, Blessed, or Martyr . . . does not apply to the persons, but emanates from customs and opinions, and should not be assumed to have a rigorous meaning." See Fr. Agustín de Vetancurt, *Teatro mexicano,* 4 vols. (Madrid: José Porrúa Turanzas, 1941), Vol. IV, pp. 4–5. This work was originally written in the seventeenth century.

1. Asunción Lavrin and Edith Couturier, "Dowries and Wills: A View of Women's Socioeconomic Role in Guadalajara and Puebla, 1640–1790," *Hispanic American Historical Review* 59, 2 (May 1979): 280–84.

2. Antonio Domínguez Ortiz, *The Golden Age of Spain, 1516–1659* (New York: Basic Books, 1971), pp. 199–228; John Elliott, *Imperial Spain, 1469–1716* (New York: St. Martin's Press, 1964), pp. 87–99; Tacisio de Azcona, O.F.M., *La elección y reforma del episcopado español en tiempos de los Reyes Católicos* (Madrid:

Consejo Superior de Investigaciones Científicas, Instituto "P. Enrique Flores," 1960); Josefina Muriel, *Conventos de monjas en Nueva España* (Mexico: Editorial Santiago, 1946), pp. 16–17.

3. Melquíades Andrés, *Los recogidos: Nueva visión de la mística española, 1500–1700* (Madrid: Fundación Universitaria Española, 1976); Francisco de Osuna, *Tercer abecedario espiritual* (Madrid: La Editorial Católica, 1972).

4. Francisco de Osuna, *Tercer abecedario espiritual;* Estudio histórico by Melquíades Andrés, p. 58; Sor Josefa de la Concepción de Castillo, *Obras completas,* 2 vols. (Bogotá: Talleres Gráficos del Banco de la República, 1968), Vol. I, *Su Vida,* cap. 22, p. 75.

Sor María Petra de Trinidad, a lay nun at the Capuchine convent of San José de Gracia in Querétaro, wrote some spiritual works that are only known through excerpts quoted by her confessor and biographer. The following passage on prayer indicates the influence of *recogimiento:* ". . . for then the soul begins to withdraw and to enter so gentle a state of calm that I can't find the words to explain what I feel. And this state of calm makes my body so weary and faint that I know the moment is near. It presses me to such a degree that my senses are suspended . . . I need only raise my eyes to the sky, see a flower, or something similar, to place myself in God's presence." See José Ignacio de Cabrera, *Gloriosa exaltación de la mystica piedra maravilla: Sermón fúnebre . . . en las honras de la R.M. Soror María Petra Trinidad, religiosa lega del convento de Señor San José de Gracia y Pobres Capuchinas de la ciudad de Santiago de Querétaro* (Mexico: Imprenta de la Biblioteca Mexicana, 1762), pp. 25–26.

5. Melquíades Andrés, *Los recogidos,* pp. 21–56.

6. To illustrate the negative attitude women's education elicited even among intellectuals, let us quote the opinion of Dr. Juan Huarte de San Juan, author of a widely read work, *Examen de ingenios,* first published in Baeza in 1575, and which by 1582 had already been translated into Italian and French. Huarte was a doctor, and he examined the nature of the human intellect in this work. On women he had the following to say: "Females, due the frigidity and humidity of their sex cannot reach a great depth of talent [*ingenio*]. We see them talking with some appearance of ability on easy and light subjects, with well-studied and common terminology. But, if they go further into letters, they cannot learn more than a little Latin, and this being the work of memory. It is not they who are to be blamed for this lack of intelligence [*rudeza*], but the coldness and humidity that made them women; those qualities, as we have already proved, contradict talent and ability." Their destiny was to be mothers, and nobody doubted that. See Alvaro Huerga, *Historia de los alumbrados,* 2 vols. (Madrid: Fundación Universitaria Española, Seminario Cisneros, 1978), Vol. II, p. 360.

7. Antonio Núñez, *Cartilla de la doctrina religiosa* (Mexico, 1708), p. 1.

8. Antonio de Miqueorena, *Vida de la V.M. Josefa de la Purificación* (Puebla, 1755).

9. Juan Benito Díaz de Gamarra y Dávalos, *Vida de la R.M. Sor María Josefa Lino de la Santísima Trinidad, fundadora del convento de la Purísima Concepción de San Miguel de Allende, obispado de Michoacán* (Mexico: Imprenta de Alejandro Valdés, 1831).

10. Francisco de Sosa, *Biografía de mexicanos distinguidos* (Mexico: Oficina Tipográfica de Fomento, 1884), p. 202.

11. Pedro Salmerón, *Vida de la Venerable Madre Isabel de la Encarnación, Carmelita Descalza* . . . (Mexico: Francisco Rodríguez Lupercio, 1675).

12. Ana María Josefa de la Purificación, *La obligación de nuestra hermandad* . . . (Mexico, 1797).

13. Francisco Pardo, *Vida y virtudes heroycas de la Madre María de Jesús, religiosa profesa en el convento de la Limpia Concepción de* . . . *N. Señora de la Ciudad de los Angeles* (Mexico: Viuda de Bernardo Calderón, 1676).

14. Nicolás de Jesús María, *El Christo A B C de la virtud y cartilla de la santidad. Sermón panegírico en la solemne profesión* . . . *de* . . . *la M. Ignacia Gertrudis de San Pedro* (Mexico, 1726). See also Fr. Joseph de la Vega, *Oración espiritual a Sor María, novicia de 5 años en el religioso convento de San Felipe de Jesús de religiosas capuchinas de esta ciudad de México* (Mexico, 1691). This nun visited the convent from the time she was three. Once, after a temper tantrum upon refusing to leave, she was allowed to stay. At age five she started wearing the habit of a novice, professing fourteen years later, when she came of age to do so.

15. Fr. Diego Díaz, *Sermón solemne en la profesión de la madre María Magdalena de la Soledad* . . . *en el convento de Nuestra Señora de la Concepción, Regina Coeli de Antequera* (Mexico, 1694). Other examples of early and decided vocation are available. Agustina Nicolasa María de los Dolores professed in the discalced Capuchines of Mexico City in 1705. This novice was heiress to a dowry estimated at one hundred thousand *doblones*. Her parents opposed her decision, but Bishop Ortega y Montañez lent Agustina Nicolasa his support and persuaded her parents to allow her to profess. See Joaquina María Zavaleta, *Copia de la carta escrita sobre las virtudes de la M.R.M. Agustina Nicolasa María de los Dolores, abadesa de dicho monasterio* (Mexico: Imprenta Nueva de la Biblioteca Mexicana, 1755). See also Fr. Miguel de Torres, *Vida ejemplar y muerte preciosa de la Madre Bárbara Josepha de San Francisco* (Mexico, 1721). This woman professed after becoming a widow, but she had been under the direction of a confessor since age six and had lived a very cloistered existence within her own house before professing: José María Gómez y Villaseñor, *Sermón predicado el día 3 de marzo de 1803, en la solemne profesión de religiosa de coro* . . . *de Sor María Manuela de la Presentación* (Guadalajara, 1803).

16. Juan Antonio de Mora, *Admirable vida y virtudes de la Venerable Madre Sor María Inés de los Dolores* (Mexico, 1729).

17. Another excellent example is that of Sor Luisa de Santa Catarina, who was under the influence of Fr. Juan L. Aguado. See José A. Ponce de León, *La Azucena entre espinas: Vida y virtudes de la V. Madre Luisa de Santa Catarina* (Mexico, 1750); José María Munibe, *Carta edificante que descubre la vida religiosa y ejemplares virtudes de la R.M. Inés Josefa del Sagrado Corazón de Jesús* (Mexico, 1805). The confessor helped this young woman rescind a marriage vow, ordered her to make a vow of chastity, and authorized her to take discipline regularly.

18. "[A]l desembarazo y quietud que pedía mi estudiosa intención eran repugnantes los ejercicios y compañía de una comunidad" and "muchas repugnantes a mi genio, con todo, para la total negación que tenía al matrimonio, era lo menos desproporcionado y lo más decente que podía elegir en materia de la seguridad que deseaba de mi salvación. . . ." *Respuesta a Sor Filotea de la Cruz*, Vol. 4, *Obras completas*, ed. by Alfonso Méndez Plancarte and Alberto G. Salceda (Mexico: Fondo de Cultura Económica, 1957), pp. 445, 446. English version from Margaret Sayers Peden's translation, *A Woman of Genius* (Salisbury, Conn.: Lime Rock Press, 1982), pp. 41, 49.

19. P. Diego Calleja, S.J., *Vida de Sor Juana* (Mexico: Antigua Librería Robredo, 1936), p. 50. The citation is from P. Juan de Oviedo, S.J., *Vida del P. Antonio Núñez de Miranda, S.J.* (Mexico, 1702), cap. V. Early in the sixteenth century, Cardinal Cisneros, one of the first reformers of the church, had stated the need to place "humanistic studies in the service of religion." See Elliott, *Imperial Spain*, p. 94.

20. Asunción Lavrin, "In Search of the Colonial Woman in Mexico: The Seventeenth and Eighteenth Centuries," in Asunción Lavrin, ed., *Latin American Women: Historical Perspectives* (Westport, Conn.: Greenwood Press, 1978), pp. 23–59; Juan Luis Vives, *Instrucción de la mujer cristiana* (Buenos Aires: Colección Austral, 1940); Fr. Alonso de Herrera, *Espejo de la perfecta casada* (Granada, 1636).

21. Anon., *Vida de Sor Mariana Josefa Nepomuceno* (Mexico, 1808).

22. José A. Ponce de León, *La Azucena entre espinas*; Fr. Juan López Aguado, *Florido Huerto: Sermón . . . a la muerte de . . . Luisa de Santa Catarina* (Mexico, 1738).

23. Ibid., p. 56.

24. Antonio Núñez, S.J., *Cartilla de la doctrina religiosa*, p. 2; *Plática doctrinal . . . en la profesión de una señora del convento de San Lorenzo* (Mexico, 1710).

25. Archbishop Francisco Javier Lizana y Beaumont, *Carta pastoral . . . que escribe a sus amadas hijas las religiosas de toda su filiación* (Mexico, 1803).

26. Asunción Lavrin, "Religious Life of Mexican Women in the XVIII Century," Ph.D. dissertation, Harvard University, 1963, chaps. III, V.

27. Asunción Lavrin, "Ecclesiastical Reform of the Nunneries in New Spain in the Eighteenth Century," *The Americas* 22 (October 1965): 182–203.

28. Pedro Salmerón, *Vida de la Venerable Madre Isabel de la Encarnación*, p. 19v; Francisco Pardo, *Vida y virtudes heroycas de la Madre María de Jesús*, p. 30. *Devociones* were special friendships between lay men and nuns, very popular in seventeenth-century Spain and Spanish America.

29. Antonio Núñez, S.J., *Distribución de las obras ordinarias y extraordinarias del día . . . conforme al estado de las señoras religiosas* (Mexico, 1712).

30. Archbishop Fr. Joseph Lanciego y Eguilaz, *Carta pastoral a sus amadas hijas las religiosas de toda su filiación* (Mexico, 1716).

31. "Coloquio que compuso la R.M. María Vicenta de la Encarnación para la profesión de su discípula la hermana María de San Eliseo, Carmelita Descalza en el convento de Santa Teresa la Antigua, 1804," Manuscript collection of the University of Texas, Austin.

32. José Ignacio de Cabrera, *Gloriosa exaltación*.

33. "Juana Inés de la Cruz, la más indigna e ingrata criatura de cuantas crió vuestra Omnipotencia," *Petición, que en forma causídica presenta al Tribunal Divino la Madre Juana Inés de la Cruz, por impetrar perdón de sus culpas*. In *Obras completas*, eds. Alfonso Méndez-Plancarte and Alberto Salceda, Vol. IV (Mexico: Fondo de Cultura Económica, 1957), p. 520.

34. "A todas pido perdón por amor de Dios y de su Madre. Yo, la peor del mundo. Juana Inés de la Cruz." "Documentos en el Libro de Profesiones del Convento de San Jerónimo," Document 413, in *Obras completas*, Vol. 4, p. 523.

35. Ezequiel A. Chávez, *Sor Juana Inés de la Cruz, ensayo de psicología*, 2d ed. (Mexico: Editorial Porrúa, 1970).

36. *Cartas en las cuales manifiesta a su confesor las cosas interiores y exteriores de su*

vida la V.M. Sor Sebastiana de la S.S. Trinidad, Manuscript at the Biblioteca Nacional de México, Archivo Franciscano; José E. Valdés, *Vida admirable y penitente de la V.M. Sebastiana Josepha de la S.S. Trinidad* (Mexico, 1765; Ignacio Saldana, *Sermón fúnebre en las exequias de Sor Sebastiana de la S.S. Trinidad* (Mexico, 1758).

37. "que de mi no hay que fiar, que me veo tal que me quiziera quitar la vida, por no poder tolerar la violencia con que sin temor me rindo a mi apetito y anda todo perdido, y no se que me valga para verme libre de mi" V.M. Sebastiana de la S.S. Trinidad, *Cartas*, p. 40. On p. 2: "No me entra cosa, que me pueda consolar; y alli bramo sin poder mas; pero disimulando las amarguras con que vivo, y asisto al choro, que a veces me cuesta trabajo detener las lagrimas; y si esto es voluntad de Dios me de conformidad, y ensanche este oprimido corazon, que me rebienta el pecho de lo que lo reprimo."

38. Ibid., p. 91.

39. Juan A. de Mora, *Admirable vida*, p. 69.

40. Sor María de Santa Clara, *Subida al Monte de Mhirra* (Mexico, 1747).

41. "Cesaron las enfermedades sin preceder medicinas sólo como naturalmente. . . . Todo era quietud, sosiego, gozo, y como quien cansado de un largo camino en que padeció grandes peligros, hambre, cansancio y todas calamidades, llega a su amada patria, se tira a descansar, y demás de eso se regala con la prenda que más ama." "Vida de la Madre María Marcela, religiosa Capuchina del Convento de Querétaro, copiada por una religiosa Brígida en 1848," Manuscript at the Biblioteca Nacional, Mexico, Archivo Franciscano, fol. 121.

42. ". . . solo palacio y dilatado campo donde el alma y el corazón se dilatan y esparcen con tal consuelo que está el alma como la piedra en su centro . . ." ". . . hallé a mi Dios dentro de mi misma; hallávalo en todas las criaturas, no veía cosa que no me llevara a Dios, las flores, los árboles, los frutos, el agua, el Sol . . . los buelos de el alma eran continuos . . ." Ibid., fols. 99 and 122.

43. María Anna Agueda de San Ignacio, *Devociones. Impresas por orden y a expensas del Illmo. Sr. D. Domingo Pantaleón Alvarez de Abreu* (Puebla, 1758). The rest of her works are in her biography, written by Fr. Joseph Bellido, *Vida de la V.R.M. Maria Anna Agueda de S. Ignacio, primera priora del religiosísimo convento de Dominicas Recoletas de Santa Rosa de la Puebla de los Angeles* (Mexico, 1758).

44. "Asi la Esposa amante que no se aparta de la vista de su amado, renace a una nueva vida de gracia, y crece tanto en ella, que viene a una Presencia de Dios unitiva, que es cosa admirable, y gracia muy particular, y aun se llega a una total transformación." María Anna Agueda de San Ignacio, *Devociones*, p. 169.

45. "el alma se halla como libre de sus pasiones, y sin impedimento pasa a unirse con su amado de suerte, que no solo siente el alma la unión divina, aun en el cuerpo siente que le tiene poseído su amado. . . . Todo parece fuego en el fuego. . . . La voluntad inflamada, ama sin saber cómo, porque es sobre todo del mismo Dios encaminada, y en él mismo transformada viviendo, pero no ella; vive pero no su Vida, vive la Vida de su amado, y puede muy bien decir lo que San Pablo: 'Vivo yo; pero no yo, porque vive en mí Christo.'" Ibid., 245–47.

46. Melquíades Andrés, *Los recogidos*, pp. 14–15, 31–32, 73–105.

47. Ibid., pp. 96, 105.

48. Francisco Pardo, *Vida y virtudes heroycas*. See also Fr. Félix de Jesús María, *Vida y virtudes, y dones sobrenaturales de la Ve. Sierva de Dios, Sor María de Jesús* (Rome, 1756).

49. Pedro Salmerón, *Vida de la Venerable Madre Isabel de la Encarnación*, op.

cit., fol. 9v. Sor Melchora had professed in 1606. Another example of an unknown author, though a published one, is, María de la Antigua, whose work *Estaciones en la Pasión del Señor,* was printed in 1699.

50. Sor Juana Inés de la Cruz, *Obras completas,* pp. 996–1023.

51. Fr. Agustín de Vetancurt, *Teatro Mexicano: Descripción breve de los sucesos exemplares . . . ,* 4 vols. (Madrid: José Porrúa Turanzas, 1961). See Vol. IV.

52. Carlos de Sigüenza y Góngora, *Parayso occidental, plantado y cultivado por la liberal y benefica mano . . . en su magnifico Real Convento de Jesus Maria de Mexico* (Mexico, 1648), pp. 88, 125.

53. Francisco Pardo, *Vida y virtudes heroycas,* pp. 74, 137, 140. This nun would put absinthe in her food to make it bitter and punish her palate, avoiding anything sweet. One wonders whether some of her visions were not due to the abuse of this drug.

54. Juan Benito Díaz de Gamarra y Dávalos, *Vida de la M.R. Sor Maria Josefa Lino,* p. 56.

55. "Carta escrita por la Señora Sor María Teresa, Abadesa en el convento de Capuchinas de la Ciudad de la Puebla de los Angeles . . . dando noticias . . . de la Vida y Virtudes de la Señora Doña Leocadia González Aranzamendi, y en la Religión Sor María Leocadia, fundadora del referido convento de Capuchinas," in *Compendio de las Ejemplares vidas del P. José de Guevara de la Ca. de Jesús, y de su tía la Sra. Da. Leocadia González Aranzamendi, naturales de la Imperial ciudad de México* (Madrid, 1754).

56. Antonio Núñez, *Distribución de las obras ordinarias,* p. 18.

57. José María Gómez y Villaseñor, *Sermón predicado el dia 3 de marzo de 1803 en la solemne profesión de religiosa de coro . . . de Sor María Manuela de la Presentación,* p. 16. This nun was Doña María Manuela Fernández de Barrena y Vizcarra, a rich heiress from Guadalajara.

58. Ibid.

59. Alonso Núñez de Haro y Peralta, *Sermones panegíricos y pláticas espirituales,* 2 vols. (Madrid, 1807), Vol. II, p. 300.

60. Antonio Núñez, *Distribución de las obras ordinarias,* p. 37.

61. P. Diego Calleja, *Vida de Sor Juana,* p. 52. The quotation originally appeared in P. Juan Oviedo, S.J., *Vida del P. Antonio Núñez,* chapter V. In 1763, Sor María Josefa de San Ignacio, a nun in the convent of Jesús María, Mexico, paid for the reprinting of Sor Juana's *Protesta de la fe,* which she allegedly wrote with her blood. It is difficult to ascertain whether she was extolling Sor Juana's dramatic gesture or using this text as a model of religious faith. In either case, it is significant that of all of Sor Juana's actions, this was the one most vividly remembered by some of her sisters in religion. See *Protesta de la fe, y renovación de los votos religiosos que hizo y dejó escripta con su sangre la M. Juana Inés de la Cruz, monja profesa de S. Geronymo de México* (Mexico: Herederos de la viuda de D. Joseph de Hogal, 1763).

CHAPTER 4

Tricks of the Weak

JOSEFINA LUDMER

We will not use labels or universalizing generalizations to discuss women's writing. In other words, we reject tautological readings. It is well known that, historically, the apportioning of emotions, functions, and faculties (transformed into a mythology, fixed in language) has dealt women the constructs of pain and passion versus reason, the concrete versus the abstract, interiority versus the external world, reproduction versus production. To read women's language and literature in these terms is merely to read what has always been, and continues to be, inscribed in their social space. One means of breaking that circle, a circle that merely confirms the difference of the socially differentiated, is to posit an inversion; that is, to read women's discourse for the ways in which abstract thinking, science, and politics filtered into it through cracks in the familiar.

Let us speak of places. On the one hand, a critical commonplace: Sor Juana Inés de la Cruz's *Respuesta a Sor Filotea de la Cruz* (Response to Sor Filotea de la Cruz); on the other, a specific place: the place occupied by a woman in the field of knowledge under particular historical and discursive circumstances. Commonplaces (classic texts, which always seem to say whatever one wishes them to say, texts that docilely accommodate mutations) hold a certain interest in that they form the battleground where inimical systems and interpretations are debated; their periodic revision provides us with a means of gauging the transformations that reading has undergone over time (a fundamental objective of critical theory). The specific place entails a different kind of discord: the relationship between the space this particular woman has chosen and occupies and that granted her by the institutions and word of the other. One must consider both the realm of social relationships and the production of ideas and texts: we shall read in Sor Juana's letter tricks of the weak, of one in a position of subordination and marginality.

As is well known, the *Respuesta* is Sor Juana's response to the letter sent to her by the bishop of Puebla (signed with the name "Sor Filotea de la Cruz"), who had taken it upon himself to publish a polemical piece by Juana (against Antonio de Vieyra's theological and polemical sermon on the favors of Christ) under the title of *Carta atenagórica* (Athenagoric Letter). Juana responds and expresses her gratitude for the publication. She narrates certain episodes of her life related to her passion for knowledge and concludes with a polemical discussion of a maxim of St. Paul's which states that women should remain silent in church, since it is not permitted them to speak.

Sor Juana's text is a vast machine of transformations running on a very few elements: the matrix of the letter contains only three—two verbs and the negative: *saber* (to know), *decir* (to speak or say), *no*. Modulating and interchanging them in an unlimited *ars combinatoria*, conjugating the verbs and shifting the negative, Juana composes a text that works through the relationships, posited as contradictory, between two spaces (places) and two actions (methods): one of each must be ruled by the negative if the other is present. To know and to say or speak, Juana demonstrates, constitute opposing fields for a woman: whenever the two coexist, they occasion resistance and punishment. Saying that one doesn't know, not knowing how to say, not saying what one knows, placing knowing over not saying—this series unites the apparently distinct sectors of the text (autobiography, polemic, quotations) and provides the basis for the two essential movements that sustain the tricks we shall examine: first, the separation of the field of knowing from that of saying, and second, the reorganization of the field of knowing in accordance with the field of not saying (remaining silent).

THE SEPARATION OF KNOWING FROM SAYING

Juana writes to the bishop that what delayed her response was not knowing how to respond with "algo digno de vos" (something worthy of you) and "no saber agradeceros" (not knowing how to express my appreciation) for the publication of her text. Juana states right off that she *doesn't know how to say*. Not knowing leads to silence, is directly related to silence. Here, however, it is a matter of a relative and positional not knowing: not knowing how to speak to one in a superior position, a not knowing that clearly implies recognition of the other's superiority. This ignorance is thus a specific social relationship transferred to discourse: Juana doesn't know how to speak from a position of subordination. The voices of the highest authorities support her: Saint Thomas "callaba porque nada sabía decir digno de Alberto" (had not spoken because he knew no words worthy of Albertus); "[a la] madre del Bautista se le suspendió el discurso" (speech deserted the mother of John the Baptist) when she was visited by "la Madre del Verbo" (the Mother of the Word); and Juana adds: "Sólo responderé que no sé qué responder; sólo agradeceré diciendo que no soy capaz de agradeceros" (I shall respond only that I do not know how to respond; I shall thank you in saying only that I am incapable of thanking you). This, too, is a (common)place, a rhetorical locus known as "affected modesty"— which interests us less per se than for its exaltation of the other, so excessive as to produce a not knowing how to say.

Juana's letter contains at least three texts: (1) the text written directly to the bishop; (2) what has been read as her intellectual autobiography; and (3) the polemic regarding St. Paul's maxim that women remain silent in church. Three zones in constant contradiction, three significant registers that transform the meaning of the utterances. Everything addressed to the bishop implies full acceptance of her socially assigned subordinate role, and the intention to remain silent, not to say, not to know (in the confession addressed to the bishop she states, for example, that she had entered religious life to "sepultar con mi nombre mi entendimiento y sacrificárselo sólo a quien me lo dio" (bury my reason along with my name, sacrificing them only to He who bestowed them upon me), since she had asked God to disabuse her of her intelligence, "dejando sólo lo que basta para guardar su Ley, pues lo demás sobra, según algunos, en una mujer; y aun hay quien diga que daña" (leaving only that which is needed to keep His law, for there are those who would say that all else is unwanted in a woman, and there are even those who would hold that such knowledge does injury). Yet in the body of the autobiographical text she confirms, almost immediately, that she entered religious life due to the "total negación que tenía al matrimonio" (total antipathy I felt for marriage). In the biography she writes that she remains silent, studies, and knows—thus creating another textual space, her own, stripped of rhetoric, in which she writes what is not said in the other zones. Her story, narrated as the history of her passion for knowledge, strikes the reader as a typical popular autobiography, or autobiography of a marginalized figure: an account of the practices of resistance vis-à-vis power. (We also note the insertion of one lesser genre, autobiography, within another, the letter.) The first scene of her story, which serves as the point of departure for her epistemophilia, is of particular interest. She tells us that she tricked the teacher ("le dije que mi madre ordenaba me diese lección," I told her that my mother had meant for me to have lessons) and that she kept it silent from her mother: "y supe leer en tan breve tiempo, que ya sabía cuando lo supo mi madre . . ." (and I learned so quickly that before my mother knew of it I could already read . . .), "y yo lo callé" (and I kept the secret). Her first encounter with writing, as narrated in the biography, thus comprises a *not saying that she knows*.

Maternal and superior authority are closely related, both being figures who occasion not saying: the bishop, because one doesn't know how to speak to him, and the mother "y lo callé, creyendo que me azotarían por haberlo hecho sin orden" (and I kept the secret, fearing that I would be whipped for having acted without permission). Silence constitutes Juana's space of resistance vis-à-vis others' power. Such also is the case with the sacred writings Sor Filotea advises her to study: Juana repeats that she doesn't speak because she doesn't know—not speaking, once again, for fear of punishment; impossible for her to speak of sacred matters due to her "temor y reverencia" (fear and reverence) and the risk of heresy: "Dejen eso para quien lo entienda, que yo no quiero ruido con el Santo Oficio, que soy ignorante y tiemblo de decir alguna proposición malsonante o torcer la genuina inteligencia de algún lugar" (Leave these matters to those who understand them; I wish no quarrel with the Holy Office, for I am ignorant and I tremble that I might express some proposition that will cause offense or twist the true meaning of some scripture). (A digression: here we can see the relationship between the *Respuesta* and the only text, as Juana tells us in the *Respuesta*, that she has written for her own pleasure, the *Sueño* or *Primero sueño* [First Dream]. From one point of view the *Respuesta* can be read as a gloss of the *Sueño*, to the degree that the poem sets forth a theory of knowledge and of epistemological impulses, as well as positing the impossibility of attaining the Absolute. Both the *Respuesta* and the *Sueño* open with the theme of muteness and silence; silence also constitutes the terminus of the poem: at the peak of understanding—perplexity, silence.)

We thus have three cases of superiority: the mother, the bishop, and the Holy Office. All three command fear and generate not saying: not saying that one knows (to the mother), saying that one doesn't know how to say (to the bishop), not saying because one doesn't know (the realm of theology). In the first case she was caught up in the process of knowing; in the second, she writes the *Respuesta* and exhibits her knowledge through quotations; the third directly involves the *Carta atenagórica*, (whose publication led to the writing of this letter. Juana progressively disabuses herself of the public word, a zone that becomes associated with the mechanisms of discipline: her not saying camouflages apparently forbidden practices. Juana thus decides that to *publish*, the highest form of saying, does not interest her. That space the culture posits as its valued and dominant zone is precisely where Juana says, "I don't know," I won't say, I abstain, underscoring yet again that saying, writing, publishing (the three now forming a series) are demands originating from others and associated with violence, with coercion: "Y, a la verdad, yo nunca he escrito, sino violentada y forzada y sólo por dar gusto a otros; no sólo sin complacencia, sino con positiva repugnancia" (And, in truth, I have written nothing except when coerced and constrained, and then only to give pleasure to others; not alone without pleasure of my own, but with absolute repugnance).

Public saying is a space occupied by authority and violence: the other grants and retracts the word. The bishop publishes (and she, while expressing her gratitude, protests: I don't want to publish, I'm forced to do so); the bishop writes (and she: I don't know how to respond to you); the bishop orders the study of sacred matters (and she: I don't know, I'm afraid). Juana, as a woman, says that rather than she being its mistress, the word is granted, retracted, and demanded (as is confession) from her. This gesture, of the superior granting the word to subordinates, is of special interest: in Latin America it gives rise to a whole literary tradition. Beginning with gauchesque literature and embracing *indigenismo* as well as the various incarnations of regionalism, we find the fictitious gesture of granting the word to those defined by their lacks (lacking land, lacking writing) and of bringing their particular language to light. This gesture issues from the superior culture and is the responsibility of the educated, who disguise and mute their own voices in the fiction of transcription to propose an alliance to the weak and subordinate against the common enemy. It is very possible that the bishop's publication of Sor Juana's letter derived precisely from his need to confront others. With this, the bishop, who in writing to Juana disguises himself as Sor Filotea de la Cruz, transfers to the letter the gesture of publishing the word of the weak: he covers up his name and sex, making way for the woman's word, and publishes Juana's writing, giving it a title (while she, in her poems, grants the word to the Indians). But both granting the word and identifying oneself with the other involve the same imperative: the weak must accept the superior's project. The bishop, who in assuming a woman's name places himself

90

on a horizontal plane with Juana, desires to win her back to religion, to persuade her to abandon what is unsuited to religion. He calls himself Filotea (lover of God), because from this position he can write to Sor Filosofía (philosophy, lover of knowledge, author of the letter worthy of Athena's knowledge). The bishop's pseudonym, his publication of the text-polemic, define his project regarding Sor Juana. And it is here where she erects her chain of negations: not to say, to say that one doesn't know, not to publish, not to dedicate herself to sacred matters. The double gesture combines acceptance of her subordinate position (the woman "shutting her trap") and her trick: not to say but to know, or saying that one doesn't know but knowing, or saying the opposite of what one knows. This trick of the weak, which here separates the field of saying (the law of the other) from the field of knowing (my law), combines, as in all tactics of resistance, submission to and acceptance of the place assigned to one by the other, with antagonism and confrontation, retreat from collaboration.

Juana sets knowing and saying in a contradictory relationship: from this basis issues the chain of contradictions that multiply throughout the text. Her own place is that of studying and knowing; if writing is a "fuera ajena" (alien force), "lo mío es la inclinación a las letras" (what is mine is the inclination to learning); I don't study in order to say, teach, or write, but rather "para ignorar menos" (to be less ignorant). And she fills the space of knowing with silence: books are mute ("sosegado silencio de mis libros," the quiet silence of my books; "teniendo sólo para maestro un libro mudo," having for a master no other than a mute book, she says, in complaint); her readings begin with St. Ambrose, St. Augustine's teacher, and progress in silence. It is from this other web, no longer the space of not saying but of its praxis, that Sor Juana writes about women's silence.

THE SECOND MOVEMENT: KNOWING OVER NOT SAYING

This movement involves a reorganization of the field of knowledge. In order to discuss Paul's maxim regarding women's silence in church, Sor Juana constructs a doctrine of reading (not her own, not revulsive, but strictly Scholastic) which negates the division between profane and otherworldly knowledge, a tree of knowledge (like that of Raimundo Lulio) at whose peak are found the sacred texts. In order to reach these texts and theology, as the bishop counsels her, Juana states that "hay que subir por los escalones de las ciencias y las artes humanas; porque ¿cómo entenderá el estilo de la Reina de las Ciencias quien aun no sabe el de las ancillas?" (one must climb the steps of the human sciences and arts; for how could one undertake the study of the Queen of Sciences if first one had not come to know her servants?). And she enumerates them: logic, rhetoric, physics, arithmetic, geometry, architecture, history, law, music, astrology. These sciences are all linked. In her biographical account, she lists the difficulties experienced in studying these (subordinate, the only means of attaining the heights) sciences: for three months she was forbidden to study, but—the gesture of resistance—"aunque no estudiaba en libros, estudiaba en todas las cosas que Dios crió, sirviéndome ellas de letras, y de libro toda esta máquina universal" (though I did not study in books, I studied all the things that God had wrought, reading in them, as in writing and in books, all the workings of the universe). It is thus always possible to annex another space for knowledge. One can separate neither sacred from profane knowledge nor the study of books from the study of reality. While cooking she has discovered "secretos naturales" (natural secrets): "Veo que un huevo se une y fríe en la manteca o aceite y, por el contrario, se despedaza en el almíbar" (I see that an egg holds together and fries in butter and in oil, but, on the contrary, in syrup shrivels into shreds). And finally, since the field admits no divisions, it is impossible to separate women from men in terms of knowledge—which only accepts the difference between the fool, the uneducated, and the proud, and the wise and the learned. Juana has found a space beyond sexual difference. And her knowledge, acquired in silence, enables Juana to reinterpret St. Paul's maxim regarding the silence that a woman must hold in church: in early churches women taught each other doctrine, and the murmurs of their knowledge distracted the Apostles as they preached. This is why Paul ordered them to remain silent. "No hay duda que para la inteligencia de muchos lugares es menester mucha historia, costumbres, ceremonias, proverbios y aun maneras de hablar de aquellos tiempos en se escribieron, para saber sobre qué caen y a qué aluden algunas locuciones de las divinas letras" (There is no doubt that for the comprehension of many Scriptures one must be familiar with the history, customs, ceremonies, proverbs, and even the manners of speaking of those times in which they were written, if one is to apprehend the references and allusions of more than a few passages of the Holy Word). Here Juana teaches us a lesson in literary and ideological criticism. Dogmatic truths and hierarchical systems, she says, erase the traces of history in the text: from concrete and particular circumstances was derived an eternal and authoritarian dogma, a transcendental law regarding the difference of the sexes. Such is Juana's knowing and saying with respect to women's silence.

Finally, she accepts the dictum that women not speak from the pulpit or in public readings but defends education and private study (she defends her own verse works and polemic against Vieyra). She thus accepts the private sphere as "proper" to the woman's word and respects the prevailing division; at the same time, she constitutes the woman's sphere as that of science and literature, whence she negates the sexual division. Her stratagem (another characteristic tactic of the weak) consists in changing, from within one's assigned and accepted place, not only its meaning but the very meaning of what is established within its confines. As does a mother or homemaker who says, "I accept my place, but as a mother or homemaker I will engage in politics or science." It is always possible to claim a space from which one can practice what is forbidden in others; it is always possible to annex other fields and establish other territorialities. And this practice of transference and transformation reorganizes given social and cultural structures: the combination of respect and confrontation can establish another truth, another approach to science, and another subject of knowledge. To the question of why there have been no women philosophers, one can answer that women have not engaged in philosophy from the space delimited by classical philosophy but rather from other zones; and if one reads or listens to their discourse as a philosophical discourse, one can effect that transformation of thought. The same holds true for science and for politics.

The letter and the autobiography provide the forum for Juana's erudite polemic. Now we can understand these lesser genres (the letter, the autobiography, the diary), mediating between the literary and the nonliterary and termed the genres of reality, as the space favored by women's literature. They display a matter of essential importance: that those regional spaces that the dominant culture has extracted from the realms of the daily and the personal and has constituted as separate fields (politics, science, philosophy) exist for women precisely in the realm of the personal and are indissociable from it. And if the personal, the private, the quotidian are included as points of departure and perspectives in other discourses and practices, they cease to be merely personal, private, and quotidian: such is one possible result of the tricks of the weak.

NOTE

Translated by Stephanie Merrim. English citations from the *Respuesta a Sor Filotea de la Cruz* follow Margaret Sayers Peden's translation of this work, *A Woman of Genius* (Salisbury, Conn.: Lime Rock Press, 1982), with sporadic modifications to fit the context and emphasis of Ludmer's essay.

CHAPTER 5

Mores Geometricae: The "Womanscript" in the Theater of
Sor Juana Inés de la Cruz

STEPHANIE MERRIM

> How we are fallen! fallen by mistaken rules, . . .
> And if some would soar above the rest
> With warmer fancy, and ambition pressed,
> So strong the opposing faction still appears,
> The hopes to thrive can ne'er outweigh the fears
> —Lady Winchilsea, b. 1661, quoted in Virginia Woolf,
> *A Room of One's Own*

No reader of Sor Juana Inés de la Cruz could fail
to be struck by the woman's drama, of inherent abilities thwarted by
cultural structures, which she so lucidly exposes in her autobiographical *Respuesta a Sor Filotea de la Cruz* (Response to Sor Filotea de la
Cruz). The woman's drama that Sor Juana ciphers, wittingly or not,
into her major dramatic works (two *comedias: Los empeños de una casa*
[The Trials of a Noble House] and *Amor es más laberinto* [Love Is the
Greater Labyrinth]; and three *autos sacramentales* or Eucharistic dramas: *El mártir del Sacramento, San Hermenegildo* [The Martyr of the
Sacrament, Saint Hermenegildo], *El cetro de José* [Joseph's Scepter],
and *El Divino Narciso* [The Divine Narcissus]),[1] on the other hand, has
gone largely unperceived. Critical attention in this regard has focused
almost exclusively on the autobiographical elements built into Leonor's
famed speech from the first act of *Los empeños de una casa*, in which the
character declaims Sor Juana's own life story of intellectual precocity
and prodigious achievements as well as beauty [IV, pp. 36–39]. For
the rest, scholars have tended to view Sor Juana *qua* playwright as an

94

imitator of Calderón and other Golden Age dramatists, as a writer ruled by her *empeños* (debts) to the house of male literary convention. For example: "In her plays she matched herself against Lope de Vega and Calderón, the earlier Spanish masters of the century. The results are flawlessly crafted works in which, as must have been her aim, the woman never shows, for she hides behind a male mask which is firm and rigid and lifeless."[2]

This study will both bear out and refute the preceding statement. Certainly, as is the case with so many women writers, Sor Juana voices a personal script from behind the mask of male theatrical conventions. Her script, however, does not enunciate the overtly "feminist" message that Sor Juana's pronouncements in the *Respuesta* regarding women would lead us to expect. The *Respuesta,* we cannot forget, is a response to an act of persecution.[3] So, too, the hidden blueprint or "womanscript" of Sor Juana's theater responds to the profoundly problematical experiences of a church/woman writer in seventeenth-century Mexico, ineluctably formed by received values and norms. Reflecting and refracting this problematic, I will argue, Sor Juana kept writing the *same* play—be it *comedia* or *auto sacramental*—which repeatedly enacts the drama of the divided woman, the dark versus the light heroine. Hardly subversive, indeed almost self-punishing, the script militates against the former, who displays attributes of the woman writer. Thus, it shall become clear that to see in the Leonor of *Los empeños de una casa* a transparent autobiographical representation of Sor Juana is to perceive but half the drama, and none of the battle.

As the female Icarus, a true daughter of Daedalus—artificer of the labyrinth—which Sor Juana will prove to be, her "womanscript" is intricate and more implicit than explicit. To expose it shall thus require a series of literary tools, to be elaborated in the first part of this study. Here I shall discuss certain of the received norms that so configured Sor Juana's writing. Next we pass to theoretical, and geometrical, premises: the play of "threes" and then "twos" in her dramatic works. Together they will allow us to articulate the paradigmatic "womanscript" that underlies Sor Juana's plays. In the main body of our exposition we will closely examine the variants of the script as they appear in each individual play, as well as its resonance in other of her works.

RECEIVED NORMS

"How we are fallen! Fallen by mistaken rules," reads a line from this essay's epigraph. In seventeenth-century colonial Mexico such "mistaken rules" for women issued in part and persistently from the (patriarchal) religious thought that would seep into literary conventions. In her *Women in Colonial Spanish American Literature: Literary Images*, Julie Greer Johnson discusses the resonance of misogynistic church doctrine and concludes, "The most continually influential component in the creation and transmission of attitudes towards women . . . was the Catholic church."[4] The religious legends, which hold woman to be diabolical, fallen, and agent of the Fall, are well known to us all and hardly warrant detailed presentation. Eve: the Devil's accomplice, incurring sin in exchange for knowledge; *Eva–Ave María*, the sinner redeemed in Mary. The Fall: origin of all suffering, characterized by Sor Juana in a paraphrase from Genesis as the source of female-male strife as well: "Quebrantará, altiva, / tu cuello orgulloso; / y a su carcañal / le pondrás estorbos" (Arrogant, the woman will break your prideful neck, and at her heel the man will place obstacles) [*El cetro de José*, III, p. 205]. In sum, woman as morally weak, easily tempted, often motivated by evil. The association of woman, presumptuousness, Devil, and knowledge, as we shall see, would prove particularly compelling for Sor Juana.

These mistaken rules, albeit muffled and transfigured, manifest themselves in the plays of Sor Juana's most immediate model, Pedro Calderón de la Barca, as well as in those of other Golden Age dramatists. Speaking broadly of Golden Age theater, we might assert that whereas the male characters generally function as bearers and defenders of the social (honor) code and order, female characters—"she-Devils" of sorts—subvert and disrupt them. Woman as *clinamen*: her actions or the love and jealousy she inspires not only shake up the rigid social structure but also provide the charge that motivates the dramatic action.[5] As Ruth El Saffar so incisively notes, "It is the male world, with its clear positioning and ranking system, that is threatened in play after play of Calderón. . . . It is always the affairs of the heart that disturb the system."[6] In these plays the woman's domestic spaces—houses, rooms—become laboratories where honor is put to the test, and household objects, such as the glass cupboard that seals off the widow Angela's hidden chamber in *La dama duende* (The Phantom Lady), serve as symbols of honor's fragility: "pues ya dices / que no ha puesto por defensa / de su honor / más que unos vidrios, / que al primer golpe se quiebran" (since you say that to defend his honor he has only some glass panes, which break at the first blow).[7] We therefore note the ironic fact that, in terms of both her spaces and her person, the woman, who wielded so little real (i.e., extra-textual) power, assumes great textual power.[8] The Golden Age honor play, in part due to the woman's function as *clinamen*, gave rise to the development of unusually strong female protagonists, particularly the *mujer varonil* (manly woman) who assumes masculine traits, and a host of variants, including the very popular *mujer esquiva* (reluctant woman) who shuns marriage.[9]

We should not, however, too readily attribute the greater latitude allowed the female character in Golden Age drama to truly enlightened attitudes toward woman on the part of the male dramatists. For one, the female characters' flight of self-assertion proves to be short-lived in that the end of the play generally has her reconciled to the social structures she defied, snuffing out her self-will. No male dramatist, for example, allows the *mujer esquiva* (a prototype so dear to Sor Juana) legitimate reasons for asserting her independence; she always marries at the end.[10] Secondly, we cannot fail to understand the role of women in these plays as a function or mere pawn of the larger aims of Golden Age drama. As is widely known, to an important degree Golden Age theater attempted to reaffirm threatened national values: "From the start, the comedia offered the Spanish populace ways to invoke threats to the . . . system and to see those threats rebutted."[11] The woman as *clinamen*, a light and fictive threat, thus largely serves a plot, and social, function. Well may we then conclude that male dramatists were less interested in redefining attitudes toward women per se than in the essential textual function "she" fulfilled, of problematizing and eventually reaffirming collective values.

Now, much as the scenario of Golden Age drama may have been intended to reflect a larger agenda, to the modern reader—and very likely to Sor Juana—its treatment of women remains deeply unsettling. For example, Jean Kennard notes in an analogous context that "the qualities we have been invited to admire in these heroines [have] been sacrificed to structural neatness."[12] With reference to Sor Juana, as a woman highly dependent on the structures of church and court for her well-being she could not fail to feel the weight of both, related, sets of patriarchal norms. If despite herself, Sor Juana would function as something of a ventriloquist, through whom received norms would speak. The colonization of her voice, and sense of woman and self, by these other voices manifests itself in the divisions—and divisiveness—that underwrite her dramatic production.

3'S

These divisions will be played out within the geometrical configurations Sor Juana adapts from Calderón. Calderonian drama, it has been said, entails "a stylization of the nationalistic theater of Lope."[13] The quintessentially baroque stylization of earlier theater found in Calderón's plays depends for its striking effects on what could be considered mathematical contrasts, that is, on symmetries, oppositions, *claroscuros*, and *enredos* (dramatic entanglements), frequently framed by *love triangles* where two rivals compete for the affections of a single individual. The theater of Sor Juana, which so stylizes the already stylized works of Calderón as to anticipate the lighter, highly choreographed Rococo drama of the eighteenth century, invariably takes triangles as its modus operandi. Such dramatic triangles, in her *comedias*, often reflect the ironic symmetries or so-called triangular "encontradas correspondencias" also found in Sor Juana's "Fabio" sonnet sequence [I, poems 166–71].[14] "Whom should I love?"—the basic argument of the sonnets runs—"He who loves me but whom I scorn, or he whom I love, but who scorns me?" Rivalries and scorn: not only love but hatred and jealousy (*celos*) link the apices of the triangles and fuel the dramatic machinery of both Calderón's and Sor Juana's theater. Indeed, according to Sor Juana's conflictive picture of secular love, *celos* reign supreme, serving as testimony and necessary condition of love: "Son crédito y prueba suya; / pues sólo pueden dar ellos / auténticos testimonios / de que es amor verdadero" (They're a guarantee and proof of it; because only they can give authentic testimony that it is true love) [I, Romance 3, p. 9].

The triangles just described, bonded in equal measure by love and jealousy, easily put us in mind of the triangles of mimetic desire that René Girard explicates in his *Deceit, Desire and the Novel*.[15] Whereas Girard propounds the triangles as a basic structuring pattern of the Western novel, I shall, presently, conjugate them with Sor Juana's plays. For now, however, let us briefly summarize those aspects of Girard's theory relevant to the subsequent discussion.

Much as we "think we move in a straight line toward the object of our desires and hates," asserts Girard, "the space of desire is Euclidean."[16] For Girard, this indirect route, the *triangle of desire*, is motivated by "mimesis," here defined as the imitation of another. The triangle of desire comes into existence when a subject desires an object that is either remote or ideal. The desired object being unattainable, a "mediator" intervenes between subject and object. This mediator, while also desiring the same object, shares certain of the object's attributes, which fact renders the mediator desirable to the subject. Hence, the mediator comes to assume the dual function of (1) the subject's *rival,* impediment to the attainment of the object, and (2) the subject's *model,* arousing the subject's mimetic, or imitative, desire. The mediator, in sum, paradoxically inspires both hatred and imitation. Finally, as the reader may have surmised, Girard's triangles of mimetic desire bear metaphysical implications, which Ruth El Saffar concisely summarizes:

> To fully appreciate the implications of Girard's analyses, the important point is to see that the love triangle is an emblem of misplaced desire for God. Lacking an Absolute Other on which to attach itself, the desire is displaced onto a secondary other [the mediator] who then acquires the attributes of God, and in seeming absolute renders the desiring self ancillary and trivial by comparison.[17]

A similar metaphysical dimension will eventually, and significantly, assert itself in Sor Juana's theater.

2'S

Two triangle-based plays by Calderón, *Los empeños de un acaso* (The Trials of a Chance Occurrence, ca. 1639) and *Eco y Narciso* (Echo and Narcissus, 1661), provided direct antecedents for Sor Juana's best-known dramas. It is interesting to note that whereas male-dominated triangles prevail in the Calderonian dramas, female-dominated triangles (i.e., two women competing for one man) occupy center stage in Sor Juana's versions. More than one critic has oberved that the female rivals carry the action in these plays by Sor Juana, determining the movements of the male characters.[18] Now, Girard would focus our "triangular" attention less on the subject-object relationship than on that of the subject-mediator, which largely emerges here as the relationship between two female characters. "Everything becomes clear," he writes, "when one sees that the loathed rival is actually a mediator."[19] Certainly, much will become clear. Yet, to understand the full dynamics of the relationship between the two female rivals, we must turn to the now familiar angel/monster problematic presented by Sandra M. Gilbert and Susan Gubar in their magisterial *The Madwoman in the Attic.*[20] Given that its broad outlines conform to the script found in many other works, the angel/monster polarization in Sor Juana's plays may not strike us as unique or remarkable; remarkable indeed, however, is the unexpected presence of this characteristic woman writer's pattern in the works of our seventeenth-century Mexican nun.

In the programmatic first two chapters of their book, Gilbert and Gubar explore the eighteenth- and nineteenth-century woman writer's "anxiety about her own artistry, together with the duplicity that anxiety necessitates,"[21] an anxiety both personal and textual. Male attitudes associating authorship with (patriarchal) authority, Gilbert and Gubar contend, engender in the woman writer an "'anxiety of authorship'. . . built from complex and often only barely conscious fears of that authority which seems to the female artist to be by definition inappropriate to her sex."[22] Male authors have traditionally (we have seen the biblical roots in Mary and Eve) polarized their female characters into the extremes of otherness, angel and monster. Women writers, struggling with the "anxiety of authorship" that renders their creative inclinations conflictive, have often "found it necessary to act out male metaphors in their own texts, as if trying to understand their implications."[23]

The woman writer encodes and (melo)dramatizes her own problematic in the male metaphors, appropriating them for her own specific purposes. We thus typically encounter in women's writings two competing heroines or polarized doubles, the angel and the monster, who may be understood as reflections of the writer's divided self. Not unlike the dark and light heroines of early romance or the good and bad twins of American cinematic melodrama,[24] the angel embodies "female" virtues of passivity and submissiveness while the monster reflects assertiveness. Significantly, in this "Snow White" script, the monster (the scheming Wicked Queen, "a woman of almost infinite creative energy")[25] will display traits of the *creative woman*. The creative and rebellious monster-madwoman may seek to destroy the angel woman; often, like the Wicked Queen, she herself is destroyed in the attempt. Returning from textual to the writer's personal duplicity, Gilbert and Gubar would have us see the madwomen as characters who enact the woman writer's "own, covert authorial anger."[26] Similarly, of the monster as the author's double and her tragic dénouement, they write:

> Of course, by projecting their [the women writers'] rebellious impulses not onto their heroines but into mad or monstrous women

(who are suitably punished in the course of the novel or poem), female authors dramatize their own self division, their desire both to accept the strictures of patriarchal society and to reject them.[27]

THE "WOMANSCRIPT"

The woman writer works both within and from without established norms. Somewhat analogously, the "womanscript" of Sor Juana's theater will both conflate and personalize the terms of our foregoing discussion. Let us now collapse (at least three of) her plays into one, profiling the outline of the "womanscript" that unites them.

In the three plays largely centering on female-dominated triangles (*Los empeños de una casa, Amor es más laberinto, El Divino Narciso*), an idealized female heroine commands the love of an idealized male hero. The hero and object of desire embodies virtue to such a degree that he functions as a model, even a displaced or actual divinity: in Sor Juana's Christian (as versus Girard's existential) universe, the Absolute Other must remain a real, and not misguided, possibility. The idealized heroine—mediator and angel—shares certain of his attributes, whether in latent or already actualized form. The love of the potential doubles, the mediator and the object of desire, begs to be realized. Yet between the two (ill-)fated lovers intervenes the second female, monster agent of division and, fittingly, other half of the divided woman. Rival of the angel, she too desires the object. The monster woman, who in these plays invariably displays boundless creative energies, will deploy them in plots and schemes designed to separate mediator from object and/or to win the object for herself.

As befits the ambivalences of Sor Juana's own situation, in her plays the relationship between the two women is highly complex, combining elements of both monster-angel (polarization) and subject-mediator (imitation). Echoing the theme of Icarus so integral to Sor Juana's *Sueño*, the monster woman—artificer, presumptuous daughter of Daedalus—embodies pride, the *soberbia* that Sor Juana terms in her *Ejercicios devotos* (Devotional Exercises) "el primero de los pecados" (the foremost sin) [IV, p. 479; we recall here the creative woman's "anxiety of authorship"]. Like Icarus, her prideful and transgressive creative schemes to destroy the angel woman's happiness inevitably and didactically end in failure. Faithful to the conventions of Golden Age theater, the creative monster woman—often a *mujer esquiva*—

will meet with defeat, and the angel will be reunited with her equally virtuous lover.

Yet angel and monster are not so diametrically opposed as such a dénouement would suggest; rather, they emerge as echoes, as it were, of each other. For one, though ultimately incarnating the virtue of humility, the angel woman also commits some transgression in seeking to achieve love. Following the dictates of dramatic convention, as well perhaps as her own convictions, Sor Juana allows both the angel and the monster heroines to assert their free will: both flex their Icarus's wings, but the humble angel will be redeemed and the presumptuous monster punished. The creative woman's transgression, however, dominates the play. Secondly, as their mutual transgressions evidence, monster and angel share properties that shape them into distorted doubles. Rewarding the light heroine with the affections of both the object of desire and the audience, the didactic thrust of the play—if not the dark heroine herself—implicitly casts her light double as the mediator, object of imitation, and substitute object of desire.

Is this a *woman*script? the reader will in all likelihood ask. In each case, the values of the play, such as the fact that the monster woman acts out of jealousy and hatred, or the play's economy, its need for heroes, heroines, and villains, might well seem sufficient to justify the developments and structures we encounter in Sor Juana's theater. It is only, however, when we look beyond these received values and norms to the infrastructure of her plays that we see their special nature. The repeated association of the villain(ess) with creative strategies, the subtle interplay of the female doubles, and the dynamics of the female-dominated triangles all distinguish Sor Juana's plays and render their hidden agenda a womanscript.

Variants of this baroque script—so fraught with *claroscuros*, as tangled as any *comedia de enredos*—of the self-punishing creative woman appear in the three dramas listed above. In each, elements are added, subtracted, or receive further definition. The two other plays, male-dominated *autos sacramentales*, develop certain elements that will culminate in *El Divino Narciso*, a rewriting *a lo divino* (into religious terms) of the secular womanscript that plays out the script's deepest and fullest implications. Let us now turn to the plays themselves, examining first the *comedias* and then the *autos sacramentales*.

LOS EMPEÑOS DE UNA CASA (THE TRIALS OF A NOBLE HOUSE)

Both the parallel triangles of *Los empeños de una casa* and the chiaroscuro oppositions they entail pit the tempered and reasoned love of the "light" male and female protagonists, Don Carlos and Doña Leonor, against the *loco amor* (mad love) of their shadier counterparts, Don Pedro, his sister Doña Ana, and, less prominently, Ana's somewhat violent suitor, Don Juan.[28] Enamored of Leonor, Pedro has plotted to lure her to his house, which interrupts her elopement with Carlos. Ana picks up the strings of the subversive plot entrusted to her by her brother and weaves them into an ever more mad and vertiginous web, a labyrinth of housebound *enredos* fueled by jealousy. For Ana, rather childishly smitten from afar with Carlos ("no sé si es gusto o capricho," I don't know if it's genuine liking or just a whim [IV, p. 32]) and a *mujer esquiva* who scorns Juan, the lover who loves her, will contrive to win Carlos from Leonor. Though hard-pressed by the trials (*empeños*) to which Ana's unreasoned love subjects them, neither Leonor nor Carlos, in their perfection, fully succumbs to jealousy of the other. Leonor, paragon of beauty and intelligence ("una dama de perfecciones tan sumas," a lady of such supreme perfection [IV, p. 28]), would rather take herself to a covent than betray Carlos. Carlos, whose perfection is established early on by Leonor's lengthy panegyric in Act I, Scene II ("y en todo, en fin, tan perfecto," and in everything, in sum, so perfect [IV, p. 41]), refuses to be taken in by circumstantial evidence against Leonor: "Calla, Castaño, la boca, / que es muy bajo quien sin causa, / de la dama a quien adora, / se da a entender que le ofende" (Stifle yourself, Castaño, because it is very vulgar with no provocation to make it known that the woman you love has offended you) [IV, p. 91]. By the end of the play, needless to say, Carlos and Leonor win, each other, while the plotters, Pedro and Ana, lose: Pedro is consigned to solitude and Ana, disencumbered of her fantasies, to the rather unsavory Juan, who at one point physically assaulted Leonor.[29]

The emerging womanscript of this early drama of Sor Juana's thus contains two congruent triangles and a male *and* female plotter. In each triangle, a "dark" plotter—Pedro, Ana—competes with a "light" rival—Carlos, Leonor—for the love of a "light" object of desire, hence the parallel characterization of Leonor and Carlos. For having initiated the plot, which crossed destined lovers, and contributing to it intermittently, Pedro receives the most severe punishment allowed by *come-*

dia norms, remaining unmarried. Nevertheless, as Juan José Arrom notes, it is his sister Ana's scheming that dominates the play:

> It is she who bears, in her restless hands, the threads of the plot. As accessory to the conspiracy that her brother Don Pedro has hatched, Doña Ana constantly finds herself at the center of the action, directing or protecting the movements of each one of the pieces in this amorous chess game.[30]

As this remark clearly indicates, displaying notable creative ingenuity Ana becomes the mistress of ceremonies and director of a play-within-a-play, arranged to keep Carlos from Leonor. She forms a conscious plan for her play ("pues ya será hora / de lo que tengo dispuesto / porque mi industria engañosa se logre," since now the time has come to do what I have planned, which will allow my deceitful skills to achieve their aim [IV, p. 87]) and cunningly manipulates people, spaces, music, and props in mounting this drama. Much in the way that Sor Juana as author disposes characters to serve her will, Ana has her maid Celia execute the plan which she directs from behind the scenes. Ana "manda" (commands) and "ordena" (orders): the space of the house becomes the scenario in which Ana, the creative woman, exercises the free will she felt was curtailed by her relationship with Juan ("sin dejar a qué aspirar / a la ley del albedrío," which left nothing for the law of free will to aspire to [IV, p. 31]).

Regrettably, however, Ana abuses her free will and that of others, which is why her flight turns into a "Fall." Like the Devil-Eco of *El Divino Narciso*, Ana acts as agent of division, being she who dis-orders and dis-locates. Ana keeps the light hero from the light heroine, interposing grates between Carlos and the others, placing them all in non-communicating spaces. She inserts Leonor and Carlos in an enchanted labyrinth in which they lose their sense of reality and identity: Carlos exclaims, "¡Cielos! ¿qué es esto que escucho? / ¡Es ilusión, es encanto / lo que ha pasado por mí? / ¿Quién soy yo? ¿Dónde me hallo?" (Heavens, what is this that I hear? What has happened to me—is it an illusion? A spell? Who am I? Where am I?) [IV, p. 99]. Indomitable ("nada a mí me desanima," nothing daunts me [IV, p. 46]), knowing she errs ("conozco que estoy errando / y no me puedo enmendar," I know that I am erring but can't mend my ways [IV, p. 32]), motivated by jealousy, Ana has become a *mujer varonil*, but a misguided one. Leonor's father, Don Rodrigo, had attempted to squelch his daughter's free will: "de si Leonor querrá o no [marry Pedro], / eso no es impedimento, / pues ella tener no puede / más gusto que mi precepto" (whether Leonor wants to [marry Pedro] or not is no obstacle, since she can have no wishes other than my own) [IV, p. 111–12]; similarly, Ana has made the house a prison, from which Leonor (and Carlos) long desperately to escape: "Celia, yo me he de matar / si tú salir no me dejas / de esta casa, o de este encanto" (Celia, I'll kill myself if you don't let me out of this house, or this spell) [IV, p. 125]. Ana, we see, in deploying her creative energies, has, like Icarus, gone out too far.

To better understand the nature and dimensions of Ana's transgressions, let us compare them to the very similar strategies of the Phantom Lady Angela in Calderón's *La dama duende* (written in 1629), a play much more akin to Sor Juana's than his *Los empeños de un acaso*. Here, the young widow Angela has been consigned to a hidden apartment (sealed off by the symbolic glass cupboard referred to earlier) by her brothers in their zealous attempt to protect the family's honor.[31] When Manuel becomes a guest in the house and piques her love interest, Angela exercises this free will in a creative form and contrives stratagems to win Manuel's love which directly parallel those of Ana. She takes on the persona of the "phantom lady," manipulates the idiosyncratic spaces of the house to her advantage, and "directs" a play-within-a-play, all of which dis-order Manuel's rational sense of things. Yet in the end *her* creative stratagems, always wrought in a good-natured spirit of play, achieve their goal, and Angela weds Manuel. What is the Phantom Lady, asks Manuel, "Angel, demonio o mujer?" (Angel, demon or woman?). Clearly this play allows the woman to employ "demonic" dis-ordering energies—albeit in a spirit of love untinged by jealousy since there is no rival for Manuel's favors—and still be the angel, Angela. As Edwin Honig concludes, "*The Phantom Lady* presents a woman's rebellion against the code's autocratic male principles as she seeks to achieve the liberty to love whom she pleases. . . . She finds freedom in a state of bondage by using stratagems to such effect that actual bondage becomes illusory and illusory freedom becomes real."[32] Within the parameters of Golden Age drama, then, this play appears favorably disposed towards the woman and her creative efforts, allowing her to triumph.

Such are the outcome and the attitudes one might naturally expect to find in Sor Juana's *Los empeños de una casa*. And, in part, one does—in the person of Leonor, who, light angel and mediator, represents Sor Juana's idealized mask. Sor Juana, as noted at the outset, places her own story of a woman endowed with exceptional intelligence and beauty in the mouth of Leonor ("Sol", Sun, and "alma de perfecciónes", soul of perfection). Leonor tells that story with notable modesty, lamenting the betrayals of fame which, in fact, have resulted in her transgressions (her elopement) and fallen condition: "donde en un punto me hallo / sin crédito, sin honor" (to the point where I find myself without a reputation, without honor) [IV, p. 43]. The biographical parallels between Sor Juana and Leonor, we can now see, prove particularly telling in that they implicate Sor Juana herself in the web of identifications that will unite Ana and Leonor.

For here the angel begins to shade into the distorted double of and mediator for the monster. In terms of transgression, the two women's stories are didactically parallel, if syncopated. Leonor, induced to presumptuousness by fame, has transgressed, has modestly confessed her transgression, and will be redeemed. On the other hand, the play shows Ana in the throes of her transgression; she will atone, as has the mediator, only in the last scene. Yet, most significant of all, the play has Ana manifest and put into action precisely that intelligence which is verbally imputed to Leonor (and shared by Sor Juana). In other words, the angel is imputed these qualities, but the monster enacts them. When Ana "directs" her play-within-a-play, Leonor is reduced to its passive victim, who at no point utilizes her alleged mental acuity to extricate herself from the labyrinth. Ana and Leonor, we see, are both *polarized*, into redeemed angel and punished creative monster, and covertly *equated* as the two halves of a divided self. We might therefore conclude that in creating these, the first female characters devised by a female playwright in the New World, Sor Juana's keen awareness of the conflicts faced by the creative woman may well have impeded her from writing a play so staunchly favorable to this figure as Calderón's *La dama duende*.

AMOR ES MÁS LABERINTO (LOVE IS THE GREATER LABYRINTH)

Though a lesser *comedia* than *Empeños* (as Octavio Paz has noted, "the critics have vilified this comedy"),[33] *Amor es más laberinto* nevertheless presents intriguing developments in Sor Juana's womanscript. The play's double authorship, its first and third acts by Sor Juana and the second by poet and priest Juan de Guevara, renders its course as confused as the mythical labyrinth of Crete—"de tan intrincadas vueltas / y entretejidas lazadas / que el discurso las ignora" (of such intricate turns and interwoven snares that their [dis]course is unknown) [IV, p. 211]—

whose tale it starts off by telling. Beneath the shifting premises of the play, however, lies Sor Juana's characteristic womanscript which, forcibly rerouted by the second act, struggles to assert itself in the third, taking on a new form somewhat more favorable to the creative woman. Like Ariadne's thread, then, the latent womanscript will guide us through the inconsistent "vueltas" or twists of the play.

We can readily speculate that Sor Juana chose the mythological basis of the play for its congruence with the terms of her own script (note the similarity in titles: *Los empeños de una casa*, house; *Amor es más laberinto*, labyrinth). The appeal that the Theseus-Ariadne myth, and particularly its heroine, may have held for Sor Juana is easy to picture: Theseus has come to Crete as a victim of Minos, its vengeful king, to be devoured by the minotaur who stalks the labyrinth invented by Daedalus. When Theseus and Minos's daughter Ariadne fall in love, she provides him with the thread that guides him out of the labyrinth, her plot thus foiling her father's scheme. For reasons not entirely clear in the myth, the ungrateful Theseus will abandon Ariadne and, much later, marry her sister Phædra. Sor Juana may well have interpreted this enigmatic about-face in accordance with the scenario of *Los empeños*, where the resourceful creative woman is punished for her hubris.

Sor Juana's rearrangement of the myth and arrangement of the elements in the play's first act bear out its similarity to *Empeños*. Ariadna and Fedra appear together here and are equated: "Y como sois Fedra y tú, / aun más que en la sangre hermanas / en la belleza, os festejan / con iguales alabanzas" (and since Fedra and you are sisters in beauty even more than in blood, they celebrate you with the same praises) [IV, p. 208]. Added to the myth, each has her own original love interest, though Ariadna's feelings for Baco appear to be stronger than Fedra's for Lidoro. Teseo, object of desire, makes his appearance in Scene III with a lengthy speech to the king establishing his own achievements, valor, and humility. Though the king remains unmoved, here Ariadna and Fedra both fall in love with Teseo, which effects a schism between the two heroines. Struck by a mad love (an "Amor tirano," "que sabes hacer más daño que herir," a tyrannical love, which can cause more damage than mere pain [IV, p. 244]), and thus immediately jealous of Fedra, Ariadna "infers" that Fedra will try to free Teseo. Ariadna's heart becomes "varonil" (manly) [IV, p. 244], her "altivez" (pridefulness) manifests itself [IV, p. 244], and she comes up with a plot to free him first: "Yo he de librarlo, pues tengo / para que se libre, ardid" (It is I who will free him, for I have a plan) [IV,

p. 245]. Other entanglements, forming triangles of *encontradas corres-pondencias* (ironic symmetries) with Baco and Lidoro, take us to the end of the first act—by which point Sor Juana's rewriting of the myth has unmistakably laid the groundwork for her mimetic triangles, female doubles, and creative plotting heroine.

Guevara's act disrupts this framework: as if it were a dramatic *payada* or contest, Sor Juana has tangled up the play and hands it over to Guevara, who sorts out the lines only further to entangle them. In a much more elaborate and concept-ridden poetic style, Guevara largely abandons characterization to devote himself to generating *enredos*. These entanglements of mistaken identities center on the clandestine nocturnal encounters of all the characters, after Teseo's escape from the labyrinth, in a palace *sarao* or dance. That is to say, Guevara skirts the heart of the myth—Theseus's escape from the labyrinth with Ariadne's aid—to turn the play into a conventional palace *comedia*, thwarting Sor Juana's conceivable attempt to showcase Ariadna as a scheming woman. Departing further from the myth to produce new complications, Guevara leaves Teseo in love with Fedra and lamenting his debt to Ariadna. With this act, then, the play justifies its title. Love is the greater labyrinth (even greater than the labyrinth of Crete): everyone is caught up in these labyrinthine tangles, no individual controls or escapes them.

Sor Juana rescues the play from its palace frivolities and attempts, rather unconvincingly, to get it back on (her) track. She returns to what remains of the terms of the myth, Minos's vengeful attitudes—to be discussed shortly—and Teseo's two lovers. Reestablishing Ariadna as the schemer, Sor Juana invents a new scrape for Teseo, his murder of Lidoro, from which Teseo's servant begs the ingenious Ariadna to extricate them: "pues sólo tu ingenio, creo / que nos podrá dar favor" (for I believe that only your wiles can save us) [IV, p. 319]. The resulting plan is that they take flight from Crete. At this point, the two female protagonists, who throughout the second and third acts of the play have been equated by their consistently twin speeches, will again individuate themselves. This rather anomalous disruption of the doubles picks up the themes of "manly" and "mad" love from the first act by having Ariadna boldly propose flight to Baco, mistaking him for Teseo [IV, p. 329]. Fedra, on the other hand, unpresumptuous (like Teseo) and "womanly," must be cajoled into transgression:

con decirlo tú me excusas
el que yo te lo proponga,

porque no sé qué se tiene
el disponer amorosas
resoluciones, que suena
siempre mejor en la boca
del galán que de la dama
. . . .
porque proponer es cosa
en que se aja la hermosura
o el respeto se abandona
[IV, p. 324]

(in saying it yourself you save me from having to propose it to you,
for I don't know what there is about making amorous arrangements
that sounds better coming from the man than the woman . . . propo-
sitions are something in which beauty is tarnished or respect forsaken)

In another speech, the second of Fedra's two principal moments of
individuation in the play (we are also given indirectly to understand
that she has selflessly sacrificed Teseo's love for his safety, entrusting
him to Ariadna), she echoes Leonor's recognition of her transgression:
"¡Válgame Dios, qué resuelto / y valiente es el Amor, / pues a una mujer obliga / a tan temeraria acción, / como que deje a su patria / y que
abandone su honor / por seguir a un hombre!" (Heaven help me! How
resolute and valiant is Love, for it forces a woman to take such fearful
actions as leaving her country and forsaking her honor to follow a man!)
[IV, p. 331]. Only with these thin and fleeting maneuvers taken from
the repertoire of her womanscript does Sor Juana establish Fedra as the
light heroine and mediator, worthy, unlike Ariadna, of Teseo's love.

The chiaroscuro of the two heroines remains faint because Ariadna,
who receives the most sympathetic treatment of Sor Juana's three monster women, will not be dealt an altogether negative fate. Like Ana, it
is true, she will have to resign herself to her original love and to losing
the object of her desire. Yet this play has two focuses, the personal
(love *enredos*) and the public (Minos's desire to avenge his son's death
through that of Teseo).[34] Though Minos's honor has indeed been af-
fronted, Sor Juana presents his thirst for revenge as blind, rigid, and
cruel. In this sphere, Ariadna, for once a positive *mujer varonil*, serves
as a laudable agent of dis-simulation in keeping Teseo from suffering
the same fate as the prince of Crete, in a sense from becoming his
double. Teseo, the play's model, appreciates Ariadna's efforts: "hizo
empeño de librarme / con finezas tan heroicas, / con industrias tan
agudas / y acciones tan generosas" (she endeavored to free me with

such heroic kindness, with such keen skill, and with such generous actions) [IV, p. 322]. Like Fedra (and sounding remarkably like a "modern" hero), he deals sensibly with jealousy: "que muy bien puede un amante / . . . ser fino con la que quiere, / sin ser grosero con otra" (well can a lover . . . be kind to the one he loves without being rude to the other) [IV, p. 322]. Ultimately, thanks to Teseo's appreciation, Ariadna will save her father's life: since she saved Teseo's life, the Athenian armies spare her father's (says Teseo, "pues él dio / el sér a quien me dio vida," for he gave life to she who gave me mine [IV, p. 349]). Thus, Ariadna, mistress of the labyrinth, emerges as the heroine in the play's public sphere; the monster succeeds in becoming an angel-mediator, but only in another dimension.

THE *AUTOS SACRAMENTALES*: *EL MÁRTIR DEL SACRAMENTO, SAN HERMENEGILDO* (THE MARTYR OF THE SACRAMENT, SAINT HERMENEGILDO)

Since the chronology of Sor Juana's three Eucharistic plays has yet to be established, rightly or wrongly we will treat *San Hermenegildo* and *El cetro de José* as studies for Sor Juana's most fully realized *auto*, *El Divino Narciso*. Each of the two plays with male-dominated triangles develops elements which will resurface there, in conjunction with the woman-script. Let us now briefly examine in *San Hermenegildo* the emerging figure of the martyr, so central to Sor Juana's Eucharistic plays.

In fashioning the two martyrs, Narciso and Hermenegildo, Sor Juana draws on her stock elements, modifying them to fit the divine male protagonists. In the case of Hermenegildo, the mimetic triangles fall away, replaced by a triangle that externalizes the protagonist's internal divisions, torn, as he is, between Catholicism and his Visigoth religion, Arianism. Whereas two female protagonists reflect the divided self in the plays we have examined, here a single male protagonist contains within himself the division, of which the other apices of the much simplified triangle serve only as reflectors: his father of Arianism, his wife of Catholicism. Like Sor Juana's Narciso and like Christ (both of them at once human and divine), in achieving martyrdom Hermenegildo will realize one half of his divided self (Catholicism) and violently sacrifice the other. Though ultimately and necessarily positive, martyrdom in these plays is also a punishment of sorts. Narciso will pay with his death for the loving narcissism within, Hermenegildo for his excessive religious zeal, which divides his father's kingdom.[35] Pride and presumption, we see, characterize the male protagonists as well: Hermenegildo belongs to the race of the Baltos, which means "daring" ("atrevido"). Yet *their* overreaching in the cause of faith earns them sainthood or divinity, beyond death.

EL CETRO DE JOSÉ (JOSEPH'S SCEPTER)

In the first scene of *El cetro de José,* José's (the Joseph of the Old Testament) prophetic dreams foretelling the adoration he will receive incite his brothers to accuse him of presumptuousness—but, for once, wrongly so. For this play, which ingeniously transposes the biblical story of Joseph in Egypt into a prefiguration of Christ, will equate José's dreams with God-given knowledge. *El cetro de José* also contains an allegorical stratum in which, somewhat like a Greek chorus, the figures of Lucero (Lucifer, the Devil) and his accomplices—Inteligencia (Intelligence), Ciencia (Knowledge), Envidia (Envy), and Conjetura (Conjecture)— witness and gloss the biblical story being enacted. The allegorical level contrasts José's divine revelations with the Devil's limited intelligence, thus shaping the play into a fascinating essay on knowledge which warrants closer critical attention.[36]

A simplified version of *El Divino Narciso*'s single triangle underlies the polemic on knowledge: the *Devil* and his handmaidens fear that *José/Christ* will return to *Mankind,* "el Hombre," the superior knowledge that was lost as a result of the Fall (we note that in retelling the story of the Fall here, Sor Juana does not deviate from biblical legend and attributes it to the woman [III, p. 204]). The play begins by establishing the important equation between the Devil and Knowledge. Married to a figure alternately identified as Inteligencia and Ciencia, the Devil realizes that if the feared event were to transpire, his own at present superior intelligence would lose its edge, and he would lose his power over mankind. According to Alfonso Méndez-Plancarte's explanation,

> The Devil (though an Angel who had rebelled and been expelled from Heaven) maintained intact that intelligence which pertained to his angelic nature. Man, per se, has an inferior intelligence, obscured and weakened by sin. Thus he is deprived of the Devil's keen intelligence, which the Devil is at pains to preserve.[37]

The case of José, however, shows that knowledge need not pertain to the Devil: knowledge and faith may coexist. Profecía (Prophecy), as

Divine Revelation, implants in José his dreams and counsel. "No soy yo," says José to the Pharaoh, "quien te responde. / Dios, Señor es quien te avisa" (It is not I who answers you. It is God, my lord, who warns you) [III, p. 224]. From José's scepter will issue the Eucharist, called the bread of "Eterna Sabiduría" (Eternal Wisdom) [III, p. 241], which He presents to His erring brothers. Compared to this ultimate knowledge, as mentioned above, the Devil's intelligence proves to be relative and myopic. Inteligencia confesses to the Devil that only Divine Revelation, and not she, could inform José's dreams [III, p. 226]. The Devil proves incapable of comprehending the fused tales of José and Christ ("parece que mi Inteligencia falta / o mi Ciencia se suspende," it seems that my Intelligence is failing or my Knowledge suspended [III, p. 243]. Profecía accuses the Devil's other accomplice Conjetura of "soberbia" (pride) and "arrogancia" (arrogance) [III, p. 239] and ultimately *mutes* her. These last two facts, and indeed the whole opposition of the Devil to José/Christ, take us directly into *El Divino Narciso*.

EL DIVINO NARCISO (THE DIVINE NARCISSUS)

Why, in *El Divino Narciso* is Narciso divine and Eco the Devil? Mythic tradition represents Narcissus—an unlikely Christ figure—as the prideful lover capable only of adoring his own image, and Echo as the woman muted by Juno for her devious stories and scorned by Narcissus. Sor Juana's unusual interpretation of the myth is likely to have derived its inspiration in part from Calderón's *comedia Eco y Narciso,* which shifts the sin of pride onto Eco, whom Liriope renders semimute for tempting her son Narciso.[38] In any case, Sor Juana's Eucharistic version of the myth remains shockingly catachrestic, being a female-dominated "echo" of the triangle found in *El cetro de José: Narciso/Christ* will redeem his beloved *Naturaleza Humana* (Human Nature), much as his efforts are thwarted by the *Devil-Eco,* whose attentions he spurns. Rivals for Narciso's love, Naturaleza Humana will become the mirror image for whom Narciso dies, while Eco receives the existential punishments of echolalia and a life of ceaseless suffering. Now, Ludwig Pfandl, with his unsettling analysis of Sor Juana's "neuroses," explains Sor Juana's treatment of the myth as an expiation of her own narcissism, in that she elevates Narcissus to the stature of Christ.[39] Sor Juana, we have seen, chooses her myths carefully. Here, as in *Amor es más laberinto,* the scorned (and muted) Eco may well equally have inspired her interest. Our argument will thus focus on the Devil-Eco—her sins, anti-"Narcissistic" stratagems, and echoes in other characters—as the definitive exposition of Sor Juana's womanscript.

Why is the Devil a woman? Ostensibly, the portrayal of the Devil as a woman holds no surprise, her role as temptress to sin and disruptor being a natural extension of the received biblical and dramatic norms we have already examined. Eco incarnates the same powers and sins attributed to Lucero in *El cetro de José's* conventional presentation of the Devil: Eco's helpmeets and reflectors, Soberbia (Pride) and Amor Propio (Self-Love), accompany her every move; presumptuous, she sets herself up as a false god, and considering herself Narciso's equal, she employs her considerable intelligence to outwit Him; this ultimately limited intelligence fails her when faced with the drama of the Eucharist ("Aqueso es lo que mi ciencia / no alcanza cómo será," That is what my knowledge can't manage to grasp [III, p. 91]). Yet, unlike Lucero, Eco does not remain on the sidelines as an impotent spectator and commentator. Instead, she intervenes in the action, placing her intelligence in the service of the creative strategies we will consider in their full context.

In this hyperliterary drama, a dense intertextual fabric woven of quotations from pagan and biblical sources, it is only fitting that Narciso and Eco should be equated with two strategies of figuration, Narciso with the reflections (similitude) and Eco with the *ecos* (dissimilation), that Octavio Paz has identified as obsessive currents in Sor Juana's poetry.[40] Exalting Narciso to the status of Christ, Sor Juana also assigns an exalted role to the verbal narcissism, or similitude, that Narciso eponymously symbolizes. Naturaleza Humana portrays as a divine instrument of providentialism the allegorical mechanisms, based on similitude, of the Eucharistic play itself, "pues muchas veces conformes / divinas y humanas letras, / dan a entender que Dios pone / aun en las plumas gentiles / unos visos en que asoman / los altos misterios suyos" (since often divine and human letters agree, it shows that even in pagan pens God places a tint in which His exalted mysteries can be glimpsed) [III, p. 26]. Love, for the Divine Narciso, must be similitude, exact mirroring. Accordingly, Naturaleza Humana seeks those specular waters unclouded by sin which will reflect her image as a double of Narciso's, thereby renewing His love for her. "Mi imagen representa / si Narciso repara / clara, clara" (let it represent my image, if Narcissus looks, clearly, clearly) [III, p. 56], she sings to the fountain of Mary.[41] Narciso/Christ's death for his mirror image culminates in the ultimate act of figuration, the Eucharist, which reunites in perpetual similitude Christ's body and soul.

Eco, on the other hand, applies her diabolical intelligence to acts of dissimilation. In arrogantly rebelling against God, the Devil-Eco lost all resemblance to Him; Narciso will never love one so dissimilar to Him, "Porque nunca corresponde / tu soberbia a la humildad / que apetece mi beldad" (Because your pride will never match the humility for which my beauty yearns) [III, p. 78]. Throughout the play we thus find Eco fabricating vengeful stratagems.[42] She plots to entrap Narciso ("con una estratagema conoceré si es divino," using a stratagem I will find out if he is divine [III, p. 20]). Once before, with the Fall, she had plotted Naturaleza Humana's undoing: "inventé tales ardides," she says, "formé tal estratagema" (I invented such tricks, I fashioned such a stratagem) [III, p. 36], that she succeeded in leading Naturaleza Humana astray. Now, afrenzy with jealousy, she plots to cloud the waters of the fountain with sin, thereby destroying their specular powers: "Y así, siempre he procurado / con cuidado y diligencia / borrar esta semejanza" (and thus I have always endeavored, with care and diligence, to erase that resemblance) [III, p. 37]. Like the house for Ana, the waters serve as the instrument of dissimilation; they also entail a powerful metaphor of mimesis (in Aristotle's sense) and that great art of imitation, writing.

Agent of dissimilation, Eco also becomes its victim—both facts foster her identification with the creative woman, the monster heroine. Before Eco can poison the fountain's waters, effectively implementing her strategy, she is struck mute. But not for the first time. Displacing Juno's act of revenge from the myth, provoked by Echo's *storytelling*, onto Narciso, Sor Juana's Eco explains:

> pues también alguna vez Narciso
> enmudecer me hizo,
> porque Su Ser divino publicaba
> y mi voz reprendiéndome atajaba,
> no es mucho que también ahora quiera
> que, con el ansia fiera,
> al llegar a mirarlo quede muda
> [III, p. 64]

(since Narcissus also once muted me for proclaiming his divinity, cutting off my voice in reprimand, it doesn't surprise me that he now wishes that I be struck mute when, yearning fiercely, I see him.)

114

Little as one wishes to take recourse to crude biographical parallels (which might suggest the church stifling Sor Juana's voice), Eco's explanation does argue against Pfandl's and for understanding her as a persona of the creative woman: she who wields such intelligence, she who has engaged in such prideful schemes, will be punished by having her *voice* muted by Narciso. Alienated from herself ("parece nueva pena / la que de sus sentidos la enajena," it seems new, this pain that alienates her from her senses [III, p. 64]), Eco can only express her thoughts through artifice and echolalic dissimilation (the baroque "echo device"), forming others' words into speeches that articulate her suffering. Further, only in this scene, with her crippled language, does Eco join her voice with Narciso in a prolonged duet [III, pp. 70–78]. Narciso, *"Autor del Universo"* (Author of the Universe) [III, p. 81], has indeed contrived an apt punishment for his dark creative heroine's transgressions.

The light heroine and quintessential Sor Juanian mediator, Naturaleza Humana, meets quite a different fate: her latent similarities to the object of desire actualized, she becomes Narciso's double and he hers, the mortality he shares with her causing his death. To achieve such a state of redemption, however, Naturaleza Humana must transcend her resemblance to her rival and distorted double, Eco. In *El Divino Narciso*, with its single paradigmatic triangle, the dark and light heroines unmistakably share the same formal profile. Both of them alternately act as mistress of ceremonies, Naturaleza Humana introducing the allegory of Narciso as Christ in the first scene, Eco in the third. Curiously enough, the Golden Age *auto sacramental* generally assigns this self-conscious function to the Devil,[43] which fact heightens the equation of the angel with the monster. Both Eco ("naturaleza angélica réproba," reprobate angelic nature) and Naturaleza Humana had once possessed the angelic attributes that made them beloved to God: Eco as angel, Naturaleza Humana as a pure being before the Fall. The sin of pride removed both females' resemblance to God. Narciso reminds Naturaleza Humana, "Engordaste, y lozana, / soberbia y engreída / de verte tan lucida, / altivamente vana, Mi belleza olvidaste soberana" (You swelled; and robust, prideful and conceited to see yourself so splendid, arrogantly proud, you forgot my sovereign beauty) [III, p. 59]. Eco, in attempting to obscure the fountain's waters, strives not only to defeat her rival but to maintain Naturaleza Humana, mediator, as her own darkened double.

El Divino Narciso equates its dark and light heroines only better, that is, more didactically, to oppose them. Here, as in the other plays, the syncopation of the two heroines' transgressions serves a didactic purpose. Naturaleza Humana, now humble ("la humildad / que ape-tece mi beldad," the humility for which my beauty yearns) as we have seen seeks reconciliation with Narciso; Eco persists in her prideful course. At first quite literally a dark heroine—paraphrasing the Song of Songs, Naturaleza Humana sings to Narciso, "mira que, aunque soy negra, soy hermosa, / pues parezco a Tu imagen milagrosa" (see that although I am black, I am beautiful, because I resemble your miracu-lous image) [III, p. 51]—when returned to Gracia, the sun, she is enveloped in light [III, p. 51]. Thus, much as Eco and Naturaleza Humana are equated and pretend to the same object of desire, the Devil-Eco, perpetually unregenerate, will never imitate the mediator's redeemed condition. The audience of this morality play, however, must, and such didactic effects induce them to do so.

Though the relationship is, we see, ultimately ruptured, Eco and Naturaleza Humana originally stand as mirror-image doubles. On the other hand, Eco and Narciso, God and Devil, emerge on several counts as *negative* doubles, which fact underscores the more ultimate dimensions of Eco's triangular dilemma. Marie-Cécile Bénassy-Berling notes the religious tradition of portraying Devil and God as negative doubles, as "inseparable but unequal."[44] In *El Divino Narciso*, Eco clearly embodies the self-pride traditionally attributed to Narcissus; in fact, she can be seen to *contain* Narciso in the form of her reflector Amor Propio, male shepherd. When the shepherd Narciso does him-self succumb to self-love, for his mirror image ("Su propia similitud / fue Su amoroso atractivo," His own resemblance was his loving attrac-tion [III, p. 93]), this narcissism assumes a positive aspect. Second, where Eco futilely exercises diabolical intelligence in the cause of jeal-ousy, like José, Narciso embodies a superior knowledge, allied with love: "Su disposición fue parto / de su saber infinito / que no se ostenta lo amante / sin galas de lo entendido" (His inclination was born of his infinite wisdom, for love never appears without the adornments of wisdom) [III, p. 81]. And finally, the Divine Narciso, having surren-dered his mortality to martyrdom (we recall Hermenegildo), will live on in the Eucharist, while Eco's immortality brings her endless suffer-ing. All of these ironic equations but accentuate the metaphysical im-plications of Sor Juana's triangle which the whole of *El Divino Narciso*, in rewriting the womanscript *a lo divino,* has explicitly revealed. Eco, we conclude, though poignantly "echoed" in both Naturaleza Humana and Narciso, is forbidden not only her love and voice but also the so-lace of reconciliation with divine forces.

ECHOES OF THE WOMANSCRIPT

Its metaphysical dimensions now fully in view, it becomes clear that the womanscript encompasses a fair sampling of Sor Juana's most central concerns: knowledge, God, woman, transgression, and so on. As such, it could not fail to inform other of her works. Let us now very briefly suggest the echoes of the womanscript in the *Primero sueño* (First Dream) and certain of Sor Juana's devotional writings.[45]

The ever-present theme of pride brings our terms of reference into the *Sueño*. According to the poem's last line with its "I" and feminine adjective ("y *yo* despiert*a*," and I awake; my emphasis), the *Sueño* can be taken to represent a woman's search for knowledge, inevitably problematical. The scenario of the poem evokes that of the plays. Under cover of night's freedom, the soul (*alma*, feminine, dark heroine) now "suspensa del exterior gobierno" (exempt from outer influence) [I, p. 340], pursues her most primordial inclinations in seeking her object, not a person but knowledge. This search commences under the sign of transgression—the mythical figures of lines 25–64, turned into animals in punishment for their erring ways—and results in prideful failure, its first portion equated with the flight of Icarus, the more hopeful second portion with Phaeton. Georgina Sabat-Rivers says of the latter, "instead of failing definitively, Phaeton becomes the symbol of he who dares time and again to attempt the same feat despite repeated failures."[46] Similar but distinct from the plays, then, the prideful rebellion in search of knowledge of the night heroine, who "segunda vez rebelde determina / mirarse coronada" (rebellious, determined to see herself crowned again) [I, p. 359], is potentially cyclical. The rebellion temporarily pacified, in the last lines of the poem order is restored ("quedando a luz más cierta / el Mundo iluminado", leaving the world illuminated by a more certain light [I, p. 359]), night cedes to day, and nocturnal seeker to diurnal. The poem rests its argument, if inconclusively and suggestively, in the hands of the light, and according to Calleja's famous summary "desengañada" (disillusioned) heroine[47]— who may not only have sought but also found true knowledge.

The main body of the *Sueño*, which Sor Juana describes as the only piece of work she freely wrote [*Respuesta*, IV, p. 471], thus provides a stunning portrait of the dark heroine's travails. Several of the nun's religious writings, particularly the *Ejercicios de la Encarnación* (Exercises for the Incarnation, probably written between 1684–1688)[48] and the "feminist" *villancicos* to Santa Catarina (1691), on the other hand, portray a light heroine uniquely constructed to exculpate woman in general, and their author in particular, of the sins levied against them. Sor Juana's writings on the Virgin Mary, from the *Ejercicios* to the religious documents of the penultimate year of her life (the *Docta explicación del misterio y voto que hizo de defender la Purísima Concepción de Nuestra Señora, la Madre Juana Inés de la Cruz,* 1694, Learned Explanation of the Mystery and Vow Made by Sister Juana Inés de la Cruz to Defend the Immaculate Conception of Our Lady, 1694), focus almost obsessively on Mary's exemption from sin (also seen in the fountain of *El Divino Narciso*) and her role as humankind's redeemer from sin, restorer of the lost similitude to God. This light heroine, though she has not transgressed, displays in the *Ejercicios* other characteristics of Sor Juana's most fully drawn angel woman and her own idealized mask, Leonor. She incarnates humility, love, knowledge, and reason. Sor Juana's highly personalized mariolatry places special emphasis on Mary as author, of the *Magnificat,* as teacher, as intellectual, as possessor of religious and scientific knowledge, as mistress of the House of the Imagination.[49] The autobiographical aspects built into the character of Leonor surface, even more explicitly, in Sor Juana's rendition of Santa Catarina's wisdom. She focuses on Catarina's "prueba por los sabios" (examination by the sages), so similar to her own, which emerges as a redemption of woman's intelligence: "De una Mujer se convencen / todos los Sabios de Egipto, / para prueba de que el sexo / no es esencia en lo entendido. / ¡Víctor, víctor!" (All the sages of Egypt are convinced by a woman that gender is not of the essence in matters of intelligence. Victor! Victor!) [II, p. 171]. In like manner, the third *villancico* of the Ascension, 1676 [II, p. 6], has the "cursantes" (students) voting Mary, "La Soberana Doctora / de las Escuelas divinas" (the Supreme Doctor of the Divine Schools), as victor, of knowledge, and against sin. Finally, the example of Catarina makes it clear that knowledge need not be opposed to faith: "Tutelar sacra Patrona, / es de las Letras Asilo; / porque siempre ilustre sabios, / quien Santos de Sabios hizo. / ¡Víctor, víctor!" (Tutelar and holy Patron, she is the Shrine of Arts; long may she illumine wise men, she who Wise Men to Saints converts. Victor! Victor!) [II, p. 172].

Victory, exoneration, idealized mask, *mediator:* placed over and against the continuing drama of the divided woman we have observed in the *Sueño* and in Sor Juana's theater we see that these divine light heroines constructed over a period of fifteen years express a desired or desiring self and comprise something of an act of resistance in face of the tangled complex of circumstances that undermined the realization of that self. All told, nonetheless, one perceives in Sor Juana's works what has been described as a certain "melancholy," the melancholy of a woman who "soared above the rest" but never fully forgave herself her own daring, cognizant as she may have been of the "mistaken rules" that rendered her daring presumptuous.[50] The final triangle— the last words in the convent's *Libro de profesiones* (Book of Professions) by and regarding Sor Juana—speaks compellingly if formulaically to such a perception: "A todas pido perdón por amor de Dios y de su Madre. Yo la peor del mundo. Juana Inés de la Cruz" (I beg the forgiveness of all [my sisters], for the love of God and his Mother. I, the worst in the world. Juana Inés de la Cruz) [IV, p. 523].

NOTES

1. *Los empeños de una casa* was first performed in 1683; *Amor es más laberinto,* ca. 1689; *El Divino Narciso,* in 1689. For a useful chronology of these plays, see Kathleen Shelly and Grínor Rojo, "El teatro hispanoamericano colonial," in *Historia de la Literatura Hispanoamericana,* Vol. I, ed. by Luis Iñigo Madrigal (Madrid: Cátedra, 1982), p. 336. The chronology of Sor Juana's other two Eucharistic plays has been less precisely established. Octavio Paz, in *Sor Juana Inés de la Cruz o las trampas de la fe* (Barcelona: Seix Barral, 1982; published in the English translation of Margaret Sayers Peden by Harvard University Press in 1988 under the title of *Sor Juana*), situates the composition of *El mártir del Sacramento, San Hermenegildo* between 1680 and 1688 and *El cetro de José* between 1680 and 1689 (p. 452).

All references in this study are taken from the four-volume *Obras completas de Sor Juana Inés de la Cruz,* ed. by Alfonso Méndez-Plancarte, Vol. IV by Alberto G. Salceda (Mexico: Fondo de Cultura Económica, 1951–57), and are included in the body of the text, with volume and page numbers indicated. The four volumes are divided in the following manner: Vol. I, *Lírica personal;* Vol. II, *Villancicos y letras sacras;* Vol. III, *Autos y loas;* Vol. IV, *Comedias, sainetes y prosa.*

2. Rachel Phillips, "Sor Juana: Dream and Silence," *Aphra* 3, 1 (Winter 1971–72):35.

3. Such has been the consecrated interpretation of the *Respuesta.* Another trend characterizes the bishop of Puebla, to whom the *Respuesta* is directed, less as Sor Juana's persecutor than as her accomplice, aiding the nun in a moment of crisis. For a discussion of the debate, see p. 290 of Georgina Sabat de Rivers's "Sor Juana Inés de la Cruz," in the volume edited by Iñigo Madrigal cited in note 1, and pp. 172–76 of Marie-Cécile Bénassy-Berling's *Humanisme et Religion chez Sor Juana Inés de la Cruz: La femme et la culture au XVIIe siècle* (Paris: Editions Hispaniques, 1982). Whatever the immediate relationship between Sor Juana and the bishop of Puebla, I contend that the *Respuesta* remains a powerfully argued self-defense against years of accumulated and/or perceived injuries. In my "*Narciso desdoblado:*

Narcissistic Stratagems in *El Divino Narciso* and the *Respuesta a Sor Filotea de la Cruz*" (*Bulletin of Hispanic Studies* 64, 2 [April 1987]:111–17), I examine the rhetoric and argumentation of this self-defense.

4. Julie Greer Johnson, *Women in Colonial Spanish American Literature: Literary Images* (Westport, Conn.: Greenwood Press, 1983), p. 186.

5. I use the term *clinamen* not in the sense attributed to it by Harold Bloom in *The Anxiety of Influence* (where it represents poetic misreading), but according to Michel Serres's suggestive definition on p. 51 of *Hermes: Literature, Science, and Philosophy*, ed. by Josué Harari and David F. Bell (Baltimore and London: Johns Hopkins University Press, 1982): "the minimum angle of the laminar flow [that] initiates a turbulence—the moment when an atom in a laminar flow deviates from its path, collides with another atom, and initiates the formation of things and ultimately of worlds."

6. Ruth El Saffar, "Unbinding the Doubles: Reflections on Love and Culture in the Work of René Girard," *Denver Quarterly* 18, 4 (Winter, 1984):14.

7. Pedro Calderón de la Barca, *Obras completas*, Vol. II, ed. by Angel Valbuena Briones (Madrid: Aguilar, 1960), p. 242.

8. See Julia Fitzmaurice-Kelly's "Woman in Sixteenth-Century Spain," *Revue Hispanique* 70, 157 (June 1927):557–632, for a detailed discussion of Golden Age Spain's attitudes toward women; and Asunción Lavrin's "In Search of the Colonial Woman in Mexico: The Seventeenth and Eighteenth Centuries," in her edited work *Latin American Women: Historical Perspectives* (Westport, Conn.: Greenwood Press, 1978), pp. 23–59.

9. In *Women and Society in the Spanish Drama of the Golden Age: A Study of the Mujer Varonil* (London: Cambridge University Press, 1974), Melveena McKendrick discusses at length the *mujer varonil* and the various offshoots to which this character gave rise. On p. 313, she states that the *mujer esquiva* was by far the most popular of these variants.

10. Ibid., p. 171. See chap. 5 of McKendrick's study, devoted to the *mujer esquiva*. Unlike the *mujer esquiva*, McKendrick also informs us, the *mujer varonil* could triumph, when she acts in "manly" ways to defend (manly) honorable causes.

We find echoes of the *mujer esquiva* in Sor Juana's noted statement in the *Respuesta* that she preferred conventual life to marriage, as well as in the *esquivez* of her theater's protagonists.

11. Anthony J. Cascardi, *The Limits of Illusion: A Critical Study of Calderón* (London: Cambridge University Press, 1984), p. 119.

12. Jean E. Kennard, *Victims of Convention* (Hamden, Conn.: Archon Books, 1978), p. 14.

13. Angel Valbuena Prat, *Calderón* (Barcelona: Editorial Juventud, 1941), p. 19.

14. Irving A. Leonard, in "The Encontradas Correspondencias of Sor Juana: An Interpretation," *Hispanic Review* 1, 23 (January 1955):33–47; and Raquel Chang-Rodríguez, in "Relectura de *Los empeños de una casa*," *Revista Iberoamericana* 104–5 (July–December 1978):409–19, discuss the mechanisms and meanings of the "encontradas correspondencias" in Sor Juana's works. Both critics see these oppositions as metaphorically representing Sor Juana's conflict between divine and secular knowledge. Clearly, my reading takes another direction.

15. René Girard, *Deceit, Desire and the Novel: Self and Other in Literary Struc-*

ture, trans. by Yvonne Freccero (Baltimore and London: Johns Hopkins University Press, 1965). See particularly the first two chapters.

16. Ibid., p. 74.

17. Ruth El Saffar, *Beyond Fiction: The Recovery of the Feminine in the Novels of Cervantes* (Berkeley: University of California Press, 1984), p. 5.

18. See George Lemus's comparison of Sor Juana's *Los empeños* to its Caldero-nian namesake on p. 22 of his "El feminismo de Sor Juana Inés de la Cruz en *Los empeños de una casa,*" *Letras femeninas* 11, 1–2 (Spring–Fall 1985). Similarly, María Ester Pérez, in comparing the two authors, notes, "in Sor Juana's works, it is the female characters who take the lead," in *Lo americano en el teatro de Sor Juana Inés de la Cruz* (New York: Eliseo Torres, 1975), p. 86.

19. René Girard, *Deceit,* p. 14.

20. Sandra M. Gilbert and Susan Gubar, *The Madwoman in the Attic: The Woman Writer and Nineteenth-Century Literary Imagination* (New Haven: Yale University Press, 1979).

21. Ibid., p. 82.

22. Ibid., p. 51.

23. Ibid., p. xi.

24. Several years before Gilbert and Gubar, in his *Anatomy of Criticism* (Princeton: Princeton University Press, 1957) and more fully in *The Secular Scripture: A Study of the Structure of Romance* (Cambridge, Mass.: Harvard University Press, 1976), Northrop Frye discussed the light and dark heroines of romance, mentioning, as well, the recurrence of these polarized heroines in romantic literature (*The Secular Scripture,* p. 83). The parallels between Frye's discussion, Gilbert and Gubar's, and our terms of reference here are highly suggestive. Frye's notion of the light heroine as she who is accommodated to the natural cycle and marries, versus the dark heroine who is sacrificed or escapes sacrifice and remains a virgin (thus, according to Frye, keeping her identity intact) would seem to hold particular resonance for our argument regarding Sor Juana's theater. See pp. 83–86 and 143 of *The Secular Scripture* for a discussion of these issues. The reader will also find in Lucy Fischer's "Two Faced Woman: The 'Double' in Women's Melodrama of the 1940's," *Cinema Journal* 23, 1 (Fall 1983): 24–43, a discussion of light and dark twins, the former embodying male constructs of the female, the latter defying them, which follows lines remarkably similar to Frye's and Gilbert and Gubar's. A similar polarization, it seems, persists from medieval romance to the present day.

25. Gilbert and Gubar, *Madwoman,* p. 38.

26. Ibid., p. 77.

27. Ibid., p. 78.

28. As Joseph A. Fuestle, Jr., writes in "Hacia una interpretación de *Los empeños de una casa* de Sor Juana Inés de la Cruz," *Explicación de textos literarios* I (1972):145, "Carlos and Leonor's love is a reflection of perfect love, an intellectual and reasoned love, in contrast with the 'mad love' of doña Ana." Raquel Chang-Rodríguez discusses Don Carlos in similar terms on pp. 410 and 412 of her article cited in note 14 above.

29. George Lemus, on p. 25 of his article cited in note 18 above, argues that Ana receives no punishment for her scheming. Yet he goes on, curiously enough, to characterize Juan as "an austere, domineering man, ready to use force when the woman doesn't want to obey his advice."

30. José Juan Arrom, *Historia del teatro hispanoamericano: Epoca colonial* (Mexico: Ediciones de Andrea, 1967), p. 84. Feustle and Lemus make similar observations.

31. Although little is made of it in Calderón's play, it is Angela's brothers who have gone out too far and, in terms of Golden Age drama, merit punishment. They believed their family honor to be at risk when Angela, laudable *mujer varonil*, dared go to court to defend her late husband's reputation. With this, Angela was fulfilling an honorable "masculine" duty; her brothers have, tacitly, kept her from acting like a "man," not a "woman."

32. Edwin Honig, *Calderón and the Seizures of Honor* (Cambridge, Mass.: Harvard University Press, 1972), p. 110.

33. Octavio Paz, *Sor Juana*, p. 437; Eng. version, p. 330.

34. As distinct from *Los empeños*, and moving towards the single triangle of *El Divino Narciso*, in this play we find two plotters but only one triangle (Aridana-Fedra-Teseo).

35. The lines, both geometrical and of the plot, grow somewhat confused in this play as Sor Juana attempts strictly to follow (rather than to adapt, as with the myths) the historical story. Since it would be Hermenegildo's brother Recaredo who eventually united the divided kingdom, he is characterized rather secondarily as something of a mediator, combining temperateness and Christian faith. We therefore find here a glimmer of the polarized and doubled female heroines, but without the full monster characteristics or attendant triangular circumstances of the female-dominated plays.

36. *El cetro de José* has received only summary critical attention. If nothing else, its polemic on knowledge and faith bears implications not only for *El Divino Narciso* but also for the *Sueño*.

37. Méndez-Plancarte, *Obras completas*, Vol. III, p. 608.

38. On p. lxxiii of his introduction to Vol. III, Méndez-Plancarte notes that Calderón's *Eco y Narciso* was "so famous and well-known that Sor Juana, in recreating this myth *a lo divino*, uses literal yet implicit quotes from it that the audience undoubtedly recognized."

39. Ludwig Pfandl, *Sor Juana Inés de la Cruz: La décima musa de México*, trans. by Francisco de la Maza (Mexico: UNAM, 1963), pp. 213 ff. Pfandl finds key evidence of Sor Juana's "narcissistic" tendencies in her stated disinclination toward marriage. For example, he writes: "Such women [i.e., narcissistic], whose psychological constitution definitely qualify them as so-called intersexuals . . . love themselves, idolize themselves, want to be loved without returning that love" (p. 155). With regard to *El Divino Narciso*, Pfandl boldly asserts: "In the fable of Narcissus she perceived the image and likeness of her own interiority; thus, her sacramental play *The Divine Narcissus* admits an interpretation which alludes to Sor Juana herself" (p. 238).

40. Paz, *Sor Juana*, p. 320; Eng. version, p. 246.

41. On pp. 220–24 of her book already cited, Bénassy-Berling discusses the fact that in what she views as Sor Juana's platonic system, divine love is equated with reciprocal love. She quotes San Juan de la Cruz's "Subida al monte Carmelo" (Ascent to Mount Carmel) as a possible source for the nun's attitude: "Love creates similarity between lover and what is loved" (p. 224).

42. Sergio Fernández writes, "Since the hero despises her, Eco exchanges her love for hatred and takes recourse to stratagems, to tricks characteristic of a low, markedly feminine [sic], condition." "Los autos sacramentales de sor Juana Inés de

la Cruz," in his *Homenaje a Sor Juana, a López Velarde, a José Gorostiza* (Mexico: Sepsetentas, 1972), p. 90.

43. Angel L. Cilveti, *El demonio en el teatro de Calderón* (Valencia: Albatros Ediciones, 1977), p. 45.

44. Bénassy-Berling, *Humanisme et religion,* p. 392.

45. As I discuss in my *"Narciso desdoblado"* article, cited in note 3 above, Sor Juana employs her dis-simulated *yo,* now divided into the light and dark personae of her own being, as a central stratagem of her self-defense in the *Respuesta.* Though related to our purposes, this argument is too detailed to be presented here.

46. Georgina Sabat de Rivers, *El "Sueño" de Sor Juana Inés de la Cruz: Tradiciones literarias y originalidad* (London: Tamesis, 1976), p. 81. See also her contribution to this volume (chapter 7) for a discussion of Phaeton and the ending of the *Sueño.*

47. Cited by Octavio Paz in his "Homenaje a Sor Juana Inés de la Cruz en su tercer centenario (1651–1695)," *Sur* 206 (December 1951): 38.

48. According to Méndez-Plancarte, *Obras completas,* IV, p. 663.

49. See Electa Arenal's "Sor Juana Inés de la Cruz: Speaking the Mother Tongue," *University of Dayton Review* 16, 2 (Spring 1983), pp. 93–106, for a discussion of Sor Juana's special mariolatry.

50. Octavio Paz writes in *El laberinto de la soledad* (Mexico: Fondo de Cultura Económica, 1959, p. 91): "Se advierte la melancolía de un espíritu que no logró nunca hacerse perdonar su atrevimiento y su condición de mujer" (One notes the melancholy of a spirit that never managed to forgive its own daring and position as a woman).

CHAPTER 6

Where Woman Is Creator of the Wor(l)d.
Or,
Sor Juana's Discourses on Method

ELECTA ARENAL

> even my sleep was not free from this continual movement
> of my imagination, but rather my mind asleep labors even
> more freely and unfettered, discoursing and composing
> verses, examining with greater clarity and calm the day's
> offering of images and occurrences, of which I could make
> a lengthy catalogue for you, and of some reasonings and
> thoughts I have reached asleep better than awake . . .
> —*Response to Sister Filotea de la Cruz,* 1691

> ¿qué cosas dijera yo,
> andando de texto en texto
> buscando la conexión?
> (what might I not say, moving from text to text seeking
> the connection?)
> —Letra XX, "Dedicación de San Bernardo," 1690

Sor Juana Inés de la Cruz was a person of astonishing consciousness. Literarily, she turned the world upside-down and inside-out with such baroque aplomb that it has taken until the twentieth century for us to rediscover the breadth of her art and the depth of her feminist epistemology. Scientifically, she turned the world right-side-up and outside-in with such empirical understanding of linguistic strategies that she became a sober and ironic herald of the Age of Reason. Enthusiastic about recombinations of old and new methods of inquiry that had led to the development of physics, mechanics, optics, astronomy, physiology, and medicine, she pondered them philosophically and made them central metaphors for her intellectual autobiography in verse: *Primero sueño,* also known as *El sueño* (First Dream).[1]

El sueño is, in part, the product of a vision not unlike Descartes's in which he glimpsed a fusion of theology, poetry, and science. But some of Sor Juana's ideas, such as her conception of a chain of being and her objection to the aggressive exploitation of nature, are much more like those of the little-known Ann Finch, Viscountess of Conway (1631–1679), who broke with Descartes and the Cambridge Platonists over the issue of dualism, influenced Leibniz, and "based her [monadic vitalist] system on the interdependence of all creatures under God."[2] It is to such seventeenth-century women philosophers and scientists that Sor Juana must be compared for a better analysis of her scientific thinking and the circumstances under which it evolved.

El sueño will be the focus of this introductory study of Sor Juana's constitution of herself as a speaking subject in her own text.[3] What I want to argue is that in Sor Juana Inés de la Cruz's poetry and prose we find prefigurements of the theoretical modes of twentieth-century feminist scholars, especially literary critics. An analysis of these prefigurements can provide both richer readings of the great seventeenth-century writer and points of comparison and contrast for the testing and sharpening of our own interpretations, deconstructions, reconstructions, and re-visions.[4] The coincidence of modern women writers with Sor Juana in their critique of patriarchy lies in similarities of consciousness, method, and subject. They are all reacting to largely the same (male) cultural heritage and to many of the same books: two thousand years separate Plato from Sor Juana; three hundred separate her from us.[5] As I establish a dialogue between recent texts and those of Sor Juana, I will also indicate how the Mexican nun set up dialogues within and between her own texts, and between her writings and those of predecessors and contemporaries. The study of her intertextuality,[6] of her "tactics of revisionary mythopoesis,"[7] in sum, of her feminisms,[8] is an important task facing contemporary *sorjuanistas.*

Like a baroque concerto, *El sueño* is made up of a multiplicity of voices in a complex weave of rhythms, tonalities, and melodies.[9] Sor Juana favored the word *concierto* (concert) for its musically and semantically connotative properties.[10] This and other musical analogies are among the terms she uses, sometimes to flaunt, others to conceal, her overriding interest in the reorchestration of sounds and silences. Traditional scores were too discordant and disconcerting to the ears of (female) intelligence. To many of her texts, we could say, she provides program notes useful for "listening" to *El sueño,* one of her most original compositions and certainly her most difficult.

Of the numerous possible examples I have chosen a few that illuminate my readings of the poem and the thesis of this essay. In the first, music is a framing metaphor. Music, a field in some ways less "gendered," because more abstract, than those related to language, was, with mathematics, among Sor Juana's preferred subjects of study and literary elaboration. "La armonía de la creación del mundo" (The harmony of the world's creation), an illustration in the *Musurgia Universalis,*[11] one of the many books by Athanasius Kircher that she owned, depicts the six days of creation, each identified by a scene or a symbol in a circle, issuing from the pipes of an elaborate organ. Sor Juana invented her own linguistic variations on the theme in a *loa* (poem in praise) written for the birthday of the man who held the principal chair in theology at the university.[12] The *loa* reveals Sor Juana's deconstructive and reconstructive as well as in-structive practices, that is, the way she ludically took apart inherited religious schema, substituting and reinserting characters, with the aim of correcting injustices and teaching her superiors.[13] The character Música (Music) comments, mediates, and orchestrates the strains played by Naturaleza (Nature), Ciencia (Knowledge), Agrado (Affability), Discurso (Discourse), Entendimiento (Understanding), Nobleza (Nobility), and Atención (Attentiveness), bringing them into harmony. Because time and again Sor Juana is concerned with the inclusion of conflictual and contradictory voices, and with resolution without suppression, we see this as a demonstration of her dexterity with a feminist dialogic process. Most important for our present intentions is Discurso's first *parlamento* (speech), addressed to Naturaleza, and Música's comment which terminates the rhyme scheme:

> Discurso. A tus pies, ¡oh fecunda y más hermosa
> madre del universo generoso!
> viene el Discurso, que es quien sólo sabe
> de las prendas hacer unión süave;
> y así siguen mis huellas,
> Música. ¡para hacer un compendio de todas ellas![14]

> (*Discourse:* At your feet, Oh! Fertile and most beautiful mother of the generous universe kneels Discourse, the only one who knows

how to bring qualities into an easy union and thus they follow my
lead,
Music: that we may achieve a compendium of them all!)

One might quake (from a safe distance, with laughter; with fear, in the
proximity of inquisitional mentalities) just imagining the august ecclesiastics at the Colegio of San Pedro as they heard those lines. Nature
here usurps the place of God the Father; the harmony of creation is
recognized as a construct of discourse. What protected her from the
consequences of such thinly veiled sacrilege? Perhaps the levity expected on such a festive occasion, the musical accompaniment (about
which we know nothing), the cloak extended by the conventions of
Baroque rhetoric, and the lightness of the genre. Sor Juana often employed so-called minor genres for the treatment of forbidden or dangerous subjects. With ingenious charm she also frequently displaced male
elements in the traditional hierarchy of conceptual values, replacing
them with females, or a female and a male, or an abstraction. For many
years intrigued and friendly or resentful but circumstantially constrained
ecclesiastics heard and saw her religious and secular works. Despite formulas of humility and feigned denials expressed in the *Respuesta* and
elsewhere, Sor Juana was expert enough to address and debate prominent theologians as well as to compose liturgical entertainments for
hundreds of both lordly and lowly worshippers.[15]

Few people, probably, had read *El sueño* before it appeared in the
second volume of Sor Juana's writings (Sevilla, 1692). Together with
the *Neptuno alegórico* (Allegorical Neptune), *El Divino Narciso* (The
Divine Narcissus), and the *villancicos* (carols) to Santa Catarina, it is
her most imaginative and accomplished act of literary daring.[16] Part of
the daring, the "atrevimiento" Sor Juana lauds so often in the *Sueño*'s
figure of Phaeton,[17] resides in her willingness to mock and reverse convention, often, as we shall see, re-presenting herself emblematically in
those brazen reversals. She takes the risk, in addition, of calling attention to what she is doing with shadow play. The poet joins adjectives
and adverbs of praise or of derision to descriptions of daring, thus
adding verve and surprise to the wor(l)ds she is recreating. She calls
Phaeton "modelo" (model) in one line and "ejemplar pernicioso" (per-
nicious example) in the next [I.803–4]. Part of the surprise is that
sometimes she doesn't reverse at all but employs a meaning so close to
convention that her critical stance is almost imperceptible. Both of
these procedures work in the verses that follow the densely mythologi-

cal description of the body (Minerva's tree) falling asleep, its fruits, pressed and distilled, being readied for the dream. Sor Juana reincarnates or reinscribes the (her) sleeping body in many forms before the end of the poem. After Minerva it (she) becomes three storytelling sisters:

> Y aquellas que su casa
> campo vieron volver, sus telas hierba,
> a la deidad de Baco inobedientes
> —ya no historias contando diferentes,
> en forma sí afrentosa transformadas—,
>
> [I. 39–43]

(And Minyas' daughters—rashly / opposed to Bacchus's will— / whose home, for their conceit, / was turned to barren field / and thread to vine and weed, / themselves no longer storying at their loom / transformed in horrid shapes, / forever lurking featherless [Harss 35–42])

In Ovid's *Metamorphosis*, Sor Juana's source, the three daughters of Minyas (Moon Man), refused to attend the festival of Dionysus. Rather, "rejecting the orgiastic call of the new god [they] stayed at their loom, spinning out the customary stories that accompanied them at their labors."[18] Sor Juana chose the version in which the vengeful Bacchus turns them into bats rather than the one in which they became maenads. Only on the surface is she reproducing the "official story" of classical convention. Despite punishments against their intelligence, grace, and beauty, resisting women, throughout the poem, persevere.

Sor Juana's thought is to be found in the contexts, subtexts, and intertextualities of her writing. Discourse analysis of *El sueño*'s lexical and grammatical components reveals it as both more and less personal a poem than we have supposed up to now. In the shade of the "usurping" queen of night, portrayed as fearful of her own shadows [I.911–16] speaks an intellectual who has for nearly thirty years protested the usurpation of her right to exercise her mind freely—and of other women's right to exercise theirs. The author of "Hombres necios" (Foolish Men) chides men for usurping the bodies and minds of women and laughs at them for immaturely creating a monster ("coço") and scaring themselves. Sor Juana did not leave the sentiments expressed in the *redondillas* of "Hombres necios" unrepeated in *El sueño*. Indeed, she developed them under the cover of that usurping night empress.[19] They appear in the form of Ceres, Proserpina (Persephone), Arethusa, and Nictimene, who were all in some way ill treated, betrayed, or tricked by male relatives or lovers or husbands, and who were all rebellious. They were also all punished.

Mixing mythological allusion and scientific description, Sor Juana attempts to understand the psychic and biological components of the species to which she belongs, that "compendio misterioso" (mysterious compendium) [I. 658]. The character Música, in the *loa* cited above, tried to make a compendium of the world (Naturaleza) and its word (Discurso). In *El sueño*, Sor Juana essays no less than a compendium of human knowledge. The quadruple appearance of the word *excess* in the poem [I. 133, 500, 525, 818] exemplifies Sor Juana's use of multiple and oppositional meanings: (1) "cuidadosa / de no incurrir de omisa en el exceso" (but cautious not to incur / omission by excess [Harss 122]), Jupiter's eagle (symbol of the Virgin Mary in other poems, of Tenochtitlán, the Aztec name for Mexico City, and given the attributes of the watchful crane) highlights the poet's intuition of plurality in ways of interpreting and experiencing the wor(l)d; (2) "—que el exceso contrarios hace efectos" (such being of excess / the contrary effect [Harss 488]) reflects both proverbial and innovative meanings, because it is followed by a suggestion that scientific methods will make what is insufferable to the naked eye bearable and "visible" in new dimensions; (3) with the repetitive intensification of "ya por sobrado exceso" (whether by excess of excess) she discusses curative methods whose mechanisms are not yet understood; (4) finally, rather than feign ignorance she chooses to be punished for "el insolente exceso" (such insolent excess [Harss 815]), of having experienced and expressed as she has, the life of the mind.

Darkness and night have been interpreted too literally. But when read figuratively, they have been interpreted too much according to the patriarchal canon to be understood as I believe Sor Juana meant them. Sor Juana hardly ever—not to say never—can be taken at face value. She herself tells us so endlessly. Witness the goddess who "con tres hermosos rostros ser ostenta" (with three beautiful faces pridefully exhibits her being) [I. 15]. There are few poems in which she gives us so many clues to the intended meaning of opposites, to the multivalency of connotations. For Sor Juana, the negative polarity of darkness is the limitation put on the pursuit of knowledge and science by the powers that be. She has no simple demons or devils in this or other works—a point worth noting, because most religious men and women of her times spoke and wrote of them.

Sor Juana was above all an intellectual. She was also a woman who refused to be *mujer* (wife) to any man.[20] As a woman and an intellectual she came to the necessary conclusion that the personal was political. Most critics still forget this. I think it one of the reasons so many fine and sensitive readings miss the way in which she places domestic, familial, and personal issues on a par with those of the state.[21] Her psychological perspicacity, recognized in general, foreshadows modern feminist psychoanalytic theory. The female emblems who represent dark powers can be interpreted in their mythic and psychological dimensions. Long before Freudian, Jungian, and other psychoanalytic schools, Sor Juana projected psychic development onto classic myths. Besides, only under cover of a certain darkness (anonymity?) could most women move and speak. Another meaning, an important one in this poem, is the need to depend on other than the senses to gather information about the inner workings of things.

El sueño, then, is a dramatically intense articulation of a Mexican woman's wisdom and autonomy. Beyond words, in the interplay of discourses, she picks up the lost and ignored sounds of banned voices— those of philosophical and scientific curiosity, those of indigenous Mexico, those of women.[22] Sor Juana is summarized in the night of *El sueño*, the inner self, the real Sor Juana, seen by the eyes of the new scientific method as well as by the blind poet,[23] the self she has dared to see projected in the "gran turba" (giant crowd) and "otras infinitas, de que están los libros llenos" (infinite number of others, who fill the pages of books) who "no fueron más que mujeres doctas, tenidas y celebradas de la antigüedad por tales" (were but learned women, held and celebrated as such in antiquity) [IV. 461]. Isis, the Virgin Mary, and St. Catherine of Egypt incarnate her radical revision of the patriarchal concepts of her times. Named or suggested, all three illuminate her dream.

Isis, mother of wisdom, poetry, and music, who "tuvo no sólo todas las partes de sabia, sino de la misma sabiduría, que se ideó en ella" (not only had all the attributes of the wise, but of wisdom itself which was conceived in her) [IV. 362], is mother also of night (Harpocrates, Egyptian god of silence) who silences the "labio oscuro" (dark lips) [I. 74], in preparation for the enactment, and the speech, of *El sueño*. The Virgin Mary, "La soberana Doctora / de las Escuelas divinas / ," (The Sovereign Doctor of Divine Schools) [II. 6], is barely hidden in

the emblematic eagle, Jupiter's bird, "como al fin Reina—, por no darse
entera" (behaving finally like a Queen—in order not to abandon herself) [I. 130]. She watches over the night with "pastoral cuidado" (pastoral vigilance) [I. 140]. St. Catherine, who "fue Pirámide que al
Cielo / fué de un vuelo" (was a Pyramid that ascended to the Heavens
in a single flight) [II. 176] is thus inscribed in the first two lines of El
sueño, along with the author. Both are pyramidal shadows born of
earth—one in Egypt, the other in Mexico—"escalar pretendiendo las
Estrellas" (pretending to scale Heaven) [I. 4; Harss 3].

Formal aspects of the dialogue Sor Juana undertakes with the discourse of others (such as marginal and direct citations of classical authors, for the purpose of confirming or contradicting opinion, and par-
odic references to outmoded rhetoric) can be studied as a particularly
skillful adaption of a common Baroque practice. How she re-reads, rewrites, re-vises, and disrupts conventions and the extent and substance
of her discursive and dialogic practice are part of a long female tradition. Sor Juana knew many texts by women that neither she nor others
have ever mentioned. I find it likely, for example, that indirectly, if
not directly, she was acquainted with the work of Christine de Pizan
and of other figures of the querelle des femmes.[24] In poems comparable
to Sor Juana's famous redondilla, "Hombres necios," these European
women attempted to subvert the same symbolic and social order that
upholds double standards and surreptitious or flagrant, if foolish, mis-
ogyny. Pizan, in The Book of the City of Ladies, like Sor Juana, in many
works including El sueño, constructs "a compelling case for the female
origins of culture and civilization."[25]

I am almost certain that the Mexican Hieronymite was acquainted
with women's texts of the Carmelite reform, in addition to those of
St. Teresa of Avila, to whom she likens herself in the Respuesta for
refusing to marry.[26] It will take many years of research to reconstruct
the "dialogue of discourses" among speaking and writing women to
which Sor Juana had access and to which she contributed. Sensitivity
to the many factors involved in the unavowed but strongly gendered
language and culture in which texts are produced is especially important in Sor Juana studies, because as the "Tenth Muse" she is an icon
of that male-dominated gendering process.

Such a sensitivity would require a refocusing of research, for instance, on the relationship between Sor Juana's texts and men's texts,
both those she cites and those she doesn't (such as Erasmus). Particular
attention would be paid to assumptions about and concepts of gender
and race and social hierarchy put forward by those texts; to what can

be discovered about the contributions of women and other "others" to the creation of those texts; and to Sor Juana and to other women writers whose texts she knew, as female readers. Different understandings of the texts involved (of the practice of discourse and of power) and a more complete picture of the periods in which they were written will emerge.

But *El sueño* is, after all, also a poetic "classic," whose richness allows endless interpretation. Although reassessment of its aesthetic virtues dates from little more than fifty years ago, in a manner similar to the poetry of Góngora and Quevedo, and to the art of the Baroque in general, its place in the canon is unquestioned. On the other hand, the double vision[27] of *El sueño*, intricate enough for it to represent both the voiced and the voiceless, the dominant and the marginalized, has not been studied before now from a feminist perspective. Sor Juana employed Gracianesque[28] ingenuity—oppositional, contradictory, and witty language—in the service of a largely rationalist woman-centered ethos.

Night's darkness and silence provide a space for epistemological meditations unthinkable in clear daylight, where heresies against dogma were punished by the Inquisition.[29] On another level, of course, it is also true that there were fewer of the routine daily distractions faced generally by nuns and specifically by one engaged in producing texts for all manner of occasions. In the passage quoted in the first epigraph to this essay, Sor Juana asserts her regard for sleep/dream time as the preserve for intense and unfettered summarizing, rethinking, and imagining. The implication that she is unable to control her mind and the willingness to catalogue her confession are self-defensive strategies.[30]

More significantly, the passage also explains, for me, one of the reasons for the shadowy and subtle use of the first person. In the final line of *El sueño*, which, in truth, could be the first, the *yo* is stated most clearly. "El Mundo iluminado y yo despierta" (the world illuminated and I awake) describes the poet's state, her experience, and her objectives in the poem. Her mind is active and free (awake), and with her intelligence and imagination she sees the world in (a different) light. Under cover of night she sheds light on "invisible" things: ways of learning and knowing, the workings of the body, the "magic lantern," medical procedures, the orbiting heavenly bodies. But men commonly cannot "see" these things, as she tells us in the *Neptuno alegórico*, because, "por la mayor parte, sólo tienen por empleo de la voluntad el [objeto] que es objeto de los ojos" (for the most part they excercise their will only on [the object] that is the object of their eyes) [IV. 356]. This and other prose commentaries to the allegorical triumphal arch she had designed to welcome the new viceroy into Mexico City—the *Neptuno*—explain Sor Juana's consistently stated/unstated (that is, explicit and implicit) textuality. They provide the "program notes" I mentioned at the beginning, relevant to hearing the discourse of *El sueño*. Seeming to claim that uncultivated people cannot understand abstraction, she implies other messages which include a critique of dependence on the senses for verification of data; silent acknowledgment of the dangers, especially for a woman, of straying from dogma or of engaging in independent, political, or scientific thinking; and a protest against the objectification of the "other." Her clarity could also lead to her downfall, as the poem in question tells us so movingly:

> alto impulso, el espíritu encendía:
> —más que el temor ejemplos de escarmiento—
> abiertas sendas al atrevimiento,
> que una vez trilladas, no hay castigo
> que intento baste a remover segundo
> (segunda ambición, digo).
> Ni el panteón profundo
>
> . . . .
>
> mueve, por más que avisa,
> al ánimo arrogante
> que, el vivir despreciando, determina
> su nombre eternizar en su rüina.
>
> (I. 789–802)

(seeing, not warning dire / to unfettered pride, / but open path, from which / once fearlessly engaged, / no punishment can turn / ambition nor dissuade; / not deepest tomb, in azure pantheon—but ashen grave— / not vengeful thunderbolt / sent against arrogance / which, scorning life, his name / in ruin immortalized [Harss 789–899].)

El sueño is perhaps the most appropriate text for the exploration of the feminist foundations of Sor Juana's approach to form, a theme related to those of light and darkness we have been discussing. Architectural, geometrical, musical, and biological concepts, forms, and images structure the poem. The poem's maddening syntactical ex-tensions and re-alignments actually echo its movement through forbidden realms.

Luis Harss, in the introduction to his recent brilliant translation of the poem, understands the organic freedom Sor Juana allowed herself in composing *El sueño* by linking "variations on known themes *spiraling on themselves.*"[31] In a poem that speaks of her lost treatise on music, she wrote:

> En él, si mal no me acuerdo,
> me parece que decía
> que es una línea espiral,
> no un círculo, la Armonía;
> y por razón de su forma
> revuelta sobre sí misma,
> lo intitulé *Caracol,*
> porque esa revuelta hacía.
> (I. 64)

(In it, if I do not forget, I believe I said that Harmony is not a circle but a spiral line; and thinking of its form turned in upon itself, I titled it *Conch* because it coiled thus.)

The *Sueño* is formed like a *caracol;* it is a manual for deciphering the music of Sor Juana's spheres.

Light and darkness, substance and shadow, illusions and reality spiral through space under the aegis of the goddess of the night. We might speculate that one of Sor Juana's unavowed reversals or reapplications of meaning could make "night" the (female) counterpart of (male) "day." Day/(night) means both the roughly twelve-hour period of light and the twenty-four hour designation of the planet's revolution on its axis. Why not be able to switch the terms—which she does toward the end of the poem when night flees with her entourage to another part of the orb—by analogy with Man/(woman), to reflect the standard asymmetry, but in reverse. If I am correct about some of the other dead-ly serious and live-ly irreverent games Sor Juana played, this one would not be out of character.[32]

In *Writing Beyond the Ending*, Rachel Blau DuPlessis discusses the modes women poets use to "attack cultural hegemony," such as putting "the last first and the first last" and "writing beyond the ending." Sor Juana, with good reason, ends with what could have been—if the world around her had been different—the beginning. She begins, for the same reason, with the end of the day rather than, as might have been expected, its inception. And if, as Luis Harss also claims,[33] the

"Piramidal, funesta, de la tierra / nacida sombra" (A shadow born of
Earth / bleak pyramid) of the first two lines is an emblem of the author,
then the poem may be said to end nine lines earlier.

At that point the very "tirana usurpadora / del imperio del día"
([she] whose tyrannic reign / usurps the throne of day) [I. 911–12;
Harss 909–10], also referred to as "la que antes *funesta* fue tirana / de
su imperio" (she who had earlier been *funereal* tyrant of her empire) [I.
950–51], with her "*funesta* capa" (*funereal* cape) [I. 928; emphasis
added], decides to continue in her planetary orbit and rule elsewhere:
"en la mitad del globo que ha dejado / el Sol desamparada / segunda
vez rebelde determina / mirarse coronada" (she once again installed /
her rebel throne, restored / to westward rule over / the dark half of the
globe / forsaken by the sun) [I. 963–66; Harss 962–66]. By repeating "funesta" a second and third time near the conclusion, Sor Juana
chose to remind readers of the connection with the beginning while
protecting herself by assuming a self-abnegating posture. For the reader
she would either be unrecognizable under the abstract and nefarious
mask, or she would be seen to accept guilt and condemn herself to the
netherworld. Many other figures, besides, had contributed to the intended obfuscation.[34] Since all elements in the dream symbolize the
dreamer (in a Jungian sense), the poem re-presents the poet in each
and every one of its elements.[35] In the final nine lines of the poem she
splits off from the multiple symbolic projections of her self, from the
various voices that have helped her tell of her extraordinary intellectual journey. Divested of the night-texts, she surfaces in the last line
with a suddenly uncomplicated syntax and a suddenly clear statement
of first-person singular.

This reading does not invalidate others. The beginning and ending
of the poem continue to be marvelous renderings of dusk and dawn,
comparable to those of other Baroque poets and analogous to the
mythological paintings of her European and Hispanic American contemporaries. And it should be noted that many of these paintings are
also being deciphered and reinterpreted in the light of new evidence.[36]

El sueño, Sor Juana's story, is an allegory of Mexico as well. While
she is explicit about the first subject, the second remains shadowed and
silent, like the snow-peaked Popocatéptl and Ixtaccíhuatl volcanos at
whose feet she was born. Mexico, however, is, in addition to the poet,
the subject that opens the poem. Its synecdochal emblem is the pyramids. To further cover the tracks of this daring, she never speaks of any
but the pyramids of Egypt, although in the book by Kircher, her reference, those of both places are illustrated. Mexico sleeps in the work of

Sor Juana much of the time. When it surfaces, however, it does so full force as, for instance, in the character "América" in the *loa* to *El Divino Narciso:*

> Si el pedir que yo no muera
> y el mostrarte compasiva,
> es porque esperas de mí
> que me vencerás, altiva,
> como antes con corporales,
> después con intelectivas
> armas, estás engañada;
> pues aunque lloro cautiva
> mi libertad, ¡mi albedrío
> con libertad más crecida
> adorará mis Deidades!
>   (III. 12)

(If your pleading for my life while you show me your great mercy arouses in you a hope that I will be beaten by your proud strength— as before with physical weapons, now with intellectual arms—you are certainly mistaken: for though as a prisoner I mourn my freedom, my free will, with liberty grown still larger, will worship and adore my Gods!)

A second of several examples of the surfacing of the theme, which also indicates Sor Juana's awareness of the situation of her country, of the great debates that took place in Spain regarding the treatment of the indigenous population, of the work of figures like Bartolomé de las Casas and of the syncretistic Christianity of her Indian compatriots, can be found in a biographical and nationalistic declaration which she characteristically calls an "aside" in the epistolary *Romance* to the Duchess de Aveiro:

> Que yo, Señora, nací
> en la América abundante
> compatriota del oro,
> paisana de los metales
>   adonde el común sustento
> se da casi de balde,
> que en ninguna parte más
> se ostenta la tierra Madre.

Europa mejor lo diga,
pues ha tanto que, insaciable
de sus abundantes venas
desangra los minerales,
                    (I. 102–3)

(For I, Madame, was born in America, the abundant compatriot of gold, countrywoman of precious metals where sustenance for us all is found almost without a price, for nowhere does Mother Earth show herself more generous. Better let Europe tell it for, insatiable, it has for so long bled the minerals of its abundant veins.)

Although they come through literary filters (Quevedo, Cervantes), it is not hard to ascribe a certain sense of pride in indigenous roots and a protest against their and the earth's exploitation.

A Mexican, syncretic ontology and an extra-Christian exploration of the nature and limits of knowledge inform *El sueño*. Egypt is a stand-in for both science and Mexico. As the poet's ideas teeter between heterodoxy and heresy, she masks them with mythological scripting—several times she refers to the poem's "hieroglyphic" nature.[37] To understand how Sor Juana, using Jesuitically sanctioned images,[38] positioned herself outside the dominant discursive order at the very moment she employed its vehicles for ascribing meaning, one has merely to turn to the prose sections of the *Neptuno alegórico*.[39]

In *El sueño*, Sor Juana creates, in the words of Octavio Paz, "one of the most complex, rigorous, and intellectually rich texts of Spanish poetry."[40] The poem is the speech of the speechless: of the curious, of women, and of pre-Columbian Mexico, whose speech had been truncated, as had many of its pyramids. Under cover of night, emblematized in a multiplicity of female and male-figured myths, Sor Juana uncovers herself more transparently than ever in self-inscriptions. There she discovers the equivalent of Julia Kristeva's prediscursive, semiotic center.[41] There she posits herself both within and without the dominant discursive order(s) and delineates a feminist epistemology.

NOTES

The author would like to thank Deborah Weiner and Joe Chadwick for discussions of the poem during her stay at the University of Hawaii, Kathleen Zane for help with editing, Stacey Schlau and Keitha S. Fine for reading and commenting on the essay, and Joshua Wallman for a room with a view in which to work.

1. I follow Georgina Sabat-Rivers's use of this title, according to Sor Juana's own usage in referring to this poem in the *Respuesta*. See Sabat de Rivers, *El "Sueño" de Sor Juana Inés de la Cruz* (London: Tamesis Press, 1977). Others, including Octavio Paz in *Sor Juana Inés de la Cruz o Las trampas de la fe*, 3d ed. (Mexico: Fondo de Cultura Económica, 1985), follow the title it was given in old editions and which appears in Alfonso Méndez-Plancarte's edition of Sor Juana's *Obras completas: Primero sueño*.

All citations from Sor Juana's work are taken from Méndez-Plancarte's four-volume *Obras completas* (Mexico: Fondo de Cultura Económica, 1951) and are included in the body of the text. References to *El sueño* cite the volume number and the line(s) of the poem; references to other works cite the volume and the page number. Translations of the *Sueño*, where noted, follow Luis Harss's from *Sor Juana's Dream* (New York: Lumen Books, 1986). All others are by Electa Arenal.

2. Carolyn Merchant, *The Death of Nature: Women, Ecology, and the Scientific Revolution* (San Francisco: Harper and Row, 1983), pp. 255–68; citation, p. 260. See also Evelyn Fox Keller, "Making Gender Visible in the Pursuit of Nature's Secrets," in Teresa de Lauretis, ed., *Feminist Studies/Critical Studies* (Bloomington: Indiana University Press, 1986), pp. 67–77. Tonia Leon has allowed me to read the chapters on "Science in Spain" and "Science in Mexico" from her dissertation in progress, "Reflections of Seventeenth Century Scientific Thought in Sor Juana's 'Primero sueño'" (New York University). Our conversations about science and Mexico in the work of the poet have contributed to the development of my thinking on those subjects.

3. I have found three recent books and an unpublished paper useful in formulating the ideas presented in this essay: Toril Moi, *Sexual/Textual Politics: Feminist Literary Theory* (London and New York: Methuen, 1985); Gayle Greene and Coppélia Kahn, eds., *Making a Difference: Feminist Literary Criticism* (London and New York: Methuen, 1985); Elizabeth A. Meese, *Crossing the Double Cross: The Practice of Feminist Criticism* (Chapel Hill and London: University of North Carolina Press, 1986); Mae G. Henderson, "Black Women Writers: Speaking in Tongues," work in progress presented at the Columbia University Seminar on Women in Society, May 18, 1987.

4. Deconstruction refers to a way of reading texts and understanding culture generally associated with Jacques Derrida. Gayatri Spivak explains how French feminists "following the reversal-displacement technique of a deconstructive reading [devised] . . . a productively conflictual [method] of expos[ing] the ruling discourse" in "French Feminism in an International Frame," *Yale French Studies* 62 (1981): 177; also cited in Moi, *Sexual/Textual Politics*, p. 139. My thesis is that (1) Sor Juana, by using similar techniques—because they were the techniques, also, of Baroque rhetoric—accomplished something analogous, and that (2) the modern feminist versions of these deconstructive techniques shed light on the Mexican poet's obscured intentions, as well as on critical biases that have kept those intentions obscured for centuries. Greene and Kahn claim that "Feminist scholarship undertakes the dual task of deconstructing predominantly male cultural paradigms and *reconstructing* a female perspective and experience in an effort to change the tradition that has silenced and marginalized us" (emphasis added).

On *re-vision*, see Adrienne Rich, "When We Dead Awaken: Writing as Re-

Vision," in *On Lies, Secrets, and Silence* (New York: Norton, 1979), pp. 33–51; Annette Kolodny uses the terms "revisionist" and "revisionary rereading" in "A Map for Rereading; or, Gender and the Interpretation of Literary Texts," *New Literary History* 11, 3 (Spring 1980): 464–65.

5. Luce Irigaray, for instance, in *Speculum de l'autre femme*, presents "a close reading of Plato's cave parable in the light of . . . [a] critique of Western philosophy" (Moi, *Sexual/Textual Politics*, pp. 129–30).

6. "This process of intertextuality—the dialogic, as the Russian critic [Mikhail] Bakhtin called it . . .—undermines the aspirations of the text towards a unifying definition" (Cora Kaplan, "Pandora's Box: Subjectivity, Class and Sexuality in Socialist Feminist Criticism" in Green and Kahn, p. 164). Also, "Volosinov [Bakhtin] and [French theorist Julia] Kristeva . . . deconstruct—the old disciplinary barriers between linguistics, rhetoric and poetics in order to construct a new kind of field: *semiotics* or *textual theory*. . . . Kristeva has coined the concept of *intertextuality* to indicate how one or more systems of signs are transposed into others" (Moi, *Sexual/Textual Politics*, pp. 155–56).

7. Rachel Blau DuPlessis, *Writing Beyond the Ending: Narrative Strategies of Twentieth Century Women Writers* (Bloomington: Indiana University Press, 1985), p. 108. For a study of this tactic of realignment as employed by Sor Juana, see my "Sor Juana Inés de la Cruz: Reclaiming the Mother Tongue," *Letras Femeninas* 11, 1–2 (Primavera–otoño 1985): 63–75; and Stephanie Merrim's essay on Sor Juana's theater in this volume (chapter 5).

8. This reference to the heterogeneity of Sor Juana's feminist worldview and to her coincidence with a variety of feminist perspectives also plays on the title *The New French Feminisms: An Anthology*, ed. and intros. by Elaine Marks and Isabel de Courtivron (New York: Schocken, 1981).

9. I play with concepts and words advisedly, trying to exemplify as I explain, some of the elements of Sor Juana's *conceptismo* and her multilayered manipulation of discourse.

10. See especially the *villancicos* and *loas*.

11. Reproduced in Paz, *Sor Juana Inés de la Cruz*, p. 367.

12. Fray Diego Velázquez de la Cadena, an Augustinian, was the brother of Captain D. Pedro, Sor Juana's godfather for her profession as a nun.

13. In the third *villancico* dedicated to the Assumption (1676), she claims the Virgin Mary, "por ser quien inteligencia / mejor de Dios participa / a leer la suprema sube / Cátedra de Teología" (being the one in whom the intelligence of God best inheres, she rises to read from the supreme Chair of Theology) (II. 6).

14. Sor Juana Inés de la Cruz, *Inundación castálida* (Castalian Inundation), edition, introduction and notes by Georgina Sabat de Rivers (Madrid: Clásicos Castalia, 1982), p. 233.

15. For a study of autobiographical strategies used by other Hispanic nuns, see Electa Arenal and Stacey Schlau, "Stratagems of the Strong, Stratagems of the Weak: Autobiographical Prose of the Seventeenth Century Hispanic Convent," in Darcy Donohue, ed., *Social Bodies, Spiritual Selves: Religious Women Writers of the Golden Age* (forthcoming).

16. I do not mention the *Respuesta* because it is more directly an act of self-defense—an "apologia *pro vita sua*," as Elias Rivers calls it in the introduction to Sor Juana Inés de la Cruz, *Antología* (Madrid: Anaya, 1965), p. 11.

17. Through Phaeton's example she finds inspiration and "abiertas sendas al

atrevimiento" (paths open to daring) (1. 792). Other appearances of Phaeton are incompletely referenced in the index to Vol. IV, edited by Alberto G. Salceda, of Sor Juana's *Obras completas*.

18. Luis Harss, *Sor Juana's Dream* (New York: Lumen Books, 1986), p. 80.

19. If we keep Sor Juana's meaningfully equivocal syntax disjointed, we can see a statement of her intentions as those of one who has "usurpado / diuturna obscuridad" (1. 495–96), that is, attempted to "take over" dark days, in order to unmask the obscurantism she witnesses all around her.

20. *Obras completas*, I, p. 138.

21. It is perhaps in the *Neptuno alegórico* that Sor Juana most clearly draws a profile of the ideal "prince"—his responsibilities, duties, and objectives—placing a woman-inspired respect for wisdom over traditional views of power. In her "poemas de ocasión" (occasional poems), flowery praise of official (male) performance is complemented by recognition of the valuable attributes of consorts who balance and complete the picture. Reciprocity between the sexes in every activity is a theme of several *villancicos*.

22. At times the uncanniness of her subterfuges makes me wonder whether she, like Lady Conway, may not have known of Knorr von Rosenroth's *Kabbalah Denudata* (1677) as well as the Gnostics. Some levels of *El sueño* seem intended for initiated ears.

23. Homer. See lines 379–403.

24. Joan Kelly, "Early Feminist Theory and the Querelle des Femmes, 1400–1789," in her *Women, History, and Theory* (Chicago: University of Chicago Press, 1984). The essay first appeared in *Signs* 8, 1 (Autumn 1982): 4–28.

25. Ibid., p. 84. Sor Juana devised a sort of Guadalupan-Tonanzintlan mariolatry on one hand and a cult to Isis and other "venerated learned women" (IV. 461) on the other, which merit further study. See Sor Juana's poems to the Virgin Mary, many of the sets of *villancicos*, and most importantly the *Ejercicios devotos* and the *Neptuno alegórico*.

26. Electa Arenal and Stacey Schlau, *Untold Sisters: Hispanic Nuns in Their Own Works*, with translations by Amanda Powell (Albuquerque: University of New Mexico Press, 1989).

27. See Kelly, *Women, History, and Theory*; and the books mentioned in note 3 above.

28. Baltasar Gracián, *Arte de ingenio* (1648), a revision of his earlier *El arte de ingenio, tratado de agudeza* (1642).

29. In the *Respuesta* she claims, cagily defending her dedication to the profane (to her sacred) lyric genre, that heresies against art are not punished by the Inquisition. Did she have the daring of *El sueño* in mind? one wonders.

30. See Josefina Ludmer's essay, chapter 4 in this book. For a study of autobiographical strategies used by other Hispanic nuns, see Arenal and Schlau, "Stratagems of the Strong, Stratagems of the Weak," cited above in note 15.

31. Harss, *Sor Juana's Dream*, p. 22; emphasis added.

32. See Arenal, "Sor Juana Inés de la Cruz: Reclaiming the Mother Tongue," cited in note 7 above.

33. Harss, *Sor Juana's Dream*, p. 133.

34. Meese (see note 3), citing Julia Kristeva, Jane Gallop, and Hélène Cixous, speaks of women's need to be unclear and duplicitous: "Woman flies, steals, and crosses over, takes the words and runs," she claims (p. 147).

35. Among the mythological symbols with which Sor Juana inscribes herself are the triple-faced moon goddess (Luna, Diana, Proserpina), Ceres, Nyctimene, Minerva, Minyas' daughters, Halcyone, Thetis, Venus, Prometheus, and Phaeton. For a fuller identification and discussion of these and other figures, see Georgina Sabat-Rivers's essay, chapter 7 in this volume.

36. See Norma Broude and Mary D. Girarde, *Feminism and Art History* (New York: Harper and Row, 1982).

37. Victoria Urbano found the inspiration for it in a 1617 masque by Mira de Amescua entitled *De los sueños y fantasmas de la noche* (Of the Dreams and Phantasms of the Night), reported in "El claro despertar de Sor Juana," *Letras femeninas* 11, 1–2 (Primavera–otoño 1985): 57–62.

38. Images relating to science, for instance, had been given approval through their appearance in the works of Jesuit Athanasius Kircher.

39. In the Introduction, she explains that the ancients, especially the Egyptians, adored their deities:

> debajo de diferentes jeroglíficos y formas varias . . . [no] porque juzgasen que la Deidad, siendo infinita, pudiera estrecharse a la figura y término de cuantidad limitada; sino porque, como eran cosas que carecían de toda forma visible, y por consiguiente, imposibles de mostrarse a los ojos de los hombres (los cuales, por la mayor parte, sólo tienen por empleo de la voluntad el que es objeto de los ojos), fue necesario buscarles jeroglíficos, que por similitud, ya que no por perfecta imagen, las representasen. Y así hicieron . . . con todas las cosas invisibles, cuales eran los días, meses y semanas, etc., y también con las de quienes era la copia difícil o no muy agradable.

> (under the guise of different hieroglyphics and varied forms . . . [not] because they believed that the Deity, being infinite, would limit himself to the figure and bounds of a limited form; but rather, since their deities lacked any visible form, and it was thus not possible to show them to human eyes [mankind for the most part only exercises its will on the object of its eyes], they sought hieroglyphics which would represent them by similitude rather than by perfect images. And such was their way . . . for all invisible things, such as days, months, weeks, etc., and also for those beings whom it was difficult or not entirely agreeable to copy.) [IV, 355–56]

40. Paz, *Sor Juana Inés de la Cruz*, p. 239; my translation.

41. See Moi, *Sexual/Textual Politics*, chapter 8.

CHAPTER 7

A Feminist Rereading of Sor Juana's *Dream*

GEORGINA SABAT-RIVERS

Undoubtedly there were many more women writing works of literature in colonial Spanish America than those whose names appear in our records from Hispaniola (the present-day Dominican Republic), from Peru, and from New Spain (Mexico).[1] And it is no accident that the names preserved derive precisely from those geographical areas where, in different periods, the major cultural centers were located. It was especially in these centers that women insisted on their right to be heard and read, along with the men who did most of the writing. If our records are fragmentary and sometimes names have been lost, this is due to a strong tradition that held literature to be a realm in which women were not supposed to be active, a tradition that was reluctant to accept those women who dared to cross cultural boundaries[2] in their desire to make themselves known literarily. In Spanish America people generally followed the customs of Spain, where "Maidens and decent ladies were expected to live in the custody of severe domestic guardians—husbands, fathers, or brothers—who, in order to keep their own manly honor above suspicion, were obliged to keep their charges under lock and key, in the tradition of Arabs and Turks, or to have them always accompanied by squires or duennas."[3] Nonetheless, we need only recall that Sor Juana Inés de la Cruz, our supreme example of the Hispanic woman's effort to participate in a literary world where she could measure herself intellectually with men, is neither a unique case nor a miracle; her case is "a peak, not in a plain, but in a mountain range."[4] For reasons that may have something to do with the shift from Renaissance to Baroque norms, the fate of Sor Juana Inés de la Cruz was fortunately not the same as that of the earlier Clarinda and Amarilis, literary names that are the only way we have of identifying two excellent Peruvian poetesses (see note 1c). Sor Juana, even though her literary reputation has suffered from the critical ups and downs of *culteranismo,* never had to conceal her own name and has always been fully recognized as a major figure in Mexican and Hispanic letters.

Sor Juana, as we know, openly and deliberately refused to be involved in the activities usually assigned to her sex when, as a nun, she insisted on devoting herself fully to the life of the mind. She even proclaimed her neuter status as a virgin, free from the domination of any man, and thus established her fundamental liberty:[5]

> Yo no entiendo de esas cosas;
> sólo sé que aquí me vine
> porque, si es que soy mujer,
> ninguno lo verifique.
>   Y también sé que, en latín,
> sólo a las casadas dicen
> *uxor,* o mujer, y que
> es común de dos lo virgen.
>   Con que a mí no es bien mirado
> que como a mujer me miren,
> pues no soy mujer que a alguno
> de mujer pueda servirle:
>   y sólo sé que mi cuerpo,
> sin que a uno u otro se incline,
> es neutro o abstracto, cuanto
> sólo el Alma deposite.

(I don't understand these matters; all I know is that I came here so that, if in fact I am a woman, no one could find it out. I also know that, in Latin, only married women are called *uxor* or feminine, and that *virgin* is of common gender, neither masculine nor feminine. So I do not consider it proper to be considered a woman, for I am not a woman to serve as wife to any man; and I only know that my body, without inclining to one sex or another, is neuter or abstract, solely the dwelling of my soul.)

143

The final stanza reminds us of what Calderón himself had said (see note 1a): "So let them fight and study, for to be brave and learned is a matter of the soul, and the soul is neither male nor female." María de Zayas took advantage of this in her struggle for women in her day, as did Sor Juana later on in a poem she addressed to the Countess de Paredes (no. 403):

> Ser mujer, ni estar ausente,
> no es de amarte impedimento;
> pues sabes tú que las almas
> distancia ignoran y sexo.

(Neither being a woman nor being far away keeps me from loving you, for, as you know, souls are ignorant of distance and of gender.)

To give the title of the "Tenth Muse" to María de Zayas and to Sor Juana (and to Anne Bradstreet, too, in colonial New England), favored in those days as a way of recognizing distinction in women who had made their mark in literature, was a somewhat ambiguous act. It combined the ideas of being abnormal and of being a woman or mother, reinforced in the case of Sor Juana by her status as a nun.[6] We may wonder whether the glory accorded to this woman in her own day, in a post-Renaissance period, was due to her genius itself or to those Baroque ideas of being unusual, extraordinary, and amazing in a topsy-turvy world.[7] She herself seems to have suspected this when, after several lines of false modesty, she writes the following (no. 506):

> Si no es que el sexo ha podido
> o ha querido hacer, por raro,
> que el lugar de lo perfecto
> obtenga lo extraordinario.

(Unless it be that my sex, so peculiar, could or would be the cause for the extraordinary to be accepted as perfection.)

Many different examples can be found in Sor Juana's writings of her active concern for women's status, of her identification with her sex.[8] In fact, I think that we may say that the whole of her literary production is permeated by her feminine consciousness of her society's patriarchal character and of her exceptional status as a female writer and intellectual. I therefore cannot accept what has sometimes been asserted:

that she wished to be identified with the masculine sex. Born a woman and an intellectual, what she did do was to assert herself and demand the same rights that were conceded to enlightened men. She did not resign herself to being a female poet with no rights or opinions of her own within the paternalistic system; she was a woman who offered, who continues to offer, "a series of suggested alternatives to the male-dominated membership and attitudes of the accepted canon."[9] The conviction that she had of her own capacity and her consequent desire for recognition as a woman intellectually comparable to men led her to rectify, by her own practice, the prejudice against women and to demonstrate by example what a woman writer was capable of achieving within the level of Golden Age literature. She did all this in a way that still moves us, by not accepting her "natural" condition of being what a woman was supposed to be but by showing what a woman could become culturally. She did not write specifically for women "sewing by parlor lamp-light,"[10] but instead managed to place her books on the library shelves of her period's intellectual men. In her poetry and prose she uses the stylistic and syntactic devices found in her feminine predecessors in the New World, her "native land":[11] false modesty, catalogues of illustrious women, contradictions, indirect ways of insinuating facts, sisterhood. But our Mexican nun, taking up the battle begun by women before her, did not limit herself to the more or less subtle characteristics of feminine writing; she went much further.

On only a few occasions did Sor Juana speak out directly against men. The most famous examples of this are her quatrains beginning "Hombres necios" (Foolish Men), and even this poem can be seen as part of the pastoral tradition,[12] in combination with her feminist concerns. What really mattered to her was to give to the feminine sex a literary and intellectual status equal to that of men, as can be seen explicitly or implicitly throughout her works.

In the light of all this, and especially of recent feminist criticism focusing on the modes of expression used by the writer as woman, it is revealing to reread Sor Juana's beloved "papelillo" or "scrap of paper,"[13] her *Sueño* or *Dream*. It is true that, in this, her most important poem, she presents intellectual concerns that are not limited to woman but belong to the human race in general, concerns always considered essential to man's thought, such as how to establish knowledge of a universal sort. In so doing, she converts her protagonist, the Soul, into pure intellect engaged in reflections of a universal sort. But at the same time we can detect—and not only in the definitive last line of the poem, "el mundo iluminado, y yo despierta" (the world bathed in light, and the feminine I awake)—other emphases and characteristics that give evidence of the woman behind the pen that did the writing: "Feminine values penetrate and undermine the masculine systems that contain them."[14] Rosa Perelmuter Pérez,[15] arguing against the impersonal character of the poem, has found in the *Sueño* many deictics that indicate the more or less veiled presence of the writer as she intervenes in the poem's discourse.

The first thing to attract my attention in this rereading of the *Sueño* was the preponderance and importance of feminine characters and of feminine nouns. Naturally, in the latter case it is a matter of Spanish grammar: all of us have to use nouns of both genders. And yet it is not easy to explain the fact that this poet, perhaps unconsciously, preferred feminine nouns in a proportion far exceeding that of masculine nouns. As for the feminine characters, what is most interesting is the significance she attributes to them, their relevance within their context, and their importance. If multiplicity and variety, besides being Baroque, can be considered characteristics of women's writing, there is no doubt that Sor Juana was doubly at home as she wrote this poem.

Immediately after the opening lines, with two feminine nouns— "Piramidal, funesta, de la tierra / nacida sombra . . ."[16] (the funereal, pyramidal shadow born of the earth, that tries in vain to scale the stars [also feminine])—the moon makes her appearance, but the shadow cannot reach her either (lines 9–13):

> que su atezado ceño
> al superior convexo aun no llegaba
> del orbe de la diosa
> que tres veces hermosa
> con tres hermosos rostros ser ostenta . . .

(whose dark frown could not even reach the upper curve of the orb of that goddess who shows herself to be thrice beautiful with three beautiful faces . . .)

The moon is presented in her triple mythological role of the goddess of three faces: as Hecate in the sky; as Diana on Earth; and as Proserpina in the underworld. Thus, Sor Juana establishes, from the beginning of the poem, a universe where woman rules as a cosmic force. (And she will return to Proserpina later on, as we shall see.)

In this prologue, which we have entitled "Night and the cosmos go to sleep,"[17] the birds of night are the next to appear. Unlike other such passages in Golden Age poetry,[18] these birds are all associated with mythological figures, and all of them except Ascalaphus are female. Although all of these figures, the sinister companions of Night, are presented with negative connotations, we can perceive a tone of sympathy for the feminine characters. It is probably no accident that Sor Juana, an illegitimate daughter who hardly knew her father, lists among the birds of night a certain Nyctimene, punished by being turned into an owl for her crime of incest with her father (lines 27–28):[19]

> la avergonzada Nictimene acecha
> de las sagradas puertas los resquicios . . .

(shameful Nyctimene lurks about the cracks in the sacred doors . . .)

Our nun-poet seems to present a somewhat ambivalent image of this character. On the one hand, she tries to attenuate her crime, perhaps in a gesture of feminine solidarity, by using the adjective "avergonzada" which evokes our sympathy insofar as it suggests *arrepentida* (repentant or remorseful), which, according to the *Diccionario de autoridades*, was one of the word's meanings in the Golden Age. But, on the other hand, in the lines that follow she also calls Nyctimene "sacrilegious" as she relates her to the chaste, intellectual figure of Minerva, whose olive oil (the olive tree is referred to periphrastically as "el árbol de Minerva", Minerva's tree). Nyctimene drinks from the temple's lamps.

Let us now read closely four lines from this passage which refer to the daughters of Minyas, who worked so hard that they ignored the festivities due to the deity of Bacchus and were punished by being transformed into bats (lines 47–50):

> aquellas tres oficïosas, digo,
> atrevidas hermanas,
> que el tremendo castigo
> de desnudas les dio pardas membranas . . .

(I mean those three industrious, daring sisters who received the awful punishment of dark, naked membranes . . .)

According to the above-mentioned dictionary, *oficïoso* meant both officious and industrious. This is the ambiguity underlying Sor Juana's treatment of the three sisters: she recognizes the hardworking virtue of their overzealous vice, which cost them so dearly. The word "tre-

mendo" (awful) seems to imply that the punishment was dispropor-
tionate to the crime. This ambiguity or doubt in the mind of the poet
is emphasized by her presence in the word "digo," a rhetorical *figura
correctionis*[20] that makes us aware of the writer's self-consciousness.)

As for the figure of Ascalaphus, "el parlero ministro de Plutón"
(Pluto's garrulous minister), who betrayed Proserpina and hence was
transformed into an owl by her, I will only note at this point that the
poet has chosen a masculine character who was punished for what has
been considered to be one of the vices most characteristic of women:
being too talkative.[21]

As she follows the coming of night, which slowly covers the whole
world, preparing it for sleep, Sor Juana next speaks to us of the sea
(lines 86–94):

> El mar, no ya alterado
> . . . .
> y los dormidos, siempre mudos, peces,
> en los lechos lamosos
> de sus obscuros senos cavernosos,
> mudos eran dos veces;
> y entre ellos, la engañosa encantadora
> Almone . . .

(The sea, no longer disturbed . . . and the sleeping fish, always mute,
in the slimy beds of their dark and cavernous recesses were twice
mute; and among them, the deceptive enchantress Almone . . .)

The latter is the only fish to which the poet attributes a name, a name
that places her within a mythological tradition according to which she
was known as deceptive. At the same time, in contrast to this negative
attribute, the poet asserts the ambiguous charm of the enchantress.[22]

As we enter the section of the poem that deals with man's intellectual sleep or dream (for in Spanish the word *sueño* is related etymo-
logically and semantically to both Latin words *somnus* and *somnium*),
the poet devotes a series of beautiful lines to the evocation of sleep's,
and death's, leveling power, which ranges from the grammatically
feminine symbol of power (line 184: "la soberana tiara," the sovereign
tiara) to the grammatically feminine symbol of humility (line 185: "la
pajiza choza," the straw hut). Immediately afterward there comes to
center stage "el Alma" (the Soul), also grammatically feminine, al-

though it theoretically represents the neuter intellect which joins both sexes and genders, as for example in line 293: "su inmaterial ser y esencia bella" (her immaterial being and beautiful essence; the first noun masculine and the second feminine). But, as a matter of fact, the Soul, "de lo sublunar reina soberana" (line 439: sovereign queen of everything under the moon), which will be the protagonist of this Baroque attempt to grasp the whole cosmos in a philosophical or scientific way, is a constantly feminine character that, like Sor Juana herself, combines intelligence and beauty in "sus intelectuales bellos ojos" (line 441: her intellectual, beautiful eyes).

In the lines that follow, which deal with the lighthouse of Alexandria, feminine nouns are emphasized even more: "la terse superficie" (the smooth surface) of "la azogada luna" (the quicksilvered plateglass) upon which Fantasy does her industrious labor (lines 280–91):

> así ella, sosegada, iba copiando
> las imágenes todas de las cosas,
> y el pincel invisible iba formando
> de mentales, sin luz, siempre vistosas
> colores, las figuras
> no sólo ya de todas las criaturas
> sublunares, mas aun también de aquellas
> que intelectuales claras son estrellas,
> y en el modo posible
> que concebirse puede lo invisible,
> en sí, mañosa, las representaba
> y al Alma las mostraba.

(Thus she calmly proceeded to copy the images of all the things, and her invisible brush began to sketch, with mental, lightless colors always showy, the outlines not only of all sublunary creatures, but also of those which are bright intellectual stars, and insofar as the invisible can possibly be conceived of, within herself she skillfully represented them and showed them to the Soul.)

This whole passage is highly significant as an example of how the nun's baroque language, centered around a feminine protagonist, becomes scientifically analytical and precise.

Another feminine noun worthy of note is the pair of pyramids that, as the poet explains (line 403), "especies son del alma intencionales" (are the intentional faculties of the soul) aspiring to reach the "Primera Causa" (line 408: First Cause), a feminine noun here used to refer to a traditionally masculine God as creative power. A similarly feminine circumlocution for God the Creator is "Sabia Poderosa Mano" (line 670: the Wise and Powerful Hand). And close to God we find Thetis, a mythological sea goddess and mother figure, performing an essentially female function as she offers "sus fértiles pechos maternales" (lines 627–28: her fertile maternal breasts) to vegetation, the first level of Creation, extracting "los dulces . . . manantiales de humor terrestre" (lines 630–31: sweet springs of earthly water) as nourishing irrigation. And before finally mentioning the human being as the culmination of Creation, she refers to him or her by means of these feminine abstractions: "Naturaleza pura" (line 661: the essence of Nature), "bisagra engarzadora" (line 659: the linking hinge, that is, the mediator between God and subhuman creatures), and "fábrica portentosa" (line 677: the prodigious structure), a series of three feminine nouns displacing the usually masculine *man*. Similar feminine circumlocutions are found in "espantosa máquina inmensa" (lines 770–71: immense and fearful machine) for the cosmos, and "cerúlea plana" (line 949: blue sheet of paper) for the sky, replacing Góngora's similar but masculine metaphor (*Soledad I*, line 592: "papel diáfano del cielo").

Let us now review a few lines appearing in the section we have entitled "Intellectual Sobriety," a section particularly rich in feminine characteristics. Sor Juana, who was probably at this point following the Florentine Platonic tradition that asserted knowledge to be impossible unless revealed to the soul,[24] has by now in her poem described two different methods of seeking truth—Plato's intuitive method and Aristotle's discursive or analytical method—both of them failures. She goes on to say (lines 704–11):

> Estos, pues, grados discurrir quería
> unas veces, pero otras disentía,
> excesivo juzgando atrevimiento
> el discurrirlo todo
> quien aun la más pequeña,
> aun la más fácil parte no entendía
> de los más manüales
> efectos naturales . . .

(These levels, then, [the Soul] would try sometimes to analyze, but other times she dissented, judging it to be excessively daring for one

> to analyze everything who could not understand even the smallest, accessible aspects of the most tangible natural phenomena . . .)

She goes on to offer us two examples of those simple aspects of nature that the human mind is incapable of comprehending: the underground course of a spring, personified mythologically as Arethusa, and the feminine flower.

Arethusa, a Nereid or nymph who was transformed into a spring so that she could flee the persecution of the river Alpheus, had asked Diana, the chaste goddess, to help her escape in this way, to go underground and there to proceed (lines 715–22):

> deteniendo en ambages su camino
> —los horrorosos senos
> de Plutón, las cavernas pavorosas
> del abismo tremendo,
> las campañas hermosas,
> los Elíseos amenos,
> tálamo ya de su triforme esposa,
> clara pesquisidora registrando . . .

(as she slowed down and began to wander about—examining as a bright investigator the dark chambers of Pluto, the frightful caverns of the awful abyss, the beautiful Elysian fields so pleasant, now the wedding bed of his threefold bride . . .)

This bride is, of course, Proserpina, the daughter of Ceres, goddess of agriculture and abundance. Proserpina (Persephone in Greek) was abducted by Pluto, the god of the underworld, while she was playing on a meadow with her sisters, and was taken away to "the awful abyss." Arethusa, turned into an underground spring as she passed through "the dark chambers of Pluto," saw her down there, and when she came to the surface in Sicily she told Ceres where her daughter was. Ceres, wishing to save her favorite daughter, begged permission from Jupiter, Proserpina's father, to go down into the underworld to rescue her, but he set one condition: that Proserpina must not have eaten anything in Pluto's realm (a harsh condition discriminating against woman, strangely reminiscent of the fruit forbidden to Eve). When Ceres reaches the underworld, Proserpina was beginning to eat a pomegranate and had in fact already swallowed a few grains. The person who told Jupiter about this was Ascalaphus, later changed into an owl by

Proserpina as punishment. After all that had transpired, the only thing Ceres could settle for was to have her daughter stay with her for half of each year, spending the rest of the year at the side of the man who, by rape, had made her his bride.

It is impossible, it seems to me, to attribute to mere chance the fact that Sor Juana chose precisely such mythological characters as these to illustrate the intellectual argument of her great poem. Their relevant characteristics are the motherly love identified with Ceres, the bond of sisterhood between her and Arethusa, Proserpina's filial loyalty to her mother, and also the abundance represented by the mother figure; and these feminine figures suffer at the hands of the masculine figures who intervene in their lives. Let us read closely the following passage, in which "the bright investigator" of the underworld reports to Ceres the whereabouts of her daughter (lines 723–29):

> útil curiosidad, aunque prolija,
> que de su no cobrada bella hija
> noticia cierta dio a la Rubia Diosa,
> cuando montes y selvas trastornando,
> cuando prados y bosques inquiriendo,
> su vida iba buscando
> y del dolor su vida iba perdiendo.

> (a useful curiosity, though prolix, which yielded positive news of her beautiful unfound daughter to the Blond Goddess when, searching high and low through woods and forests, inquiring of meadows and groves, she was seeking for her beloved and was losing her life in grief.)

In addition to Sor Juana's usual emphasis on the positive characteristics of her feminine figures, here we have a striking example of her capacity to bring together in a single complex reflection two different aspects of her own personality: her concern about being a woman and her concern about being an intellectual. Let us recall what she tells us in her *Reply* to the bishop about the scientific discoveries she made while she was in the kitchen or on the playground watching girls spin a top, discoveries leading her to consider the advantages of being a woman and having access to fields of observation closed to men, to a fuller perspective on the world: "If Aristotle had been a cook, he would have written a great deal more." In this case, too, Sor Juana's ultimate purpose is to give us an example to illustrate a philosophic point about the limitations of human knowledge, an example based on observing underground water coming up from a spring. For this she chooses a feminine character, Arethusa, and brings her into a personal relationship involving intimate maternal feelings of suffering for a lost daughter.

The other example she uses to illustrate the same epistemological concerns is that of the "breve flor," or short-lived flower, a variation on a similar feminine theme: when she mentions "her fragile beauty," we cannot help thinking of the traits traditionally attributed to woman as a "weak and lovely being." It is easy for us to imagine, behind the following lines of Baroque poetry, a seventeenth-century nun bent over a flowerpot on the windowsill of her convent cell, concentrating her attention on the most beautiful carnation, and trying in vain to comprehend it (lines 733–41):

> . . . mixtos, por qué, colores
> —confundiendo la grana en los albores—
> fragante le son gala;
> ámbares por qué exhala,
> y el leve, si más bello,
> ropaje al viento explica,
> que en una y otra fresca multiplica
> hija, formando pompa escarolada
> de dorados perfiles cairelada . . .

> (not knowing why mixed colors—combining crimson with white light—adorn it with fragrance; why it exhales perfumes and unfolds in the wind its loveliest thin garment, multiplying itself in one new daughter after another, forming a frilly fringe fluted with gold streaks . . .)

She notes, incidentally, the flower's reproductive function, multiplying itself in daughters, and then immediately decides to follow the Renaissance poetic tradition of comparing the carnation's combination of red and white to women's cosmetics, using the flower as an exemplum in a sermon against the dangers of deception (lines 751–56):

> preceptor quizá vano
> —si no ejemplo profano—
> de industria femenil que el más activo

veneno hace dos veces ser nocivo
en el velo aparente
de la que finge tez resplandeciente.

(a reproof perhaps in vain—if not a bad example—of feminine wiles
that make the deadliest poison doubly noxious in the deceptive veil
of a fictitiously glowing complexion.)

These are the incidental thoughts that occur to Sor Juana as she comments on how problematic it is for human science, which cannot
understand a single, simple object, to try to comprehend the entire
universe. From the topos of the rose, traditionally compared with
woman because of her fleeting, fragile beauty and her cosmetics, the
poet moves in a sophisticated leap to epistemological questions of philosophy. This gives us insight into how an extraordinary nun in New
Spain invents a new feminine rhetoric to theatricalize everyday aspects
of women's lives, making them significantly relevant to the adventures
of scientific thought.

Let us turn now to the final section of the poem, the dramatic battle
between night and day. Before the appearance of the "father of burning
light" in line 887, Sor Juana has three feminine characters precede the
sun: Venus, the planet goddess representing intelligence, love, and female beauty; Aurora, the goddess of the dawn; and Night, also, like
Aurora, presented as an Amazon (lines 895–906):

> Pero de Venus, antes, el hermoso
> apacible lucero
> rompió el albor primero,
> y del viejo Titón la bella esposa
> —amazona de luces mil vestida,
> contra la Noche armada,
> hermosa si atrevida,
> valiente aunque llorosa—
> su frente mostró hermosa
> de matutinas luces coronada,
> aunque tierno preludio, ya animoso,
> del planeta fogoso . . .

(But first the lovely peaceful star of Venus broke the dawn, and the
fair bride of aged Tithonus—an Amazon clad in many rays, armed
against the Night, lovely while daring, brave though tearful—

showed her beautiful forehead crowned with morning light, a vigorous though tender prelude to the fiery star . . .)

Venus leads the way and helps Aurora show her ray-crowned head in an attack on Night. Aurora sheds tears of dew, in a traditional way, but Sor Juana is innovative in having her armed and brave, vigorous in her onslaught as she leads the fight against Night—also an Amazon, but dark (lines 914–16):

> y con nocturno cetro pavoroso
> las sombras gobernaba,
> de quien aun ella misma se espantaba.

(and with her fearsome nocturnal scepter she ruled the shadows, which frightened even her.)

Upon the attack of "la bella precursora signífera del sol . . . tocando al arma todos los süaves / si bélicos clarines de las aves" (lines 917–20: the fair forerunner and standard-bearer of the sun . . . sounding in alarm all the sweet yet warlike clarions of the birds), the Night "ronca tocó bocina / a recoger los negros escuadrones / para poder en orden retirarse" (lines 936–38: sounded her hoarse horn for the black squadrons to gather and be ready to retire in order). But they were unable to do so since the Sun's arrival was already imminent (955–58):

> y llegar al ocaso pretendía
> con el (sin orden ya) desbaratado
> ejército de sombras, acosado
> de la luz que el alcance le seguía.

(and so she tried to reach the west with her now shattered and disorderly army of shadows, attacked by the light that was pursuing them.)

But Night—and this is most significant—was only temporarily defeated (lines 959–66):

> Consiguió, al fin, la vista del ocaso
> el fugitivo paso,
> y—en su mismo despeño recobrada,
> esforzando el aliento en la rüina—
> en la mitad del globo que ha dejado

el sol desamparada,
segunda vez rebelde determina
mirarse coronada . . .

(Her fleeing step at last brought her in sight of the west and—re-
covering even as she fell, taking courage in defeat—in the half of
the globe that the sun has left unoccupied she decides, again rebellious, to have herself crowned as queen.)

The dramatic quality of this final scene depends primarily on the two
feminine characters, Aurora and Night. The intervention of the sun
(and Sor Juana could not have avoided considering Apollo a supremely
masculine figure), though narrated in beautiful verse, is relatively passive (lines 943–49):

Llegó, en efecto, el sol cerrando el giro
que esculpió de oro sobre azul zafiro:
de mil multiplicados
mil veces puntos, flujos mil dorados
—líneas, digo, de luz clara—salían
de su circunferencia luminosa,
pautando al cielo la cerúlea plana . . .

(The sun arrived in fact, closing the circle that he drew in gold on
sapphire blue: from a thousand points multiplied a thousand times, a
thousand golden rays—lines I mean of bright light—shone from his
luminous circumference, drawing straight edges on the sky's blue
sheet . . .)

What is emphasized in these lines is the light projected by the sun.
However, the poet avoids presenting the sun as a personal individual or
specific mythological character, as Phoebus or Apollo, while this is
precisely what she does with Venus, and especially with Aurora and
the Night.[25]
    Since woman has been credited with an ability to endure and adapt
in a flexible way, characteristics also attributed to Baroque culture,[26] I
should like to point out something that has not, I believe, been commented on before, and that is the Night's attitude toward defeat: she
undertakes the battle knowing that she is going to lose but also knowing, at the same time, as Sor Juana had remarked before apropos of

Phaeton (lines 785–826), that she can repeat her efforts interminably, like Sisyphus, "segunda vez rebelde." If the sun is a masculine character, the Night is feminine; if daytime belongs to the sun, the Night takes courage from defeat and succeeds the sun in endless rotation. This poem is a dream that will be repeated night after night, the obverse of daily activities under patriarchal vigilance. Sor Juana was fully aware of the literary tradition of the dream as reality, of the close relationship between what we do during the day and what we dream of doing at night.[27] The daylight classical brilliance of the Renaissance had given way to twilight zones of light and darkness in the Baroque period. The nun's dream is not the ethical *Bildungstraum* of Calderón's *La vida es sueño* (Life Is a Dream); it is an epistemological dream that reveals the impossibility, for human beings, of comprehending the universe and at the same time urges persistence in the face of defeat as a sufficient compensation for that impossibility.

Night as a character is given emphasis by being placed at the end of the poem; in this way the poet reinforces what she had said apropos of Phaeton. Both of these figures represent an urge to succeed and to rebel, even though in vain, to strive to comprehend the universe, which was Sor Juana's own major aim in life. This is the aspiration incarnated in these two figures. Like Phaeton and like Night, the nun decides to repeat in her poem what she indefatigably tries to do with every new day that begins, even though she accepts in advance the inevitability of defeat: during long and patient hours she studies, affirming in this way her right to existence as effort, and she does this centuries before Camus and his existentialist theories. As Octavio Paz says,[28] *El Sueño* is a poem that represents "the last example of one genre and the first of another." In a world that made no space available to woman as a thinking being, it was a woman, a nun, who, by making use of every recourse available to women, offered new solutions to the old problems of man, inscribing herself fully within a universal human problematic. With Sor Juana, Woman (with a capital W) enters the literary history of the Spanish-speaking world; after her, no one could exclude the female intellectual from Spanish American letters. If it is true that the writings of women have always been heroic,[29] it has never been truer than in the case of this extraordinary nun who concludes her long philosophical poem, unique in Hispanic literature, by asserting her faith in womankind with her single explicit reference to her feminine self, a reference made by means of the first-person singular pronoun modified by a feminine past participle, the last word of *El Sueño*:

. . . quedando a luz más cierta
el mundo iluminado y yo *despierta*.

(leaving the world illuminated by a more certain light, and me
awake; my emphasis)

NOTES

Translated by Elias Rivers.

1. The present essay was completed for this collection in December 1986. I delivered it as a keynote address at the international conference on Sor Juana and
Juan Rulfo celebrated in Oklahoma in April 1987. In the past few years I have
written four studies concerning feminine poetry in colonial Spanish America, but
only one of them has yet been published. I list them as follows for easy reference:

(a) My long chapter entitled "Lírica popular y lírica culta," with a section devoted to "Mujeres poetas de la colonia," is to be published soon by Editorial Alhambra of Madrid in Volume II of *Historia de la literatura hispanoamericana: La
Colonia,* coordinated by Giuseppe Bellini.

(b) "Contribución de la mujer a la lírica colonial," which I wrote for the first
meeting of American and Soviet specialists in colonial Spanish American literature, held in January 1986 at the Soviet Academy of Sciences in Moscow, is to be
published (along with the other papers delivered on that occasion) by Editorial
Monte Sexto of Montevideo.

(c) "Amarilis y su epístola a Lope: ¿Amor profano o admiración devota?" is a
paper I delivered at the conference of the Instituto Internacional de la Revista
Iberoamericana, held in Bonn in the summer of 1986. An English and revised version of this essay is scheduled for publication in a 1989 homage to Elias Rivers.

(d) "Antes de Juana Inés: Clarinda y Amarilis, dos poetas del Perú colonial"
(first delivered as a paper at the October 1986 congress of LASA in Boston) has
recently been published in *La Torre* (Nueva Época, dirigida por Arturo Echavarría)
I (1987): 275–87.

I shall refer to each of these four studies by citing this note, 1, followed by the
appropriate letter.

2. Elaine Showalter, "Introduction," in her *The New Feminist Criticism: Essays
on Women, Literature, and Theory* (New York: Pantheon, 1985), p. 6.

3. José Deleito y Piñuela, *La mujer, la casa y la moda* (Madrid: Espasa-Calpe,
1966), pp. 17–18. For further evidence, see Manuel Serrano y Sanz, *Antología de
poetisas líricas,* Vol. I (Madrid: RABM, 1915), pp. xi–xii: "Feminine poetry in
Spain shows characteristics that—although fundamentally universal and very human, for shyness has always been considered a virtue more peculiar to women than
to men—probably derive from a social situation that still persists in some regions
of Spain, where women live in a sort of reclusion, which many hold to be a conse-
quence of Moorish customs, but which perhaps belongs to the special psychology

of the Iberian race. The fact is that during the 16th and 17th centuries very few Spanish poetesses expressed sincerely in verse their feelings of love."

4. Luis Monguió, "Compañía para Sor Juana: Mujeres cultas en el virreinato del Perú," *University of Dayton Review* 16, 2 (Spring 1983): 50.

5. Sor Juana's poems will be identified by the numbers assigned to them by Georgina Sabat de Rivers and Elias L. Rivers in their edition of her *Obras selectas* (Barcelona: Noguer, 1976).

6. María de Zayas wrote poetry, in addition to novels, and perhaps became a nun toward the end of her life (see Deleito y Piñuela, *La mujer*, p. 42); the same title of "Tenth Muse" was given to women in the literary worlds of England and of Portugal.

7. See José Antonio Maravall, "Un esquema conceptual de la cultura barroca," *Cuadernos Hispanoamericanos* 273 (1973): 423–61.

8. See the introduction to my edition of Sor Juana's *Inundación castálida* (Madrid: Castalia, 1983), pp. 18–23.

9. Annette Kolodny, "A Map for Rereading: Gender and the Interpretation of Literary Texts," in her *Feminist Criticism: Essays on Women, Literature and Theory* (New York: Pantheon, 1985), p. 106.

10. Ibid., p. 48.

11. See, for example, the poem addressed to the Duchess de Aveiro (beginning "Grande duquesa de Aveiro") in which, after mentioning America twice, she continues to refer to it as her native land in the following words (ed. 1982, p. 222):

> Pero ¿a dónde de mi patria
> la dulce afición me hace
> remontarme del asunto
> y del intento alejarme?

(But where does my sweet fondness for my native land carry my thoughts and divert me from my subject?)

Or the poem beginning "Cuándo, númenes divinos," in which we find these more ambiguous words (ed. 1976, p. 504):

> ¿Qué mágicas infusiones
> de los indios herbolarios
> de mi patria, entre mis letras
> el hechizo derramaron?

(What magical infusions from the Indian herb stores of my native land poured their charms into my letters?)

(I cite as ed. 1982 my edition of *Inundación castálida* and as ed. 1976 the edition of *Obras selectas* edited by Georgina Sabat and Elias Rivers; I also give the first line, so that the poem may be found in Méndez-Plancarte's edition.)

12. For the pastoral tradition and further bibliography, see my chapter to be published by Alhambra and my presentation made orally in Moscow (both mentioned in note 1a and b).

13. I refer to the well-known passage in her *Respuesta* where Sor Juana says, "I

have never written anything voluntarily, but because of other people's requests and instructions; thus I do not remember having written for my own pleasure anything except a scrap of paper ["papelillo"] that they call *El Sueño*" (ed. 1976, p. 803).

14. Showalter, *New Feminist Criticism*, p. 131.

15. See "La situación enunciativa del *Primero sueño,*" *Revista Canadiense de Estudios Hispánicos* 11 (1986): 185–91.

16. For the text of *El Sueño*, I use our 1976 Noguer edition, with line numbers indicated; any emphasis is my own. The poem can also be found in Vol. I of Méndez-Plancarte's edition of the complete works or in his independent edition of the poem, *El Sueño* (Mexico: Imprenta Universitaria, 1951).

17. See our edition of 1976, p. 718, for an outline of the poem, with section titles to which I will refer.

18. For further details, see my monograph of 1976, pp. 69–72.

19. For a Freudian or Jungian interpretation of the poem, and specifically of Nyctimene, see Ludwig Pfandl's *Sor Juana Inés de la Cruz: La décima musa de México* (Mexico: UNAM, 1963), p. 214; and Rafael Catalá's "La trascendencia en *Primero Sueño*: El incesto y el águila," *Revista Iberoamericana* 44 (1978): 421–34. It should also be pointed out that Sor Juana may well have been influenced by Aztec mythology: Huitzilopochtli personifying the sun in his battle against the moon and the stars, and other Aztec gods in the form of bats and owls.

I also recall with appreciation a conversation I had with Professor Electa Arenal long ago, when we talked about Nyctimene.

20. See Perelmuter Pérez, "La situación enunciativa," p. 186.

21. We may compare the references to Ascalaphus in Góngora's *Soledad II*, ed. by Dámaso Alonso (Madrid, 1956), lines 791–93, 974–79:

> Grave, de perezosas plumas globo,
> que a luz lo condenó incierta la ira
> del bello de la estigia deidad robo . . .
> . . . .
> Con sordo luego estrépito despliega
> —injuria de la luz, horror del viento—
> sus alas el testigo que en prolija
> desconfianza a la sicana diosa
> dejó sin dulce hija,
> y a la estigia deidad con bella esposa.

> (A heavy ball of sluggish plumes, condemned to uncertain light by the anger of she who was robbed from the Stygian deity. . . . Then with a muffled crash he spreads—an insult to light, a shudder to the wind—his wings, he the witness whose prolonged betrayal left Sicania's goddess without her sweet daughter, left the Stygian god with a lovely wife.)

See also Eunice Joiner Gates, "Reminiscences of Góngora in the Works of Sor Juana Inés de la Cruz," *PMLA* 54 (1939): 1041–58.

22. "Encantadora," the word used by Sor Juana, already had a double meaning in the Golden Age: the woman who charms one with her grace, and the female magician or enchantress.

I have restored the name "Almone" that is found in the first edition. It was changed to "Alcione" (Halcyon) by Vossler, a change that Méndez-Plancarte accepted with praise (see the notes to his edition, Vol. I, pp. 578, 585). The two readings have been discussed at length by Manuel Corripio Rivero, "Una minucia en *El sueño* de Sor Juana: ¿Almone o Alcione?" *Abside* 29 (1965): 472–81; and by Audrey Lumsden-Kouvel and Alexander P. MacGregor, "The Enchantress Almone Revealed: A Note on Sor Juana Inés de la Cruz's Use of a Classical Source in the *Primero sueño*," *Revista Canadiense de Estudios Hispánicos* 2 (1977): 65–71.

, 23. For an explanation of how philosophy and science were at that time a single field of thought, see Elias Trabulse, *El hermetismo y Sor Juana Inés de la Cruz: Orígenes e interpretación* (Mexico: Regina de los Angeles, 1980), esp. pp. 21–23.

24. See Nesca A. Robb, *Neoplatonism of the Italian Renaissance* (London: Allen and Unwin, 1935), p. 17.

25. This stands in clear contrast to Góngora's treatment of the beginning of the day in his *Soledad I*, lines 179–81, and 705–13, in which the protagonist is clearly the sun, personified as such, with mention of his fiery chariot; and he is awakened, not by feminine birds but by another masculine character, Hymenaeus, god of the wedding day, who uses shining rays as door knockers to wake up the sun (his father, according to some mythological accounts). At no point is there a mention of Aurora or of any other feminine character.

26. According to Maravall ("Un esquena conceptual," p. 459), Baroque disillusion does not mean escapism but rather coming to grips with reality ("el desengaño no significa apartamiento . . . sino adecuación").

27. See my 1976 monograph, pp. 33–54.

28. *Sor Juana Inés de la Cruz o Las trampas de la fe* (Barcelona: Seix Barral, 1982), p. 474.

29. See Showalter, *New Feminist Criticism*, p. 9.

CHAPTER 8

Speaking Through the Voices of Love:
　　　　Interpretation as Emancipation

ESTER GIMBERNAT DE GONZÁLEZ

Among Sor Juana's sonnets we find a group classi-
fied as "sonnets of love and discretion." Various critics have turned
their attention to these sonnets and wondered if they arose from lived
experience or were in fact commissioned. Octavio Paz has said of
them: "As many have pointed out, her love poems must be based on
lived experience, provided . . . that what we call experience embraces
the real and the imaginary, what is thought and what is dreamed."[1]
Moreover, with her meticulous knowledge of the great Text of love poetry that runs from the troubadours to her own contemporaries, passing
through the *dolce stil nuovo*, Sor Juana engages in a love poetry that
subtly questions, from within the conventions to which she ostensibly
adheres, the very terms of that tradition. These delicate and frequent
rebellions open a critical zone within the canonical system that contains them, revealing the possibility of a meta-discursive level, that is,
a view from without and from above. As such, the sonnets conjoin Sor
Juana's experience at its fullest with her mastery of knowledge.

　　The voices converge between the lines, in the pulse of an absence
fully capable of exposing the truth of the false "I" which the poem, a

literary exercise, proclaims. This play of underlying voices has led me to focus on three of Sor Juana's love sonnets which draw on the technique of the ancient *jarchas* where a male poet speaks through the female character's words. The poet sang through the other's voice. Here, Sor Juana, a woman, speaks as a man, creating a space in which diverse voices dialogue in unison: a simultaneity that allows the discourse to assume the other's voice while still maintaining its own.

Sor Juana's three love sonnets that issue from what Méndez Plancarte calls a "male persona"[2] seem to fuel the conviction that the nun sang of loves not her own, that she constructed verses on request; exemplary in this regard, they placate the critics.[3] The construction of the poems, addressed to the females Anarda, Lisarda, and Celia, clearly distinguishes the voice of the poet (hers), from that of the lover (a male voice), which thus creates a critical space within the text itself. *What does the male lover say to his female beloved when the poet is a woman?* This whole lyric tradition partakes of a field of metaphors, paradoxes, and hyperboles ruled by conventions whose hierarchical system imposes set relationships of values and power. Nothing escapes Sor Juana: she complies with and conveys the whole corpus. She appears to yield herself to the voice of the male lover, to be erased by his direct intent, becoming an absent-presence of the utterance. On the other hand, the verbal texture can reveal what lies beneath the voice of the male lover, making her a present-absence. It lays bare that path which departs from established convention and gives way to the unpredictable, so resistent to facile interpretation: a new realm of particularity which in Sor Juana's hands becomes an independent force that contradicts the male lover in diverse and subtle ways. This decentering endows her poetic language with an unexpected flexibility. Having denied priority to the voice of convention, it avails itself of the excentric wanderings of words which have been declared free and independent of a foreseeable framework. The ostentatious display of convention, then, forms part of a game in which the expectations will not be fulfilled, because their authority as vehicles of power has been renounced. With their dislocation, a subtle rejection of authorized meaning, the possibilities of interpretation increase. What direction will be taken by the poet, purveyor both of differences and of the supplement of a new and unusual meaning that arises from the interstices of texts belonging to the lyric tradition of the male lover? The ingenious organization and accumulation of words and phrases makes available a variety of meanings, a polysemia. Individually and together they are cast into an intertextual flow. Let us now attempt to tease out the latent meaning planted by the "poet" who has marked her distance from the male lover.

As Electa Arenal has rightly observed, there is a great need for enriched readings of Sor Juana, for readings more relevant to our times.[4] Every period privileges its own way of controlling the production of intertextual meanings: given the importance that the intellectual liberation of the Mexican woman held for Sor Juana, we can establish a determining relationship between more modern concepts and those of Sor Juana, privileging the contexts that oriented her works and rendering them relevant to contemporary concerns. What interests me is the dynamic nature of the texts of the three sonnets; in the displacements of successive readings, I will therefore try to discover the interpretive system that illuminates those redoublings of meaning of the least accessible zones of the text in accordance with a modern feminist problematic.[5]

"OUR COMMON SORROW"?

SONNET 178: "Un celoso refiere el común pesar que todos padecen, y advierte a la causa el fin que puede tener la lucha de afectos encontrados"

> Yo no dudo, Lisarda, que te quiero,
> aunque sé que me tienes agraviado;
> mas estoy tan amante y tan airado,
> que afectos que distingo no prefiero.
>
> De ver que odio y amor te tengo, infiero
> que ninguno estar puede en sumo grado,
> pues no le puede el odio haber ganado
> sin haberle perdido amor primero.
>
> Y si piensas que el alma que te quiso
> ha de estar siempre a tu afición ligada,
> de tu satisfacción vana te aviso:
>
> pues si el amor al odio ha dado entrada,
> el que bajó de sumo a ser remiso,
> de lo remiso pasará a ser nada.

("A jealous lover relates the common sorrow that all suffer, and warns its cause of the ends to which the struggles of conflicting affections obtain."

I doubt not, Lisarda, that I love you, though I know you have injured me; but I am so enamored and so angered, that I prefer not the emotions I can discern.

In seeing that I both hate and love you, I infer that neither can exist in the highest degree, since hatred cannot win out without love having first given it way.

And if you think that the soul which loved you will forever be linked to your whim, I must warn you of your vain satisfaction:

For if love has given entry to hatred, what descended from the heights to a state of indifference, from indifference will pass to nothingness.)

Love sonnet 178[6] sets up the internal conflict which Catullus long ago celebrated in his poem 85—I love you and I hate you. In the first stanza, the lover presents the situation to Lisarda: in a paradoxical simultaneity, he knows not whether he loves her more than he hates her, or vice versa. There is a balance in these opposing sentiments, although in stating that he loves her, the male lover uses the verb *to doubt* in the negative, and to express his injury, the unqualified verb *to know*. The tension between love/injury, enamored/angered, is a commonplace in Renaissance poetry, frequently resolved with the recognition that love prevails. While the complexity of his emotions tormented Catullus, the situation makes Lisarda's lover uncomfortable. The rancor of his injury doesn't leave room for the amorous torments of Catullus.

The poem merely states that if hatred has appeared it is because love has lost ground. Who is to blame? How to relieve the situation? In the tercets the male lover turns his displeasure on Lisarda. He concedes that she may now be thinking about these amorous problems, but the verb *to love* is in the past tense. It is important to note that the phrase "el alma que te quiso" (the soul that loved you) introduces an impersonal distance which generalizes the sentiments expressed in the poem, as does the title of the poem in announcing, "el común pesar que todos padecen" (the general sorrow which all suffer).[7] *All* refers to jealous lovers in general, lovers whose suffering derives from the injurious actions of their ladies. Yet given, as I believe, that the text both hides and reveals itself, the conceivable generalization takes on a different dimension, referring as well to all of those female beloveds who find themselves marginalized by the discourse of their jealous lovers, beloveds who dare not venture beyond superfluous vanity. The first line of the sonnet's resolution (line 9) establishes that she can think, a favorable concession. But the proposition the beloved has thought up is merely the product of her "vana satisfacción" (vain satisfaction), against which the "prudent" lover warns her. The tense equilibrium of opposites found in the beginning of the poem is dislocated, giving way to a hierarchical logic, which menaces the primacy and victory of the male lover's love. Hatred, invading the territory of love, contaminates and diminishes it. "[B]ajó de sumo a ser remiso, de lo remiso pasará a ser nada" (what descended from the heights to a state of indifference, from indifference will pass to nothingness)—the threat of imminent hatred, of the total rupture of the couple's supposed equilibrium. The last two lines signal a temporary balance. "[B]ajó de sumo" (descended from the heights): the verb in the past tense seems to refer to the present state of the relationship—the result of the dehierarchization which has already taken place—which passes to the future tense in the last line, "pasará a ser nada" (will pass to nothingness). This temporal distinction, with its backing in the speaker's present, confirms the peculiar equilibrium of the beginning of the poem and returns us to the problem whose motivating cause is Lisarda.

As the title states: "advierte a la causa el fin que puede tener la lucha de afectos encontrados" (and warns its cause of the ends to which the struggles of conflicting affections obtain). It calls attention to the female beloved. She is the cause both of the initial love and of some action that has given rise to injury. As the title suggests, this injury is caused by jealousy. Both conflicting sentiments depend on Lisarda: her "satisfacción vana" (vain satisfaction) will reduce to nothingness that love which he seems to have awarded her. But let there be no mistake: though constructed within the given conventions, this is not a love poem but rather a poem of warning about the order that must be respected and the spheres in which each member of the couple moves— that is, the "pride, the presumption, that 'leads a woman from her state of obedience.'"[8] He knows, has no doubt, discerns, prefers, infers, warns. She, in turn, "si piensa" (if she thinks), is wrong. Which implies that after having existed in the highest degree, not only will his love descend into weakness and inertia, but she too will sink into nothingness. Whatever love he may feel becomes for Lisarda—inevitably on the losing end—an obligation and preoccupation. Without the man who loves her, she will descend to indifference and then to nothingness. After having been worshipped on the highest pedestal, she will descend to the lowest position of woman-without-man. She must accept one condition: not to arouse jealousy with her actions, to remain within the bounds of passivity. To provoke injury is to challenge the very structure of the system from within which he speaks.

The agent provocateur is the poet, the female poet: speaking a man's words, installed moreover in the recreation of a Latin tradition, she dares to question from the interstices of deprivation the very proposition that the male lover's discourse declaims. Her text inscribes itself in the margins of the conventional text, supplementing it. The mask of the male voice dissembles the possible meaning of the text. "[T]e quiero" (I love you) confronts "me tienes agraviado" (you have injured me): he gives her love, and she gives him back sorrow. The voice of the male lover, presenting himself as a victim in the first stanza, falls victim to the circle of his own logic of inferences, knowledge, discernment, and warnings. The female poet controls his descent; his discourse has condemned him.

"TEARS INEVITABLY FLOW"?

SONNET 177: "Discurre inevitable el llanto a vista de quien ama"

> Mandas, Anarda, que sin llanto asista
> a ver tus ojos; de lo cual sospecho
> que el ignorar la causa, es quien te ha hecho
> querer que emprenda yo tanta conquista.
>
> Amor, señora, sin que me resista,
> que tiene en fuego el corazón deshecho,
> como hace hervir la sangre allá en el pecho,
> vaporiza en ardores por la vista.
>
> Buscan luego mis ojos tu presencia
> que centro juzgan de su dulce encanto;
> y cuando mi atención te reverencia,
>
> los visüales rayos, entretanto,
> como hallan en tu nieve resistencia,
> lo que salió vapor, se vuelve llanto.

("Tears inevitably flow when he sees the one he loves."
  You order me, Anarda, without tears to attend the sight of your

eyes; which leads me to suspect that your ignorance of the cause, is
what has made you desire I undertake such a conquest.

Love, my lady, without my resisting, has my heart dissolved into
fire, and as does it make the blood boil below in the breast, vaporizes
into ardors through the eyes.

My eyes then seek your presence which they consider the center
of their sweet charm; and as my attention reveres you,

the visual rays, meanwhile, find resistance in your snow, and
what emerged as vapor, turns to tears.)

Love sonnet 177 contains a textual play similar to that of sonnet
178, especially in the ways it relates and adapts the knowledge and actions of the female beloved to the texture of established traditions of
amorous discourse. The poem begins, "Mandas, Anarda" (You order
me, Anarda), a command that places the female beloved on the superior plane granted her by the conventions of courtly love. Surrendered
to the command of this woman whose name is linked with flowers—
Anarda, white nard, lilies of unimpeachable purity—the male lover
voices concern over his ability to obey. In the presence of the eyes of
the beloved, his eyes can't help but weep. The disdainful beloved, exalted by the enslaved lover; the eyes, windows to the soul, provoking
reactions not limited to the dialogue of looks—these elements are undeniably aligned with the commonplaces of love poetry. They give rise
to predictable expectations, which in turn assume a dénouement appropriate to the convention, a resolution of the recurring tensions
posed by the topoi that appear in the poem.

But by the middle of the second line we encounter the unexpected.
The reason for the captivating Anarda's orders and desires is her ignorance. She demands out of ignorance. Does the lady, victim of her own
ignorance, realize that she is merely a desirable vehicle whose basic
value in the system is that of initiating in the lover an internal process
that exceeds her own control? The first stanza briefly grants her a space
only immediately to underline the impertinence of her command and
pretentious actions. The more obvious scenario is dislocated; the will
to recreate commonplaces of the tradition gives way to a new dimension, irreducibly polysemic.

The next three stanzas will present the woman as a passive object,
confirming her inability to act. Reified, recipient of beauty, attributed
a life-denying coldness, the lady lacks the one thing that would allow
her to act: knowledge. The male lover has decided to surrender himself
to the mandate of love, but despite his reverence he cannot allow the

hierarchy of knowledge versus power to be altered. He therefore seizes on the very mechanisms of the institution as his means of restitution.

First he refers to love as the cause of what goes on in his heart and declares that he hasn't resisted its devastation. The internal fire gives sign of its ardor through the vapor that escapes through the look. In the best Platonic tradition, his eyes translate his most intimate recesses. Love, not she, has initiated this process, which makes of Anarda an intermediate, if necessary, vehicle of this amorous effervescence. This is the story told by the quartets.

In the tercets the male voice takes pleasure in the individual, personal process of the transformation of ardent love into tears; although presented as something beyond his control, it would seem to respond to an all too clear cause-effect relationship. First his eyes seek out the desired presence and become enchanted by she who in this way becomes their center. Now her prisoner, he reveres her with his attention. The look is the mode of communication between the burning fire and the receiving snow, ingenious signs of his desire and her indifference. Much as she may issue orders, much as she may be the cold, disdainful lady who refuses to allow herself to be melted or pierced by the warm and illuminating rays of love, thanks to the construction of the sonnet she finds herself denied active part in the course of events. The victim of her ignorance manages to displace the beloved from her centrality at the same time as he proclaims her the center. "Buscan luego mis ojos tu presencia/que centro juzgan" (My eyes then seek your presence, which they consider the center).

The poem says little about the external beauty of the beloved: her presence is a "dulce encanto" (sweet charm), and she is associated with snow, a common topos equating rejection and disdain with the cold of the snow at the same time as it extols the whiteness of the skin.[9] What the poem does present is her deficiency: wanting to command but not knowing. Her not knowing creates the space for his knowing. While she commands in one line, his explanation requires three stanzas—stanzas charged with the task of thoroughly stripping the beloved of her centrality and her command of its possible authority. From an ingenious pseudo-scientific play of vapors, humors, and temperatures issue the subtle bonds of submission. Yet the reversal doesn't end here, but rather establishes a framework that presents the virtues of this submission, a conversion within love to the very rule that demarcates and creates hierarchies. Consequently, two opposing lines are drawn: on the one hand the submission to which Anarda believes she can subject her lover, based on the regimented discourse of convention that depicts her as the superior lady, the center to whom one yields one's will simply for what and where she is; versus the self-justified and self-justifying submission enunciated by the lover. Rather than its victim, the lover is the "unmistakable subject of his role, which he plays out until merging with it."[10] A matter which the poet exploits as a means of showing/without showing the conflict: in this closed theater converge the diverse lines that regulate the imperatives of submission, their logic nourished by the clichés of amorous expression. We know that behind this male voice which enunciates the rule, and the explanation which fortifies the rule, lies the voice of the poet, Sor Juana. Her artifices and concepts acquire a double voice as they become implicated in other possible meanings: that which purported to reestablish the hierarchy doubles back and questions the order. The poem posits a woman-object who is reproached for daring to issue orders about things she doesn't understand—this is the juncture where the voices diverge. Ignorance leads to submission and to loss of the sphere of action.

OF CHANGE AND APPETITES

SONNET 183: "Para explicar la causa a la rebeldía, o ya sea firmeza, de un cuidado, se vale de la opinión que atribuye a la perfección de su forma lo incorruptible en la materia de los Cielos. Usa cuidadosamente términos de las Escuelas."

> Probable opinión es que, conservarse
> la forma celestial en su fijeza,
> no es porque en la materia hay más firmeza
> sino por la manera de informarse.
>
> Porque aquel apetito de mudarse,
> lo sacia de la forma la nobleza;
> con que, cesando el apetito, cesa
> la ocasión que tuvieran de apartarse.
>
> Así tu amor, con vínculo terrible,
> el alma que te adora, Celia, informa;
> con que su corrupción es imposible,

ni educir otra con quien no conforma,
no por ser la materia incorruptible,
mas por lo inamisible de la forma.

("Which explains the cause of the rebelliousness, or obstinacy, of an amorous concern, by means of the principle that attributes the incorruptibility of celestial matter to the perfection of its form. Scholastic terms are carefully applied."

Provable opinion has it, that the maintaining of celestial form in its fixity, owes not to the matter being more stable but to the manner in which it is informed.

Because that appetite for change, is sated by the nobility of form; and thus, when the appetite ceases, with it cease too the possibilities of change.

So too your love, with an invincible bond, informs the soul which adores you, Celia; and thus its corruption is impossible,

and to another it need not conform, not because the matter is incorruptible, but because the form cannot be lost.)

Sonnet 183 compares the love relationship that ties Celia and the speaker to the principle, explained in scholastic terms, regarding the unchangeable form of celestial matter. The bonds of love inspired by Celia have the ability of giving definitive form ("informar"—inform, form) to this love because they offer permanence within change.[11]

In sonnet 183, as in the others we have analyzed, Sor Juana assumes the voice of a man. The poem starts off with certainty: it is a provable opinion. It departs from a firm premise:[12] heavenly matter is not more stable but rather is formed in a privileged fashion which renders it insusceptible to becoming.[13] Change[14] obeys an appetite;[15] the fact that appetite is a weakness unknown to the heavens eliminates the possibility for change in essential things. The manner in which matter is informed provides the basis for comparison between the scholastic concepts and the relationship between the two lovers.

The tercets compare Celia's love with celestial matter;[16] her love's matter is also informed[17] or formed in a privileged fashion by the soul of the speaker. Though not celestial, this matter will remain incorruptible thanks to the unrenounceable form the lover imposes on it "con vínculo terrible" (with an invincible bond).

It may well be that Celia's sentiments, given shape by the love that another professes her, will attain the category of unchangeable, permanent, celestial matter—not because her love itself is an incorruptible entity but because the manner in which it has been formed, enacted, is unrenounceable and cannot be lost.

Matter is the indeterminate and determinable principle; form is what gives it substance. The lover's discourse, tinged with a somewhat pedantic erudition, insists on the importance of the scholastic notion of being "informed"; that is, the state in which potency has received, united with, and been specified by a formal element. The first stanza indicates that celestial form remains immutable, not due to its matter but rather because of the manner in which it is informed. Analogously, the poem insists that love, which imparts unity to the lovers by binding them together, responds not to incorruptible matter—by which is meant Celia's love—but rather to the form *his* soul has succeeded in imparting to their relationship. The prime matter—her love—remains potential and subject to the changes that can entail decadence, corruption, deterioration, unless it is informed in such a matter as to attain the privileged characteristics of the celestial order.

Scholasticism conceives the universe as a stratified order of ascending categories. All being is actualized in change, except God, who is a constant because He never has and never will undergo change, nor beginning or end. By virtue of her lover's adoration, this matter that is Celia's love becomes actualized within the immutability of the divine order: it cannot give way thanks to the fact that the presence and imparting of a substantial form has granted it permanence within change. The loving devotion of her male lover has accorded her a transubstantiation; the transformation of her properties has wrought a conversion that renders her capable of halting any other change. This unrenounceable form has halted deterioration.

Where, in this universe of vertical categories, do we find the orchestrating presence of Sor Juana? In controlling the discourse through the man's voice, she assumes a certain superiority. From her privileged position, knowing and the knowledge she controls raise her to a metadiscursive level from which she exercises a new power; interpretation as emancipation. Celia doesn't understand the invariable intensity of her love; she receives "information" which assigns her a place in the highest celestial sphere. We emphasize that what allows Celia to attain the celestial environs is the love accorded her by the lover. Her love in and of itself must be completed; it is a mere potency. When touched, when informed, by his adoration, it is realized, actualized, elevated, despite the fact that in human terms her love is condemned to immutability. With the greatest subtlety and complexity, under the guise of a game that permits her a show of scholastic knowledge, Sor Juana here displays an erudition that she questions by reinterpreting it.

In all three sonnets the position of each member of the pair depends on a system organized according to the coordinates of love. When one partner declares the other's ignorance of the processes that organize the system, he sets up a hierarchy based on inequality. It is this imbalance which the poem would express and redress. The ignorance here reproached assumes a crucial importance, underlining women's undeveloped intellectual potential, what keeps them from rebelling. Sor Juana "scoffs at the idea, current in her day, that women are intellectually inferior. As stupidity is not confined to women, neither is intelligence an attribute only of men."[18]

The male voice, fortified by the conventions of love poetry, partakes of a canonical order more attached to the law than to the beloved. From her position beyond this lover made of words, product of writing, the poet launches a scheme that shakes the hierarchy of oppositions. The play of voices allows us a glimpse of the zone that regulates the polysemia and establishes a logic of supplementarity within the very syntax to which it subscribes.

With its adherence to literary conventions and traditions, Sor Juana's poetic discourse could easily be viewed as an arena for received norms and socially accepted forms of power.[19] With its appropriation of the norm, her language could be taken as a function of the machinery of domination—expressing the reality of the oppressor, showing his world and point of view; its adherence to the canon would be no more than the transparent translation of respect for the ruling order into a language that partakes of its power. Yet Sor Juana's oeuvre contains poems such as the three we have analyzed, in which we catch sight of the search for an emancipating language, or at least a language with flashes of emancipation. Though submerged in a cultural context that forms and conditions them, making them "formulas set in rhyme",[20] the poems contain a layer of self-awareness critical of those modes of thought and reflection, which enriches and enables other readings.[21]

It is interesting that although these poems subtly indicate the oppressiveness of the traditional language of love, which subjugates as it caresses, they present the lady, the beloved, as victim less of a system than of her own ignorance. From within language itself, they reveal the possibilities of entering the sphere of equality through an increased awareness of the prime factor that makes subjection possible: ignorance. If in other poems Sor Juana expresses the problems that arise from thinking, knowledge, and questioning, in these three poems, with their play of possible voices, she underscores the urgency of knowledge as a means of surmounting such problems. In the first two, the intimate and very personal circumstances of jealousy or the lover's sentiments, as adapted to poetic convention, emphasize the innocent ignorance of the beloved, which allows her to be threatened or marginalized. The co-presence of the poet, capable of fully grasping the subtleties of the amorous relationship described in the poem, makes itself felt more decisively and conclusively in the third poem. Sonnet 183 leaves the more intimate sphere of love poetry to penetrate the world of knowledge: the terms of Scholasticism. The poet's knowledge rules the lover's voice. Her presence allows for a balance with no negative implications, one whose strength lies in the discourse itself: reciprocity prevails; it involves both voices. To attain this equality, through her meta-discourse[22] the poet has mounted a scenario that opens a space for emancipation, erasing the lines that demarcate hierarchical and confining orders.

Sor Juana's art: subtly installing itself in the rules of convention, questioning those rules by means of their own legitimating knowledge (Scholasticism, the traditions of love poetry), shaking the dialectic of hierarchies and power which lies at the heart of the lover's discourse, in order to contrive a warning against ignorance in the beloved[23] and a denunciation of the lover's discursive strategies.

NOTES

Translated by Stephanie Merrim.

1. Octavio Paz, *Sor Juana Inés de la Cruz o Las trampas de la fe* (Barcelona: Seix Barral, 1982), p. 371. I follow here, and in all quotations from this work, the English translation by Margaret Sayers Peden, *Sor Juana*, (Cambridge, Mass., and London: Harvard University Press, 1988), giving page references to the Spanish and English versions—here, Eng. version, p. 280.

2. Sor Juana Inés de la Cruz, *Obras completas*, ed., prologue, and notes by Alfonso Méndez-Plancarte (Mexico: Fondo de Cultura Económica, 1951), p. 535.

3. In this regard, Méndez-Plancarte writes: "And this fiction [speaking as a man] . . . supports the possibility that in certain other poems she also sang of loves not her own—even in cases dealing with women, in which it isn't clear from the grammatical gender." Ibid.

4. Electa Arenal, "Sor Juana Inés de la Cruz: Speaking the Mother Tongue,"

University of Dayton Review 16, 2 (Spring 1983), p. 93. Various recent studies treat Sor Juana's "feminism," among them Paz's *Sor Juana Inés de la Cruz,* esp. pp. 628ff; Eng. version, pp. 486ff.

5. The following texts have been most useful with regard to the subjects of female discourse and writing: Leonor Calvera, *El género mujer* (Buenos Aires: Editorial de Belgrano, 1983); Margarita Dalton, *Una aproximación a cómo se construye el discurso de lo femenino,* doctoral dissertation, Barcelona, 1985; Sandra M. Gilbert and Susan Gubar, *The Madwoman in the Attic* (New Haven: Yale University Press, 1979); Rosaldo N. Keohane and Barbara Gelpi, *Feminist Theory: A Critique of Ideology* (Chicago: University of Chicago Press, 1982); Julia Kristeva, *Desire in Language* (New York: Columbia University Press, 1980); Toril Moi, *Sexual/Textual Politics: Feminist Literary Theory* (London: Methuen, 1985); K. K. Ruthven, *Feminist Literary Studies* (Cambridge: Cambridge University Press, 1984); *Nuevas perspectivas sobre la mujer: Actas de las primeras jornadas de investigación interdisciplinaria* (Madrid: Universidad Autónoma de Madrid, 1982).

6. We reproduce the texts according to Méndez-Plancarte's edition.

7. I recognize that this title comprises a reading of the poem, which in certain ways complements my reading. See Frederick Luciani, "Sor Juana Inés de la Cruz: Epígrafe, epíteto, epígono," *Revista Iberoamericana* 132–33 (July–December 1985): 777–84.

8. Paz, *Sor Juana Inés de la Cruz,* p. 552; Eng. version, p. 426.

9. In poems by Quevedo and Herrera, among others, we find the association of snow/indifference/whiteness applied to the beloved.

10. Pierre Legendre, *El amor del censor: Ensayo sobre el orden dogmático,* trans. by Marta Giacomino (Barcelona: Anagrama, 1979), p. 17.

11. In his notes to this poem (p. 538), Méndez-Plancarte observes that "in itself it is very clear, if one understands the philosophical terms." Paz calls it an "abstruse, but admirably constructed sonnet. The Scholastic terminology makes it difficult; fortunately Méndez-Plancarte clarifies it" (Span., p. 373; Eng., p. 282).

12. Méndez-Plancarte defines this premise as "Hilemorphism (the fundamental doctrine of Aristotelian-Thomist cosmology)," p. 538.

13. "According to Aristotle's physics (a universal error in Antiquity), the Heavens—their 'Spheres' and the Stars—were incorruptible. And ancient Scholasticism (itself antiquated) explained this false supposition by saying that either their Prime Matter was different from that of the 'sublunar' bodies and capable of only one Form, or rather—although it was identical to earthly matter—because its appetite was satisfied by the eminence of any of the substantial 'celestial' forms." Ibid.

14. "Change: the actualization of a being in potency inasmuch as it is in potency; the movement of a movable being inasmuch as it is movable; the passage from (subjective) potency to act." Bernard Wuellner, S.J., *Dictionary of Scholastic Philosophy* (Milwaukee: Bruce Publishing, 1956), p. 22.

15. "Appetite: a form and especially a power that has an inclination toward an object suitable to itself or away from an unsuitable object." Ibid., p. 8.

16. "'[I]ncorruptible' love, like a star, not because of the superior nature of its will (symbolized by the Prime Matter), but because of the excellence of its object (represented by the 'celestial form'), which cannot be exchanged for any other." Méndez-Plancarte, p. 538.

17. "Information: (1) The presence and communication of the substantial form

in the potency. (2) Existing in another as in a substantial substrate." "Informed: the state of the potency when it has received and been united with and been specified by the formal element. Thus, the body is informed by the soul; the intellect is informed by a species; virtues are informed by charity." Wuellner, *Dictionary of Scholastic Philosophy*, p. 61.

18. Paz, *Sor Juana Inés de la Cruz*, p. 548; Eng., p. 420.

19. "Discourse has become the arena for the generation and propagation of historically specified norms and socially adequate forms of power." Paul Foss, "On the Value of That Text which is Not One," *Language, Sexuality and Subversion* (August 1979): 180.

20. Paz, *Sor Juana Inés de la Cruz*, p. 371; Eng., p. 280.

21. "The past shapes us. But we can become critically self-aware of those modes of thought and reflection that have helped to constitute our own thought and action." Jean Bethke Elshtain, "Feminist Discourse and Its Discontents: Language, Power, and Meaning," in *Feminist Theory: A Critique of Ideology*, p. 131.

22. I use the term *meta-discourse,* and not *subtext,* because I believe that the interpreting voice of the text, which makes for the dialogue within the text itself, rises above the enunciating presence of the male with his baggage of literary tradition and achieves a superior and all-embracing position which favors the desired equilibrium. If I understood this interpretive force as a subtext, I would be proposing a reading of respect and subordination to the order imposed by tradition.

23. Let me emphasize that I consider these poems to be warnings, and not criticisms, of women's ignorance. A warning holds the hope of a solution: in pointing out the subtle manner in which literary tradition wields guilt and paves the road toward "sweet" submission, the poet is not mocking the woman confined to the sphere of ignorance; rather, she acknowledges her, opening the only door that has allowed the female voice of the sonnets to rise to a meta-textual level in the exercise of equality: knowledge.

Bibliographical Note

STEPHANIE MERRIM

Of the thousands of pages that have been dedicated to Sor Juana Inés de la Cruz over the centuries, only a fraction display a genuine insight into the author's works and retain more than merely historical interest. The following bibliographical note contains a very personal and brief selection of works in English and Spanish that I consider to be basic research tools for the nonspecialist reader seeking a general introduction to Sor Juana. I have chosen to list here (with one or two exceptions) overviews of her works and/or times which, despite their general nature, in this reader's opinion do particular justice to their subject and its complexities. Read together, these studies should provide a well-rounded picture of Sor Juana's literary production, as well as of the literary and cultural context in which she wrote.

Research on Sor Juana from the point of view of modern feminist criticism is still in the seminal stages; the compilation of a complete bibliography of this nature remains a *studio a fare*. The works cited below, when not overtly feminist in their approach, do sympathetically advance our understanding of Sor Juana as a (woman) writer and of her larger circumstances. (The reader is advised that this bibliography represents only the editor's point of view and not necessarily that of the contributors to the volume.)

For those who wish to pursue further their investigations of Sor Juana, I also include a list of suggested bibliographies included in longer studies of the author's work.

SPANISH EDITIONS
Méndez-Plancarte, Alfonso, and Alberto G. Salceda, eds. *Obras completas*. Vols. I–IV: *Lírica personal; Villancicos y letras sacras; Autos y loas; Comedias, sonetos y prosa*. Mexico: Fondo de Cultura Económica, 1951.

Obras completas. Prologue by Francisco Monterde. Mexico: Editorial Porrúa, 1985. This edition, readily available commercially, contains the full text of Sor Juana's works but lacks notes.

Sabat de Rivers, Georgina. *Sor Juana Inés de la Cruz: Inundación castálida.* Madrid: Editorial Castalia, 1983. Modern edition of the first edition of the first volume of Sor Juana's works, 1689.

Sabat de Rivers, Georgina, and Elias L. Rivers. *Sor Juana Inés de la Cruz: Obras selectas.* Barcelona: Editorial Noguer, 1976.

ENGLISH EDITIONS/TRANSLATIONS

Harss, Luis. *Sor Juana's Dream.* New York: Lumen Books, 1986. Bilingual edition, with commentary, of the *Primero sueño.*

Peden, Margaret Sayers. *Sor Juana Inés de la Cruz, Poems: A Bilingual Anthology.* Binghamton, N.Y.: Bilingual Press/Editorial Bilingüe, 1985.

———. *A Woman of Genius.* Salisbury, Conn.: Lime Rock Press, 1982. Translation of the *Respuesta a Sor Filotea de la Cruz.*

Trueblood, Alan S. *A Sor Juana Anthology.* Cambridge, Mass.: Harvard University Press, 1988. A bilingual edition, including translations of the *Respuesta* and portions of *El Divino Narciso,* as well as an excellent selection of poetry.

CRITICAL SOURCES

Arenal, Electa. "The Convent as Catalyst for Autonomy: Two Hispanic Nuns of the Seventeenth Century." *Women in Hispanic Literature: Icons and Fallen Idols,* ed. by Beth Miller. Berkeley: University of California Press, 1983. Pp. 147–83.

> Viewing the convent as a semiautonomous culture which allowed women to develop their talents (p. 149), the study examines the achievements of visionary Castilian nun Isabel de Jesús and of Sor Juana. Arenal provides a solid introduction to Sor Juana's life and to the feminist ideological content of her works, featuring a discussion of the role of women in propagating Sor Juana's works as well as a keen reading of the subtleties of the *Respuesta a Sor Filotea de la Cruz.*

Gaos, José. "El sueño de un sueño" [Dream of a Dream]. *Historia Mexicana* 10, 1 (1960): 54–71.

> A penetrating guide to Sor Juana's most ambitious poem, its architecture and baroque aspects. Offers a reading of the philosophical implications of the dream in the *Primero sueño,* revolving around the contention that "El Sueño es el poema del sueño del afán de saber como sueño" (The *Sueño* is the poem of the dream of knowledge as a dream) [p. 67]. Gaos's interpretation rests on his apt sense of Sor Juana as an intellectual woman.

Leonard, Irving A. *Baroque Times in Old Mexico.* Ann Arbor: University of Michigan Press, 1959.

> A milestone work by a pioneer in Latin American colonial studies, particularly attractive for its dramatic reenactments of Mexican Baroque society and culture. The chapters on Sor Juana and her fellow seeker of knowledge Carlos de Sigüenza y Góngora put forth a now classic argument: that both

were precursors of the Enlightenment in the New World, constrained and oppressed by church orthodoxy. Though Leonard's treatment of Sor Juana is marred by his problematical notions of the feminine and questionable readings of Sor Juana's psyche, the analysis of the dualities that shaped her thinking and literary works remains worthy of consideration.

Muriel, Josefina. *Cultura femenina novohispana* [Women's Culture in New Spain]. Mexico: UNAM, 1982.

This voluminous yet straightforward study of the significant women and women writers of all walks of life in colonial Mexico dedicates an extensive section to Sor Juana, "La poesía femenina en el virreinato" (Women's Poetry in Viceregal Mexico). Though its approach remains more historical and thematic than literary, and its sense of Sor Juana's orthodoxy is debatable, the chapter affords a systematic exposition of Sor Juana's theology as well as of her manipulation of humanistic culture at large. Of particular note is Muriel's discussion—one of the few of its kind—of the influence of a female model, Mother María de Jesús de Agreda, on Sor Juana's works.

Paz, Octavio. *Sor Juana Inés de la Cruz o las trampas de la fe*. Barcelona: Seix Barral, 1982. English translation: Margaret Sayers Peden, *Sor Juana*. Cambridge, Mass.: Harvard University Press, 1988.

See my essay in this volume, "Toward a Feminist Reading of Sor Juana Inés de la Cruz: Past, Present, and Future Directions in Sor Juana Criticism," for a detailed discussion of this work. Also note that an appendix in the third edition of Paz's book (1983), as well as in the English translation, reprints and discusses Sor Juana's recently unearthed letter to her confessor, her *Autodefensa espiritual* (Spiritual Self-Defense).

Picón-Salas, Mariano. "El barroco de Indias." *De la conquista a la independencia*. Mexico: Fondo de Cultura Económica, 1944. English translation: Irving A. Leonard, *A Cultural History of Spanish America, from Conquest to Independence*. Berkeley: University of California Press, 1962.

With notable literary acuity and a syncretic sense of the whole, Picón-Salas examines the (Latin) American Baroque as a distinctive cultural phenomenon with regard to its Spanish models. Tracing the literary, historical, and intellectual background of the Baroque of the Indies, he brings out the relationship between the repression of the Counter-Reformation and the ornate forms of the Baroque. The chapter culminates in a schematic but incisive discussion of Sor Juana—"El caso Sor Juana Inés de la Cruz" (The Case of Sor Juana Inés de la Cruz)—as epitomizing the characteristics and spirit of the Baroque he has elaborated.

Sabat de Rivers, Georgina. "Sor Juana Inés de la Cruz." *Historia de la literatura hispanoamericana. Tomo 1: Epoca colonial*, ed. by Luis Iñigo Madrigal. Madrid: Ediciones Cátedra, 1982. Pp. 275–93.

A comprehensive and authoritative overview by the distinguished Sorjuanista of the writer's life and works (in all genres), incorporating recent scholarship on the subjects. The section on the nun's poetry—classifying the various types, situating them within their traditions, analyzing pervasive themes and significant texts—provides an indispensable point of departure for the student of Sor Juana.

BIBLIOGRAPHIES (Included in the Following Studies)

Arroyo, Anita. *Razón y pasión de Sor Juana.* Mexico: Porrúa, 1971.

De la Maza, Francisco. *Sor Juana Inés de la Cruz ante la historia.* Mexico: UNAM, 1980.

Puccini, Dario. *Sor Juana Inés de la Cruz: Studio d'una personalità del Barocco messicano.* Rome: Edizioni dell'Ateneo, 1967.

Sabat de Rivers, Georgina. Selected bibliography appended to the article in Iñigo Madrigal's *Historia de la literatura hispanoamericana,* cited above.

Chronology of Sor Juana Inés de la Cruz

VICTORIA PEHL SMITH

THE LIFE OF SOR JUANA INÉS DE LA CRUZ	YEARS	PRINCIPAL WORKS OF SOR JUANA	CULTURAL AND LITERARY EVENTS
	1648		Quevedo, *Parnaso español*
	1649		
	1650		
Born Nov. 12, 1651, in Nepantla (Mexico)[1]	1651		Gracián, *El criticón*
	1652		Soto de Rojas, *Paraíso cerrado*
	1653		Moreto, *Primera parte de sus comedias*
Learns to read from the "amiga" of Amecameca	1654		
	1655		Saavedra Fajardo, *República literaria*
	1656		Velázquez, *Las Meninas*
	1657		Polo de Medina, *Gobierno moral*
	1658	Composes a *loa* to the Holy Sacrament	
	1659		
Goes to live with her grandfather in Mexico City	1660		Calderón, *El laurel de Apolo*
	1661		The *Gaceta de Madrid* begins
Enters the court of the	1662		
Viceroy's wife, the	1663		Calderón, *Tercera parte de comedias*
Marquise of Mancera	1664		
	1665	Poetry on the death of Felipe IV	F. Santos, *Las tarascas de Madrid*
Enters the convent of the discalced Carmelites	1666		
Leaves after three months	1667		
Takes the veil at the convent of San Jerónimo	1668	Examined in the viceregal palace	
Will, February 4, 1669	1669		
	1670		María de Jesús de Agreda, *Mística ciudad de Dios*
	1671		
	1672		N. Antonio, *Bibliotheca hispana vetus*
	1673		
	1674		
	1675		Calderón, *Cuarta parte de comedias*
	1676– 1691	*Villancicos* by petition of the cathedrals of Mexico, Puebla, and Oaxaca[2]	Feijóo is born
	1677		Calderón, *Autos sacramentales*
	1678		
	1679		
	1680		
	1681		Calderón dies
	1682		Calderón, *Quinta parte de comedias*
	1683		
	1684		

Adapted from Elias L. Rivers, *Sor Juana Inés de la Cruz, Antología* (Anaya, 1965).

THE LIFE OF SOR JUANA INÉS DE LA CRUZ	YEARS	PRINCIPAL WORKS OF SOR JUANA	CULTURAL AND LITERARY EVENTS
	1685		Solís, *Historia de la conquista de Méjico*
	1686		
	1687		
	1688		
	1689	First edition of Vol. 1 of her works (Madrid), *Inundación castálida*. Includes: nine *loas* (the others are in the *Segundo volumen* [Sevilla, 1692]) and *El Neptuno alegórico* (also published before in an undated Mexican edition)	Posthumous edition of A. Hurtado de Mendoza
	1690	*Carta atenagórica* published by the Bishop of Puebla, Manuel Fernández de Santa Cruz. Three months later Sor Juana writes her *Respuesta a Sor Filotea*.	
	1691		
	1692	First edition of Vol. II of her works (Seville), *Segundo volumen*. Includes *El sueño*, published for the first time; three *autos* and their *loas* (*El cetro de José, El mártir del Sacramento, San Hermenegildo*, and *El Divino Narciso*); two comedies (*Los empeños de una casa* and *Amor es más laberinto*), with *loas* and *sarao*; and *Crisis sobre un sermón* (*Carta atenagórica*).	Torres Villarroel is born
General confession	1693		
	1694	"Protesta que, rubricada con su sangre, hizo de su fe y amor a Dios . . . al tiempo de abandonar los estudios humanos"	
Dies during an epidemic, April 17	1695		
	1700	First edition of Vol. III of her works (Madrid), *Fama y Obras póstumas*, with approval by the Jesuit Diego Calleja. Includes the *Respuesta a Sor Filotea*, published for the first time	

1. Based on a baptismal record, perhaps Sor Juana's, Paz proposes 1648 as her birth year. We have kept 1651; for more details, see Georgina Sabat de Rivers's edition of *Inundación castálida*.

2. The twelve series of *villancicos* are dedicated to the Assumption (four from 1676, 1679, 1685, 1690), the Conception (1676, 1689), St. Pedro Nolasco (1677), the Apostle St. Peter (1677, 1683), the Nativity (1689), St. Joseph (1690), and St. Catherine (1691).

CONTRIBUTORS

ELECTA ARENAL

College of Staten Island/CUNY

ESTER GIMBERNAT DE GONZÁLEZ

University of Northern Colorado

ASUNCIÓN LAVRIN

Howard University

JOSEFINA LUDMER

Universidad Nacional de Buenos Aires

STEPHANIE MERRIM

Brown University

GEORGINA SABAT-RIVERS

State University of New York at Stony Brook

DOROTHY SCHONS[†]

University of Texas at Austin

VICTORIA PEHL SMITH

Brown University

INDEX

HISP 25 20I

DATE DUE